JACKSONIAN AMERICA
1815–1840
New Society, Changing Politics

EDITED BY

Frank Otto Gatell and John M. McFaul

Prentice-Hall, Inc. Englewood Cliffs, N. J.

A SPECTRUM BOOK

To Lothar's Master

Frank Otto Gatell, coeditor of this volume in the *Eyewitness Accounts of American History* series, is Professor of History, University of California, Los Angeles. He holds a Ph.D. from Harvard University, and his other publications include *John Gorham Palfrey and the New England Conscience* and *American Negro Slavery: A Modern Reader.*

Coeditor John M. McFaul is Associate Professor of History, Long Beach State College, Long Beach, California. He received his Ph.D. from the University of California, Berkeley.

Contents

iii

IV. The Spirit and Practice of Reform 59

Part Two
THE NEW POLITICS

V. The New Rules 85

VI. The Jacksonians Take Over 115

VII. The Bank War 139

VIII. Whig Response 156

Suggestions for Further Reading   *179*

Introduction

Historians agree about very little that took place during the Age of Jackson, but there is a general consensus that changes occurring in the United States after the War of 1812 significantly altered American society. Jackson's commanding figure attracted or repelled earlier historians, who were heavily influenced by the "Great Man" school of history. Thus the Jacksonian Era, however misleading the title, has remained a separate and distinguishable part of the American past. But aside from Jackson and other individuals of considerable talent and influence—Webster, Calhoun, and Clay, for example—what distinguished the era from others? Almost everything. Although the dimensions and timing are still disputed among historians, the era can be validly linked with the emergence of a democratic spirit which ultimately displaced traditional forms of civility, decorum, and deference.

The coronation of "King Democracy" was the result of forces astir in every aspect of American life. The traditional approach has led historians to search out at the national political level those issues, voting patterns, and speeches which illustrate the democratizing of the United States. We Americans tend to think of politics as a progressive force, directing and commanding the way to the future—hopefully, to a better future. Politicians and parties are dubbed "progressive" or "reactionary" according to how well they anticipate the future or fitfully embrace the past.

This collection of readings reverses the process to explore the view that the political forces of the Jacksonian Era were more adaptive than creative. The major forces for change lay outside of the political structure. A Transportation Revolution, itself a product of new entrepreneurship and an invigorated nationalism, made most of the forms and practices still lingering from the Federalist and Jeffersonian periods old-fashioned. All parts of society felt these economic shock waves. Some reaped immediate gains; many others, most notably and alarmingly the working classes emerging in the new urban centers, did

1

not. The expanded opportunities and the manifold problems created by these changes raised significant political questions which called into question basic premises underlying the American social and political orders.

The Transportation Revolution was essentially a promissory note, a gamble on future greatness. The vastness, the complexity, and the enormous resources involved in these undertakings symbolized the expansive forces at work in America. The optimistic vision which could underwrite a massive feat like the Erie Canal also influenced the thinking about man's relationship to God and society. If Americans could build roads and canals anywhere, they wanted to believe that the road to salvation was as open to their efforts. A new religious emphasis upon an intuitive sense of the imminence of God and His placability matched the expansiveness of man's material potentialities, so easily and abundantly observable. If God was ready for man, and vice versa, and if the American Adam might create a heaven on earth, then all Christians had to fight to eliminate the last vestiges of evil and corruption from American life. From this basic premise sprang the reformist zeal and activity of the 1830s and 1840s.

These economic, religious, and social forces were propelling Americans into an uncertain future. They also put pressure upon a political structure which had worked effectively and comfortably within the rules of a deferential society. Political practices, always resistant to change, yielded in time to the democratizing forces then at work. The rate of adaptation which characterized the responses of different political groups may well indicate the degree of conservatism among varied factions and parties, but it should be remembered that nearly all groups approached the nationalizing of American politics cautiously.

Political adaptation required new rules of procedure, an abandonment of Jeffersonian gentility in favor of the politics of the common man. Some politicos may have considered this a temporary expedient, but whatever their expectations a permanent revolution in American political style resulted. Jacksonians did not initiate all these changes, but they did fashion the period's most successful national coalition, and they remained in power for most of the time between 1829 and the Civil War. The Jacksonian Democratic response to the political order was as much symbolic as substantive, yet the style was unmistakably new, especially Jackson's appeal to "the people" for ratification of his executive actions.

One substantial institution became a direct casualty of the New Politics when Jackson directed his power against the Second Bank of the United States. The Bank War of the 1830s provides the most illuminating political issue of the era. The struggle between Jackson and the Bank brought into sharp focus the advantages and the drawbacks of the New Politics. Also, political reactions to economic growth produced further economic changes, as the economic consequences of the Bank War made themselves felt on the pre-Civil War American economy.

While Jacksonians dominated the politics of the era, a loyal and sometimes successful opposition groped to find an alternate way. Whigs, more nationalist-minded than Democrats, had little trouble adapting to the new nationalizing economic forces, but political egalitarianism took a bit more getting used to. Nevertheless, Whig victories occurred enough times to keep the Democrats honest. Jacksonians had to manufacture fresh appeals to the people, and warnings that Whiggery and aristocracy were synonymous. For their part, Whigs suffered from their somewhat stodgy and well-heeled image—non-populistic traits effectively publicized by Jacksonians, but by the end of the 1830s Whigs were matching Jacksonians in their appeals to the people, compliment for compliment.

The interconnections between political institutions and basic economic, religious, and social changes are difficult to trace with certainty, but it seems clear that changing political forms brought up the rear. That the political framework would eventually be remolded was as "inevitable" as the adaptation of the American constitutional process to political parties. That adjustment, the democratizing of American politics, is sketched in the following documents as a response to the economic, religious, and social changes which shaped the politics of the Age of Jackson.

Part One

A NEW SOCIETY

I. Transportation Revolution

Americans have customarily defined progress in material terms. By these criteria the addition of thousands of miles of track and inland waterways in the nineteenth century attested to national progress and coming greatness. Spokesmen for economic nationalism after the War of 1812 prophesied that the expanding new nation would be held together by a network of internal improvements, and the political and economic energies of the society were, accordingly, committed to economic expansion.

The unqualified enthusiasm for internal improvements subsided during the depression-marked 1820s however, and orthodox Jeffersonian hesitancy about economic change, sidetracked during the Era of Good Feeling, came back in fashion. Complaints against the alleged unfair advantages going to certain regions and places, notably New York City, became common. The controversy over the changing economy and its allegedly unequal benefits became an important ingredient of the politics of the turbulent twenties, and American politicians were forced to recognize confused and often ambivalent public demands. The differing political responses to these economic changes —primarily based upon a transportation revolution—provide one of the distinctive features of the Jacksonian era.

1. DE WITT CLINTON: PROPHET OF INTERNAL IMPROVEMENTS

No one better represents the optimism of economic expansion after the War of 1812 than DeWitt Clinton, the "father" of New York's Erie Canal. After a successful career in state politics, Clinton authored the 1816 petition to the legislature favoring a canal between the Hudson River and Lake Erie. Clinton's argument rested

upon the promise of prosperity and Union, the belief that
the canal would multiply the riches of New York and
benefit the entire nation as well. Most important, Clinton
cautioned New Yorkers that only by this undertaking
could the Union be held together. The beginning of the
Canal coincided with Clinton's comeback in New York
politics. He prodded the legislature in his annual message
of 1819 to finish the Canal. The economic arguments are
similar to those in the 1816 document, but of equal interest is the tone of Clinton's appeal, especially his call
for an energetic government to serve the public interest.
Clinton's politics were nominally Republican, but his
views smacked of Federalism, too much so for the political purists in the Albany Regency. [Laws of the State of
New York in Relation to the Erie and Champlain Canals
. . . (2 vols., Albany, 1825), I: 122–24, 129, 138–41,
394–96.]

MEMORIAL

*Of the citizens of New-York, in favor of a Canal Navigation between
the great western Lakes and the tide-waters of the Hudson, presented
to the Assembly February 21, 1816, and ordered to be printed.*

The memorial of the subscribers, in favor of a canal navigation, between the great western lakes and the tide-waters of the Hudson, most
respectfully represents:

That they approach the legislature with a solicitude proportioned to
the importance of this great undertaking, and with a confidence
founded on the enlightened public spirit of the constituted authorities.
If, in presenting the various considerations which have induced them
to make this appeal, they should occupy more time than is usual on
common occasions, they must stand justified by the importance of the
object. Connected as it is with the essential interest of our country,
and calculated in its commencement to reflect honor on the state, and
in its completion, to exalt it to an elevation of unparalleled prosperity;
your memorialists are fully persuaded, that centuries may pass away
before a subject is again presented so worthy of all your attention, and
so deserving of all your patronage and support.

The improvement of the means of intercourse between different
parts of the same country, has always been considered the first duty
and the most noble employment of government. If it be important
that the inhabitants of the same country should be bound together
by a community of interests, and a reciprocation of benefits; that agriculture should find a sale for its productions; manufactures a vent for

their fabrics; and commerce a market for its commodities; it is your incumbent duty, to open, facilitate, and improve internal navigation. . . . Canals operate upon the general interests of society, in the same way that machines for saving labor do in manufactures; they enable the farmer, the mechanic, and the merchant, to convey their commodities to market, and to receive a return, at least thirty times cheaper than by roads. As to all the purposes of beneficial communication, they diminish the distance between places, and therefore encourage the cultivation of the most extensive and remote parts of the country. They create new sources of internal trade, and augment the old channels; for, the cheaper the transportation, the more expanded will be its operation, and the greater the mass of the products of the country for sale, the greater will be the commercial exchange of returning merchandize, and the greater the encouragement to manufacturers, by the increased economy and comfort of living, together with the cheapness and abundance of raw materials; and canals are consequently advantageous to towns and villages, by destroying the monopoly of the adjacent country, and advantageous to the whole country; for though some rival commodities may be introduced into the old markets, yet many new markets will be opened by increasing population, enlarging old and erecting new towns, augmenting individual and aggregate wealth, and extending foreign commerce. . . .

While we do not pretend that all the trade of our western world, will centre in any given place, (nor indeed would it be desirable if it were practicable, because we sincerely wish the prosperity of all the states,) yet we contend that our natural advantages are so transcendant, that it is in our power to obtain the greater part, and put successful competition at defiance. As all the other communications are impeded by mountains; the only formidable rivals of New-York, for this great prize, are New-Orleans and Montreal, the former relying on the Mississippi, and the latter on the St. Lawrence. . . .

Granting, however, that the rivals of New York will command a considerable portion of the western trade, yet it must be obvious, from these united considerations, that she will engross more than sufficient to render her the greatest commercial city in the world. The whole line of canal will exhibit boats loaded with flour, pork, beef, pot and pearl ashes, flaxseed wheat, barley, corn, hemp, wool, flax, iron, lead, copper, salt, gypsum, coal, tar, fur, peltry, ginseng, bees-wax, cheese, butter, lard, staves, lumber, and the other valuable productions of our country; and also, with merchandise from all parts of the world. Great manufacturing establishments will spring up; agriculture will establish its granaries, and commerce its warehouses in all directions. Villages, towns, and cities, will line the banks of the canal, and the shores of the Hudson from Erie to New York. "The wilderness and the solitary place will become glad, and the desert will rejoice and blossom as the rose." . . .

If the legislature shall consider this important project in the same point of view, and shall unite with us in opinion, that the general prosperity is intimately and essentially involved in its prosecution, we are fully persuaded that now is the proper time for its commencement. Delays are the refuge of weak minds, and to procrastinate on this occasion is to show a culpable inattention to the bounties of Nature; a total insensibility to the blessings of Providence, and an inexcusable neglect of the interests of society. If it were intended to advance the views of individuals, or to foment the divisions of party; if it promoted the interests of a few, at the expense of the prosperity of many; if its benefits were limited as to place, or fugitive as to duration, then indeed it might be received with cold indifference, or treated with stern neglect; but the overflowing blessing from this great fountain of public good and national abundance, will be as extensive as our country, and as durable as time.

The considerations which now demand an immediate, and an undivided attention to this great object, are so obvious, so various, and so weighty, that we shall only attempt to glance at some of the most prominent.

In the first place, it must be evident, that no period could be adopted in which the work can be prosecuted with less expense. Every day augments the value of the land through which the canal will pass; and when we consider the surplus hands which have been recently dismissed from the army into the walks of private industry, and the facility with which an addition can be procured to the mass of our active labour, in consequence of the convulsions of Europe, it must be obvious that this is now the time to make those indispensable acquisitions.

2. The longer this work is delayed, the greater will be the difficulty in surmounting the interests that will rise up in opposition to it. Expedients on a contracted scale have already been adopted for the facilitation of intercourse. Turnpikes, locks, and short canals, have been resorted to, and in consequence of those establishments, villages have been laid out, and towns have been contemplated. To prevent injurious speculation, to avert violent opposition, and to exhibit dignified impartiality and paternal affection to your fellow-citizens, it is proper that they should be notified at once of your intentions.

3. The experience of the late war has impressed every thinking man in the community, with the importance of this communication. The expenses of transportation frequently exceeded the original value of the article, and at all times operated with injurious pressure upon the finances of the nation. The money thus lost for the want of this com-

munication, would have perhaps defrayed more than one half of its expense.

4. Events which are daily occurring on our frontiers, demonstrate the necessity of this work. Is it of importance that our honourable merchants should not be robbed of their legitimate profits; that the public revenues should not be seriously impaired by dishonest smuggling, and that the commerce of our cities should not be supplanted by the mercantile establishments of foreign countries? then it is essential that this sovereign remedy for maladies so destructive and ruinous, should be applied. It is with inconceivable regret we record the well known fact, that merchandise from Montreal has been sold to an alarming extent on our borders, for 15 per cent. below the New-York prices.

5. A measure of this kind will have a benign tendency in raising the value of the national domains, in expediting the sale, and enabling the payment. Our national debt may thus, in a short time, be extinguished. Our taxes of course will be diminished, and a considerable portion of revenue may then be expended in great public improvements; in encouraging the arts and sciences; in patronising the operations of industry; in fostering the inventions of genius, and in diffusing the blessings of knowledge.

6. However serious the fears which have been entertained of a dismemberment of the Union by collisions between the north and the south, it is to be apprehended that the most imminent danger lies in another direction, and that a line of separation may be eventually drawn between the atlantic and the western states, unless they are cemented by a common, an ever acting and a powerful interest. The commerce of the ocean, and the trade of the lakes, passing through one channel, supplying the wants, increasing the wealth, and reciprocating the benefits of each great section of the empire, will form an imperishable cement of connexion, and an indissoluble bond of union. New-York is both atlantic and western, and the only state in which this union of interest can be formed and perpetuated, and in which this great centripetal power can be energetically applied. Standing on this exalted eminence, with power to prevent a train of the most extensive and afflicting calamities that ever visited the world, (for such a train will inevitably follow a dissolution of the Union,) she will justly be considered an enemy to the human race, if she does not exert for this purpose the high faculties which the Almighty has put into her hands.

Lastly. It may be confidently asserted, that this canal, as to the extent of its route, as to the countries which it connects, and as to the consequences which it will produce, is without a parallel in the history of mankind. The union of the Baltic and Euxine; of the Red Sea and the Mediterranean; of the Euxine and the Caspian; and of the

Mediterranean and the Atlantic, has been projected or executed by the chiefs of powerful monarchies, and the splendor of the design has always attracted the admiration of the world. It remains for a free state to create a new era in history, and to erect a work more stupendous, more magnificent, and more beneficial, than has hitherto been achieved by the human race. Character is as important to nations as to individuals, and the glory of a republic, founded on the promotion of the general good, is the common property of all its citizens.

We have thus discharged with frankness and plainness, and with every sentiment of respect, a great duty to ourselves, to our fellow-citizens, and to posterity, in presenting this subject to the fathers of the commonwealth. And may that Almighty Being, in whose hands are the destinies of states and nations, enlighten your councils and invigorate your exertions in favour of the best interests of our beloved country.

Clinton's Message to the Legislature, 1819

It is certainly more important that the productive classes of society should have good markets out of the state, than that they should be exclusively confined to indifferent or fluctuating markets in it. In the former case, wealth is diffused over the whole country, while in the latter, it is limited to a few great towns.—A wise government ought to encourage communications with those places, where the farmer and manufacturer can sell at the highest, and buy at the lowest price. And, as the acquisition of many markets increases the chances of good ones, and diminishes, in many instances, the expenses of transportation, and guards against the pernicious fluctuations of price, I look forward with pleasure to the speedy arrival of the time, when the state will be able to improve the navigation of the Susquehannah, the Allegany, the Genesee and the St. Lawrence—to assist in connecting the waters of the great lakes and of the Mississippi—to form a junction between the western canal and lake Ontario, by the Oswego river, and to promote the laudable intention of Pennsylvania to unite the Seneca lake with the head-waters of the Susquehannah.

But there are other and more important considerations connected with this subject, which enter into the very essence of our liberty and prosperity. The gloomy and comfortless doctrine, which supposes man incapable of free government, necessarily implies that he must be subject to a bad one, because it presupposes his utter incompetence to govern either others or himself. In hereditary and elective monarchies, and indeed in all governments not founded on the broad basis of equal representation, the actual ruler is the prime minister of the day, elected from time to time, by the prince, to govern the country. Whether this right of choosing be vested in an hereditary elector, or in an elector for life, appointed by a diet or a conclave, or in an elector chosen by an army of Janisaries, it is clear that it is a faint recognition of the representative principle, transferred from the body of the people to an irresponsible individual, totally unfit, from his situation and education, to exercise it with patriotism and intelligence.—Who then can doubt the superior excellence of a free government, its entire accordance with the dignity of man, and its almost exclusive devotedness to his happiness? But in the United States our liberty and our union are inseparably connected.—A dismemberment of the republic into separate confederacies, would necessarily produce the jealous circumspection and hostile preparations of bordering states: large standing armies would be immediately raised; unceasing and vindictive wars would follow, and a military despotism would reign triumphant on the ruins of civil liberty. A dissolution of the union may, therefore, be considered the natural death of our free government. And to avert this awful calamity, all local prejudices and geographical distinctions should be discarded, the people should be habituated to frequent intercourse and beneficial inter-communication, and the whole republic ought to be bound together by the golden ties of commerce and the adamantine chains of interest. When the western canal is finished, and a communication is formed between lake Michigan and the Illinois river, or between the Ohio and the waters of lake Erie, the greater part of the United States will form one vast island, susceptible of circumnavigation to the extent of many thousand miles. The most distant parts of the confederacy will then be in a state of approximation, and the distinctions of Eastern and Western, of Southern and Northern interests will be entirely prostrated. To be instrumental in producing so much good, by increasing the stock of human happiness,—by establishing the perpetuity of free government,—and, by extending the empire of improvement, of knowledge, of refinement and of religion, is an ambition worthy of a free people. The most exalted reputation is that which arises from the dispensation of happiness to our fellow creatures, and that conduct is most acceptable to God which is most beneficial to man. Character is as important to states as to individuals, and the glory of a republic founded on the promotion of the general good, is the common property of all its citizens.

2. DANIEL WEBSTER:
ECONOMIC NATIONALISM CONTINUED

Daniel Webster, after a brief flirtation with New England particularism, became one of the most prominent converts to Clinton's call for national unity through economic expansion. The following selections are from Webster's speeches at the opening ceremonies for the Northern Railroad in 1847. From that vantage point, Webster glanced back approvingly at the completed national improvements, which he attributed to free labor and corporate activity, twin faiths of his beloved Whiggery. Looking forward, Webster predicted greater triumphs from the age of steam. He used the railroad to typify American society, a new energy breaking down spatial and class barriers.

Webster, though no Henry David Thoreau, could not resist drawing attention to the intrusion of the machine upon previously untouched nature. Adopting a tone similar to that used by modern critics, Webster excoriated those who artificially disturbed nature's handiwork, but ended by reaffirming the greater virtues of progress and unity built upon national economic expansion. The allusion to these complaints, however, even to dismiss them, reveals that not all Americans easily made the adjustment to the era of steam so celebrated by Webster. [The Writings and Speeches of Daniel Webster (20 vols., Boston, 1903), IV: 107–10,115–17.]

In my youth and early manhood I have traversed these mountains along all the roads or passes which lead through or over them. We are on Smith's River, which, while in college, I had occasion to swim. Even that could not always be done; and I have occasionally made a circuit of many rough and tedious miles to get over it. At that day, steam, as a motive power, acting on water and land, was thought of by nobody; nor were there good, practicable roads in this part of the State. At that day, one must have traversed this wilderness on horseback or on foot. So late as when I left college, there was no road from river to river for a carriage fit for the conveyance of persons. I well recollect the commencement of the system of turnpike roads. The granting of the charter of the fourth turnpike, which led from Lebanon to Boscawen, was regarded as a wonderful era. . . .

I remember to have attended the first meeting of the proprietors of this turnpike at Andover. It was difficult to persuade men that it was possible to have a passable carriage road over these mountains. I was too young and too poor to be a subscriber, but I held the proxies of several absent subscribers, and what I lacked in knowledge and experience I made up in zeal. As far as I now remember, my first speech after I left college was in favor of what was then regarded as a great and almost impracticable internal improvement, to wit, the making of a smooth, though hilly, road from Connecticut River, opposite the mouth of the Contoocook. Perhaps the most valuable result of making these and other turnpike roads was the diffusion of knowledge upon road-making among the people; for in a few years afterward, great numbers of the people went to church, to electoral and other meetings, in chaises and wagons, over very tolerable roads. The next step after turnpikes was canals. . . .

. . . I cannot conceive of any policy more useful to the great mass of the community than the policy which established these public improvements. Let me say, fellow-citizens, that in the history of human inventions there is hardly one so well calculated as that of railroads to equalize the condition of men. The richest must travel in the cars, for there they travel fastest; the poorest can travel in the cars, while they could not travel otherwise, because this mode of conveyance costs but little time or money. Probably there are in the multitude before me those who have friends at such distances that they could hardly have visited them, had not railroads come to their assistance to save them time and to save them expense. Men are thus brought together as neighbors and acquaintances, who live two hundred miles apart.

We sometimes hear idle prejudices expressed against railroads because they are close corporations; but so from the necessity of the case they necessarily must be, because the track of a railway cannot be a road upon which every man may drive his own carriage. Sometimes, it is true, these railroads interrupt or annoy individuals in the enjoyment of their property; for these cases the most ample compensation ought to be made. I have myself had a little taste of this inconvenience. When the directors of the road resolved to lay it out upon the river (as I must say they were very wise in doing), they showed themselves a little too loving to me, coming so near my farm-house, that the thunder of their engines and the screams of their steam-whistles, to say nothing of other inconveniences, not a little disturbed the peace and the repose of its occupants. There is, beside, an awkward and ugly embankment thrown up across my meadows. It injures the looks of the fields. But I have observed, fellow-citizens, that railroad directors and railroad projectors are no enthusiastic lovers of landscape beauty; a handsome field or lawn, beautiful copses, and all the gorgeousness of forest scenery, pass for little in their eyes. Their business is to cut and to slash, to level or deface a finely rounded field, and fill up beautifully winding valleys. They are quite utilitarian in their creed and in their practice. Their business is to make a good road. They look upon a well-constructed embankment as an agreeable work of art; they behold with delight a long, deep cut through hard pan and rock, such as we have just passed; and if they can find a fair reason to run a tunnel under a deep mountain, they are half in raptures. To be serious, Gentlemen, I must say I admire the skill, the enterprise, and that rather bold defiance of expense, which have enabled the directors of this road to bring it with an easy ascent more than five hundred feet above the level of the Merrimac River. We shall soon see it cross yonder mountainous ridge, commonly called "the Height of Land," and thence pitch down into the fair valley of the Connecticut. . . .

And now what is the particular cause of all the prosperity and wealth which I foresee in this valley? What is it that has chiselled down these Grafton rocks, and made this road which brings my own house so near to the home of my most distant New Hampshire hearer? It is popular industry; it is free labor. Probably there never was an undertaking which was more the result of popular feeling than this. I am told that there are fifteen hundred stockholders in the enterprise, the capital being two millions and a half. That single fact would serve to show the generally diffused interest felt by the people in its success. It is but three or four years since, when, having occasion to visit my farm at Franklin, I observed a line of shingles stretching across my fields. Asking my farmer what was the meaning of all this, I was answered, "It is the line of our railroad." Our railroad! That is the way the people talked about it. I laughed at the idea at first; and, in conversation with a neighbor, inquired what in the world they wanted of a railroad there. "Why," was the reply, "the people want a ride behind the iron horse, and that ride they will have." This day they have had it. The result has proved, not that my friend was too sanguine, but that I was too incredulous.

It is the spirit and influence of free labor, it is the indomitable industry of a free people, that has done all this. There is manifested in its accomplishment that without which the most fertile field by nature must remain for ever barren. Human sagacity, skill, and industry, the zealous determination to improve and profit by labor, have done it all. That determination has nowhere been more conspicuously displayed than here. New Hampshire, it is true, is no classic ground. She has no Virgil and no Eclogues. She has a stern climate and a stern soil. But her climate is fitted to invigorate men, and her soil is covered with the evidences of the comforts of individual and social life. As the traveller pursues his way along her roads, he sees all this. He sees those monuments of civilization and refinement, churches; he sees those marks of human progress, schoolhouses, with children clustering around their doors as thick as bees. And they are bees, except in one respect. The distinction is, that whereas the insect day after day returns to its home laden with the spoils of the field, the human creature is admitted to the hive but once. His mind is furnished with the stores of learning, he is allowed to drink his fill at the fountains of knowledge, his energies are trained in the paths of industry, and he is then sent out into the world, to acquire his own subsistence and help to promote the welfare of his kind.

It is an extraordinary era in which we live. It is altogether new. The world has seen nothing like it before. I will not pretend, no one can pretend, to discern the end; but every body knows that the age is remarkable for scientific research into the heavens, the earth, and what is beneath the earth; and perhaps more remarkable still for the application of this scientific research to the pursuits of life. The ancients saw nothing like it. The moderns have seen nothing like it till the present generation. Shakspeare's fairy said he would

"Put a girdle round about the earth
 In forty minutes."

Professor Morse has done more than that; his girdle requires far less time for its traverse. In fact, if one were to send a despatch from Boston by the telegraph at twelve o'clock, it would reach St. Louis at a quarter before twelve. This is what may be called doing a thing in less than no time. We see the ocean navigated and the solid land traversed by steam power, and intelligence communicated by electricity. Truly this is almost a miraculous era. What is before us no one can say, what is upon us no one can hardly realize. The progress of the age has almost outstripped human belief; the future is known only to Omniscience.

In conclusion, permit me to say that all these benefits and advantages conferred upon us by Providence should only strengthen our resolves to turn them to the best account, not merely in material progress, but in the moral improvement of our minds and hearts. Whatsoever else we may see of the wonders of science and art, our eyes should not be closed to that great truth, that, after all, "the fear of the Lord is the beginning of wisdom."

3. QUALIFIED NATIONALISM:
A SOUTHERN SPOKESMAN

Southern complaints of northern and especially New York City domination of their trade became commonplace in pre-Civil War America. Indeed, the following selection, by William F. Maury in the Southern Literary Messenger of 1839, refers with guarded impatience to the ineffectiveness of the many southern conventions calling for direct trade with Europe. Southern explanations of northern trade dominance frequently relied upon contemptuous portrayals of a grasping, Yankee commercial spirit, a spirit obviously less desirable than the easygoing civility of the land of cotton. Maury, however, assumes that the entre-

preneurial spirit did not stop at the Mason-Dixon line. Appealing to the Benjamin Franklins of the South to be "up and doing," he attributed New York City's dominance of the shipping lanes to the enterprising spirit of selected individuals—many of them Quakers. Calling for equality of enterprise, he urged southerners to develop a fleet of steam-driven ships to compete with the New York City packets. Although Maury patiently documented the particulars of New York City's rise to trading eminence to show that it had not occurred "naturally" nor inevitably, he seems almost persuaded of that city's continued dominant role. The plea thus becomes a fatalistic appeal to southerners to make the liberating effort even though they may expect to fail. [*Southern Literary Messenger,* V (January, 1839): 3–7, 12.]

DIRECT TRADE WITH THE SOUTH

The business of commerce presents no law, which forbids the southern merchant to exchange his flour in Rio for the coffee of Brazil; or to barter in Valparaiso and Lima, his produce for the copper of Chili and Peru; and this again for teas and silks in China. That he should carry on a lucrative trade with the West or East Indies, with the Brazils, on the coast of South America, or in the Mediterranean, nothing is wanting but the nerve and capital of the South controlled and regulated by well directed energies. The example of a single capitalist in any of the southern ports, who should have a correct knowledge of the demands of trade, would not fail to gain for his town in a short time a fair proportion of direct trade, such as that enjoyed by Baltimore, Philadelphia, or Boston. . . .

With patience and the exercise of proper talents and enterprise, the shoulders of one capitalist at his own windlass would do more for Norfolk or Charleston, than all the resolutions adopted by southern conventions are likely to do. It is example, not precept, that the South requires.

We have watched these conventions with much interest; but we have ever laid down the reports of their proceedings in disappointment. The resolutions passed in convention, "not to buy northern goods when they can get southern, unless the northern are the cheapest; not to freight northern vessels when they can freight southern, unless the northern freight for less," and many others, remind us of the oath which Neptune and his crew required of us, when we first crossed the equator, viz: "never to eat brown bread when we could get white, unless we preferred the brown; and never to kiss the maid, if we could kiss the mistress, unless we liked the maid best." Unless these gentlemen have been sworn by old Neptune, and really mean to do nothing in the way of direct trade from the South, they should resolve always to kiss the maid and eat brown bread, whether they liked it or not, and commence trading on their own bottoms.

When we say that the South might, in a few years, and with no other means than individual enterprise, share with Baltimore and Philadelphia, her just quota of direct trade, we do not include as any portion of it, that great influx of European commerce, which the packet ships pour into the New York market. But this will not satisfy the South. Her vaulting ambition craves something more than the grasping hand of New York has left to Boston, Baltimore and Philadelphia. The commercial grandeur and prosperity of that city, have long attracted her attention. In view of the growing importance and immense advantages of its trade, she has become restive, and would now fain rouse up into a bold and honorable emulation her lethargic spirit of commerce. But in essaying to divert any part of the packet trade into a new channel, the southern merchants must do more than hold conventions merely to take the sailor's oath, to resolve and re-resolve to meet again.

How artificial soever the present course of trade through New York may at first sight appear, it has settled down into regular channels. In attempting to divert it from these channels, by re-opening the natural ones, or creating others, the South, before she proceeds to the undertaking, should perfectly understand the nature of every obstacle to the scheme, in order that she may take her own measures, and be fully prepared to meet and overcome every difficulty as it presents itself. She will find in New York a formidable competitor, if this city have not already reached that point of commercial grandeur which brooks no rivalry. It were well therefore to examine into the causes, which have turned the balance of trade so greatly in favor of New York, and to show by what means that city attained and maintains her commercial supremacy over all other ports in the United States. From this examination, some clue may be gained, to the only means by which the South may reasonably hope to become possessed of similar advantages. If, looking at the present, we refer to the past for information, we will be struck with the fact that commerce has dwindled away at the South, only to flourish the more at the North. If we go a step further, and attempt to trace to its origin, the cause which was adequate to such an effect, we may discover it in the circumstance, that at the South, planting was found most profitable; but at the North, commerce and navigation. Therefore the South grew the cotton, and the North carried it to market. And up to this time, each section has followed the course which circumstances rendered most expedient; and each in its favorite pursuit has taken the lead of all other countries. . . .

Among the many schemes which were originated by mercantile men to supply the continually increasing demands of their trade, none were so bold, so grand, as that of an unpretending Quaker of New York. He conceived the beautiful idea of running a line of express ships to and fro across the Atlantic, and thus gave rise to the celebrated packets of New York. As sailers and carriers they have become proverbial among seafaring men on both sides of the Atlantic. For strength, safety, fleetness and beauty; and for a combination of all the requisites of a good ship, in such admirable proportions, no nation can boast of vessels, public or private, comparable to them. They, added to her other resources, gave New York commercial advantages, in the enjoyment of which she has prospered, and is every day growing stronger, more wealthy and great. Let the South look well to the packet ships; for in them lies the strength of her competitor. They control the trade of New York with France and England. If the South would contend with the North for her portion of this trade, the race must be run with the New York packets. And before she can carry off the prize, she must put in execution a plan of intercommunication with England, which must rival, may eclipse, that carried on by the New York *liners*.

It is not our purpose to extol the North, or to disparage the South, or in any way to magnify the difficulties which the latter must encounter in every attempt to draw off from the North any considerable portion of the trade monopolized there. The sea is our home; the North and the South, the East and the West, our country. We go for the "stars and stripes," and, like the emblematic constellation in the union of the flag, we look upon the states as one harmonious whole. Therefore, when on shore, we have nothing to do with sectional jealousies, or state prejudices; though ours incline us to favor and if possible to assist the weaker party. The South has slumbered and slept over her commercial advantages, while the North has guarded hers with a jealous eye. The former is just now waking up to their importance. Her sons, by calling conventions, are striving to rouse into action the dormant energies of mercantile enterprise, that her merchants, like true and lawful champions, may boldly enter the lists for the prize of commerce. Their motto is DIRECT TRADE ON SOUTHERN BOTTOMS. With ships for steeds, their tiltyard is the sea, and nations will be spectators at the tournament. Nothing but a bold stroke can crown their cause with triumph; for they have fearful odds against them. But let them *act*. Let them lay well their plans, and come to the contest with capital and energy; and like the gallant yeoman in Ivanhoe, the South will find us ever ready to add our halloo to a good shot, or a gallant blow. The fight with New York, for her trade, cannot now be carried on under sail. That time is gone by. The contest must be carried on by steam. By prompt action, and a well timed stroke with a line of steam packets, the South may gain important advantages. But more of this anon. . . . .

Some are of opinion, that the establishment of packets was a natural consequence of the course of trade: but we think this a mistaken view of the subject; and certainly, when the project of sailing on the same day of each month, full or empty, was first broached, it was generally thought a piece of mere Quixotism. Many were the half cargoes of turpentine and cotton from New York, and salt and coals from Liverpool, which the owners, for many years, were compelled to ship on their own account, in the face of almost certain loss, in order to be ready for the appointed time of sailing. Morcover, the packets were in operation two years, before they got any decided preference from passengers. But now they serve as the *passenger train*, on the great highway between the old world and the new. The officers of the British army in Canada, and the merchants of British America, think of no other route both for coming from and going to the mother country. Merchants and travellers from the South and West, from Havana, Mexico and the West Indies, make them the great thoroughfare to England and all parts of Europe. Always sailing at their stated times, full or empty, business men began to calculate with certainty on their departure and arrival; the effect of which, in a short time, was to make New York a greater depot for produce and manufactures, and a place of resort for merchants and passengers: so that there is now less difficulty in obtaining cargoes for twelve ships per month, each of three or four times the capacity of the original liners, than there was in filling up the Amity, or the James Monroe. Thus, New York now carries on a trade in her foreign packets alone of twenty-four of *their* cargoes per month, equal to 17,000 tons, and sufficient to give constant employment to 140 ships of the size of those which commenced the Havre line. . . .

Ever since the establishment of packets, New York has been gradually swallowing up the commerce of Philadelphia and Boston with England. We have seen that their merchants now make large importations through New York. Twenty years ago, and there were almost as many ships sailing from Boston, as from New York, to Liverpool. But if one ship sailed last year from that port to Liverpool, it is more than we know. British ships too are almost entirely thrown out of the trade from New York to Liverpool. In the months of December, 1837, and January and February, 1838, fifteen packets, and about as many transient vessels, sailed for Liverpool, but not one English vessel, though freights at this time were twenty-five or thirty per cent. higher than usual.

If then the direct trade of the enterprising cities of Boston and Philadelphia have been so much crippled in their contest for its advantages with New York, on something like equal terms, and before she possessed the facilities which she now enjoys from her packet system and extended commercial relations, what may the agricultural South expect to accomplish by her commercial conventions, which meet to *resolve* and not to *act?* . . .

The practical solution of the Atlantic steam problem, by facilitating intercourse alone, will tend greatly to increase at home the power of New York, and to extend abroad her commercial sway. But let the success of Atlantic steam ships meet the just expectations of their most sanguine friends, many and great improvements must be made in the generation and application of steam, before this subtile means of navigation can compete with canvass, in the carrying trade of the ocean. For a long time to come, the steam packets must rely for their profits mainly on the transportation of passengers, small parcels, and letters.

The number of these parcels will rapidly increase. They will consist mostly of light and costly articles of merchandise, such as the demands of fashion and the change of seasons are continually calling for. If one merchant receive by steam ship the latest fashions and newest patterns from France and England, all the merchants of the same city, in self-defence, must do the same, or lose their run of custom. It is to this circumstance—to the advantages of the most rapid communication, that we wish to call the attention of those who have the will and the means to open a direct trade from the South. The trade of Bristol, like that of the South, has dwindled down into a mere skeleton of its former greatness. She has made a bold effort, and sent out her splendid steam ships, to invite commerce again to her wharves, and recover back to her piers the rich argosies of her merchants. In the example of that ancient city, let the South get understanding.

The plan talked of at the South, of sending their vessels, dragging along at uncertain periods, after foreign trade, must signally fail in the present stage of commerce. The South has not the market of the North to receive, nor the fleets of packets of New York to distribute her return, or to collect her outward cargoes; for she must have something more for commerce than raw cotton, tobacco, tar, pitch, and turpentine. The force of her own habits is against her; and to succeed in gaining her portion of direct trade, she must, as we have before said, go vigorously to work, and carry on the heat of the contest, not with the bulky trader, as might have been done twenty years ago, but with the crack liners of the present day. . . .

Those who first established the packets, have placed New York on a commercial eminence, and put a sceptre in her hand, which she delights to hold; and she will neither come down from the one, nor surrender the other, until the balance of trade be lost to her ships. The plying of steamboats across the Atlantic will but make more absolute her sway over the commerce of the United States; for, besides making New York the channel of direct communication with England, both by letter and in person, they will further aggrandize that city in her commercial importance by bringing bills on America into the English market, and setting on foot a regular system of exchange with this country, similar to that between England and all parts of Europe. And New York will be the centre of negociation for all these bills.

If the South would take away this sceptre and divide commerce with the North, she must be prodigal of her wealth, and attempt boldly— for the odds against her are fearful. The contest now cannot be carried on under sail, ship against ship; New York has become too skilful in the manœuvres of her fleets—too powerful and too swift in the chase with her packets. She must be attacked in her high places, and steam must be the weapon.

Havre is ripe for a steam enterprise across the Atlantic. That town is ready to co-operate with any city in the Union, and no doubt would receive with open arms, a proposition from the South, to run from Norfolk a line of steam packets, which, going and coming, might touch at Portsmouth, as the London packets do, to land and embark passengers. It may be perceived by the chart, that Portsmouth is but a step out of the direct track of a steamer to Havre; and that, by steam, Norfolk is only one hundred and eighty miles further than New York, from either place. But whatever be done, must be done quickly. Without the help of steam, and the improvements of the day, the commerce of the South must continue to dwindle.

The South has taken an honorable lead in Atlantic steam navigation. She it was, who, twenty years ago, sent the first steam vessel across the Atlantic, and thus acted as pioneer to the splendid steam enterprise which is now going into operation with a success that astonishes as much those in the old as it delights those of the new world.

Let the South bring her strong men to the enterprise, and get up, as we have said, her line of splendid steamers to England and France; and let the first blow be aimed to divide with New York the facilities of communication; and then withdraw from her, if she can, a part of the travel, and make the port of Norfolk the centre of exchange for New Orleans and the South. When she has done this, let her throw herself behind her cotton bags, and then with her ships make the gallant stand. And if, after all this, the proud spirit must succumb—if the South must sink into her, so called, vassalage to the North, and be *ruined* by her tribute to New York, her sons may say of her, as Wirt said of the General Armstrong privateer, "she has graced her fall, and made her ruin glorious."

4. POLITICAL PROBLEMS:
NORTHERN STYLE

*State rights theories have never been the exclusive prop-
erty of Southerners, as the following selection from
DeWitt Clinton's 1825 message to the New York Legislature demonstrates. After lauding the internal improvements undertaken by other states—emulating New York's
example in building the Erie Canal—Clinton complained
of the encroachments of the national government. There
were, of course, special interests involved, as there usually
are when the principle of state rights is invoked. Clinton
quickly pointed out that the state of New York built and
operated the canal, and that the national government, using the commerce clause of the Constitution, proposed to
tax and license canal traffic. But Clinton argued that more
than an economic threat to New York State existed: the
proper balance must be maintained between national and
state governments.*

*Clinton was one of many public figures of that era who
called for a balanced federalism. Most politicians had to
stake out some position on the respective powers of state
and national governments. A laissez-faire policy, though
consistent and simple, attracted few men in public life
since they recognized the necessity of governmental action
to stimulate economic growth. The question remained,
what kind of balance should be struck, and over what
issues?* [New York Laws in Relation to Canals, I: 238–41.]

I cannot refrain, upon this occasion, from congratulating you and
our country, on the propitious spirit which is generally diffused through
the other states, in favor of internal improvements. The state of Ohio
has now under consideration, a stupendous project for uniting the Ohio
river with Lake Erie, which may justly be considered a prolongation or
continuance of our Erie canal, and which will connect the Hudson with
the Mississippi, and convert a most important portion of the United
States into one vast island. I shall welcome the commencement, and
hail the consummation of that work, as among the most auspicious
events in our history. It will open to our trade the luxuriant valley of
the Mississippi, and its auxiliary rivers. It will immeasurably enhance
the value and usefulness of our works, concentrate the commerce of
the east and the west in our great emporium, and bind the union together by indissoluble ties. The state of Ohio is distinguished for
fertility of soil, benignity of climate, moral power, and prospective re-

sources. The revenue from the canal will pay, in a reasonable time, the interest of the sum expended for its completion, and form a large surplus applicable to the speedy extinguishment of the debt; and there can be no doubt, but that the necessary funds may be procured in this state, on easy and satisfactory terms.

I cannot pass over, in silence, the attempt which has been recently made to bring the boats navigating our canals, within the operation of the statutes for regulating the coasting trade of the United States, by requiring from such boats enrolment and license, and the payment of tonnage duties. The canals are the property of the state, are within the jurisdiction of the state, have been constructed by the state, and can be destroyed by the state. They have been made at its expense, after the general government had refused all participation and assistance. It cannot well be perceived how the regulation of commerce "with foreign nations, and among the several states, or with the Indian tribes," can authorise an interference with vessels prosecuting an inland trade, through artificial channels. The coasting trade is entirely distinct from a trade through our canals, which no state in the union, nor the general government itself has a right to enjoy, without our consent. The consequences of such assumptions would be, if carried into effect, to annihilate our revenue arising from tolls, to produce the most oppressive measures, to destroy the whole system of internal improvements, and to prostrate the authority of the state governments.

A just exposition of the laws of the United States, cannot authorise their application to such cases. But if a different interpretation should prevail, then it becomes a very serious question indeed, whether the state can enforce its laws imposing tolls. The supreme court of the United States has solemnly adjudged, that a coasting license from a collector is a grant of the right of navigation. If so, and that right being derived from a law of congress, it will be contended that it cannot be prohibited nor controlled by any state law; the right, to be complete, must be enjoyed without restraint. The state cannot demand a toll, as the price of the enjoyment of such a right, if it has not the power to prohibit such enjoyment altogether.

It may be further remarked, that the power to regulate commerce, among the states, under which the act regulating the coasting trade was passed, is held, by that high tribunal, to be exclusively in congress. If so, and if that act, or any other act, which congress may pass, under that power, can be applied to the canals, it would follow, as a consequence, that our laws imposing tolls, are void from the beginning. The state has no power to adopt them; and in this view of the subject, it would seem to be immaterial whether any license be taken out under the act of congress.

The supreme court has also declared, that the power to regulate commerce includes a power to regulate navigation, as one means of carrying on commerce. The same remark may be made, with equal force, concerning any kind of transportation, whether by land or water, the power to regulate commerce applying to the one as well as to the other. If congress can declare, that a boat passing between different parts of the same district, within the same state, shall take a license, why can it not direct that a wagon shall take one, under similar circumstances? When we shall have arrived at this point we shall begin to have some adequate notion of the extent to which this claim may be carried.

I shall say no more on this subject at this time. I will not entertain a doubt but that the national government will command the abandonment of a claim so unfounded and pernicious; and I am persuaded that it has been preferred without due reflection, and without instructions from superior authority. But if this course shall not be pursued, it will then be your duty to take that stand which the rights and safety of the people imperiously demand.

The considerations which grow out of this occasion, and the complaints which have been made in different states about alleged encroachments of the national government on their constitutional powers, point to the most formidable dangers that can menace the stability of the union and the welfare of our country. Without a general government, we shall neither have union at home nor respect abroad. We shall be arrayed into separate confederacies, or exist as insulated states, maintaining large standing armies, wasting our resources in intestine wars, the dupes of foreign intrigue, and the victims of civil discord. Without state authorities, there can be no civil liberty and no good government; for it is utterly impossible that so extensive a country can be bound together, unless as a confederation or a military despotism. Every true friend of America will strive to maintain these respective authorities in full purity and vigor, without detracting from the powers of the one to add to those of the other, nor extending the facilities of either beyond their legitimate dimensions. Each possesses a portion of the delegated authority of the people, and each is supreme within the sphere of its constitutional powers. The apprehensions entertained by some of our distinguished statesmen at the formation of the national constitution, have entirely failed; and instead of the predominance of a controlling power in the states, the centripetal force of the general government has had perhaps too great a preponderance. The offices of the latter exceed those of the former, in rank, power, number and emolument: its patronage is commensurate with its superior resources; and it touches, in its relations and ramifications, every chord of ambition; presents the most spacious theatre for the display of great talents, and for the gratification of lofty aspirations. It also possesses a decided advantage over the state governments in the arrangement of its judicial authority. In all controversies relative to the due exercise of their powers, this department of the national government is a tribunal of dernier resort, without any amenability to the people or the states, with a compensation that cannot be diminished, under a tenure that will endure for life, and with no other responsibility than liability to impeachment for high crimes and misdemeanors, under which any decisions, however erroneous, can never be classed, because an error of judgment can never be adjudged a crime.

Natural justice prescribes that no man should be a judge in his own cause, and that between contending sovereignties neither should pronounce the law of the case. A new tribunal ought to be constituted, to decide upon the powers of the national and state governments, and to keep them within legitimate boundaries. I know of none that can be formed with a character so imposing, with a responsibility so imperative, and with a position so dignified, as the senate of the United States. Composed of the most distinguished and talented men of the several states, its decisions would be formed with integrity and ability, and received with respectful acquiescence. As a co-ordinate branch of congress, and as a component part of the executive power, it would be a safe guardian of the just authority of the national government; and as a representation of the states with a periodical change of members, it would be their natural and efficient protector against un constitutional invasions. In these suggestions, I have not the most distant intention of violating the habitual respect which I entertain for the supreme judiciary of the union.

5. POLITICAL PROBLEMS: SOUTHERN STYLE

Internal improvements promised economic expansion and spurred hopes for a strengthened Union, but the proposal that the federal government pay for these ventures stirred the wrath of a vociferous southern minority. The following speech by John Randolph of Roanoke, Virginia, in 1824 is typical of long-standing objections of southern particularists to a program of federal support for internal improvements. Anticipating the Jacksonian critique of the 1830s, Randolph objected to the scramble for special privileges which such a program would produce. After rejecting the notion of any special claims on the part of the West for such programs, Randolph upheld the pristine Jeffersonian view of strict constitutional interpretation. And prophetically, Randolph raised the ominous question of

*federal encroachment upon the South's particular interest
—slavery. The apprehensive and defiant Virginian called
upon his southern brethren to stay on the "windward side
of treason" but to resist strongly any surrender of the state
rights principle in favor of expedient laws which might
increase national power. [Annals of Congress, 18th Cong.,
1st sess., 1298–1311.]*

In the course of the observations which the gentleman from Kentucky saw fit to submit to the Committee, were some pathetic ejacula-
tions on the subject of the sufferings of our brethren of the West. Sir,
our brethren of the West have suffered, as our brethren throughout the
United States, from the same cause, although with them the cause
exists in an aggravated degree—from the acts of those to whom they
have confided the power of legislation; by a departure—and we have
all suffered from it—I hope no gentleman will understand me as wishing to make any invidious comparisons between different quarters of
our country—by a departure from the industry, the simplicity, the
economy, and the frugality of our ancestors. They have suffered from
a greediness of gain, that has grasped at the shadow while it has lost
the substance—from habits of indolence, of profusion, of extravagance
—from an apery of foreign manners, and of foreign fashions—from a
miserable attempt at the shabby genteel, which only serves to make
our poverty more conspicuous. The way to remedy this state of suffering is to return to those habits of labor and industry from which we
have thus departed. . . .

With these few remarks, continued Mr. R., permit me now to recall the attention of the Committee to the original design of this
Government. It grew out of the necessity, indispensable and unavoidable, in the circumstances of this country, of some general power,
capable of regulating foreign commerce. Sir, I am old enough to remember the origin of this Government; and, though I was too young to
participate in the transactions of that day, I have a perfect recollection
of what was public sentiment on the subject. And I repeat, without
fear of contradiction, that the proximate, as well as the remote cause
of the existence of the Federal Government, was, the regulation of
foreign commerce. Not to particularize all the difficulties which grew out
of the conflicting laws of the States, Mr. R. referred to but one, arising
from Virginia taxing an article which Maryland then made duty-free
—and to that very policy, said he, may be attributed, in a great degree,
the rapid growth and prosperity of the town of Baltimore. If the old
Congress had possessed the power of laying a duty of ten per cent. *ad
valorem* on imports, this Constitution would never have been called
into existence.

But, we are told that, along with the regulation of foreign commerce, the States have yielded to the General Government, in as broad terms, the regulation of domestic commerce—I mean, said Mr. R., the commerce among the several States, and that the same power is possessed by Congress over the one as over the other. It is rather unfortunate for this argument, that, if it applies to the extent to which the power to regulate foreign commerce has been carried by Congress, they may prohibit altogether this domestic commerce, as they have heretofore, under the other power, prohibited foreign commerce.

But why put extreme cases? This Government cannot go on one day without a mutual understanding and deference between the State and General Governments. This Government is the breath of the nostrils of the States. Gentlemen may say what they please of the preamble to the Constitution; but this Constitution is not the work of the amalgamated population of the then existing confederacy, but the offspring of the States; and however high we may carry our heads, and strut and fret our hour, "dressed in a little brief authority," it is in the power of the States to extinguish this Government at a blow. They have only to refuse to send members to the other branch of the Legislature, or to appoint Electors of President and Vice President, and the thing is done. . . .

. . . From the commencement of the Government to this day, differences have arisen between the two great parties in this nation—one consisting of the disciples of Mr. Hamilton, the Secretary of the Treasury, and another party who believed that, in their construction of the Constitution, those to whom they opposed themselves exceeded the just limit of its legitimate authority—and Mr. R. prayed gentlemen to take into their most serious consideration the fact that, on this very question of construction, this sect, which the framers of the Constitution foresaw might arise, did arise in their might, and put down the construction of the Constitution according to the Hamiltonian version. But did we at that day dream, said Mr. R., that a new sect would arise after them, which would so far transcend Alexander Hamilton and his disciples, as they out-went Thomas Jefferson, James Madison, and John Taylor, of Caroline? This is the deplorable fact: such is now the actual state of things in this land; and it is not a subject so much of demonstration as it is self-evident—it speaks to the senses, so that every one may understand it. . . .

. . . Are gentlemen aware of the colossal power they are giving to the General Government? Sir, I am afraid, that that ingenious gentleman, Mr. McAdam, will have to give up his title to the distinction of the *Colossus of Roads*, and surrender it to some gentlemen of this Committee, if they succeed in their efforts on this occasion. If, indeed, we have the power which is contended for by gentlemen under that clause of the Constitution which relates to the regulation of commerce among the several States, we may, under the same power, *prohibit*, altogether, the commerce between the States, or any portion of the States—or we may declare that it shall be carried on only in a particular way, by a particular road, or through a particular canal; or we may say to the people of a particular district, you shall only carry your produce to market through *our* canals, or over our roads, and then, by tolls, imposed upon them, we may acquire power to extend the same blessings and privileges to other districts of the country. Nay, we may go further. We may take it into our heads—Have we not the power to provide and maintain a navy? What is more necessary to a navy than seamen? And the great nursery of our seamen is (besides fisheries) the coasting trade—we may take it into our heads, that those monstrous lumbering wagons that now traverse the country between Philadelphia and Pittsburg, stand in the way of the raising of seamen, and may declare that no communication shall be held between these points but coastwise; we may specify some particular article in which alone trade shall be carried on. And, sir, if, contrary to all expectation, the ascendency of Virginia, in the General Government, should again be established, it may be declared that coal shall be carried in no other way than coastwise, &c. Sir, there is no end to the purposes that may be effected under such constructions of power. I here beg of gentlemen to recollect—I particularly call upon the very few members of this House, who happen to be interested in the navigation of the river on which I reside, (the Roanoke,) to say, whether, after we have, with many efforts and a great expense, with the loss of at least half of our capital, effected the navigation of that river, it would be competent to this Government to seize upon our feeders, to assume jurisdiction of Lake Drummond, &c., and, for the accomplishment of some wild scheme—not more preposterous and ridiculous than some others I could name—drain the waters of that lake into the Atlantic ocean, and abolish our canal. If we should chance to encounter the displeasure of the Government, under these constructions of power, they may say to every wagoner in North Carolina, you shall not carry on any commerce across the Virginia line, in wagons or carts, because I have some other object to answer, by a suppression of that trade. Are gentlemen prepared for this?

There is one other power, said Mr. R., which may be exercised, in case the power now contended for be conceded, to which I ask the attention of every gentleman who happens to stand in the same unfortunate predicament with myself—of every man who has the misfortune to be, and to have been born, a slaveholder. If Congress possesses the power to do what is proposed by this bill, they may not only enact a sedition law—for there is precedent—but they may emancipate every slave in the United States—and with stronger color of reason than they can exercise the power now contended for. And where will they find the power? They may follow the example of the gentlemen who have preceded me, and hook the power upon the first loop they find in the Constitution; they might take the preamble —perhaps the war making power—or they might take a greater sweep, and say, with some gentlemen, that it is not to be found in this or that of the granted powers, but results from all of them—which is not only a dangerous, but *the most* dangerous doctrine. Was it not demonstrable, Mr. R. asked, that slave labor is the dearest in the world— and that the existence of a large body of slaves is a source of danger? Suppose we are at war with a foreign Power, and freedom should be offered them by Congress as an inducement to them to take a part in it—or suppose the country not at war, at every turn of this federal machine, at every successive census, that interest will find itself governed by another and increasing power, which is bound to it neither by any common tie of interest or feeling. And, if ever the time shall arrive, as assuredly it has arrived elsewhere, and, in all probability, may arrive here, that a coalition of knavery and fanaticism shall, for any purpose, be got up on this floor, I ask gentlemen, who stand in the same predicament as I do, to look well to what they are now doing— to the colossal power with which they are now arming this Government. The power to do what I allude to is, I aver, more honestly inferrible from the war-making power, than the power we are now about to exercise. Let them look forward to the time when such a question shall arise, and tremble with me at the thought that that question is to be decided by a majority of the votes of this House, of whom not one possesses the slightest tie of common interest or of common feeling with us. . . .

Should this bill pass, one more measure only requires to be consummated; and then we, who belong to that unfortunate portion of this Confederacy which is south of Mason and Dixon's line, and east of the Alleghany mountains, have to make up our mind to perish like so many mice in a receiver of mephitic gas, under the experiments of a set of new political chemists; or we must resort to the measures which we first opposed to British aggressions and usurpations—to maintain that independence which the valor of our fathers acquired, but which is every day sliding from under our feet. I beseech all those gentlemen who come from that portion of the Union to take into serious consideration, whether they are not, by the passage of this bill, precipitately, at least without urgent occasion, now arming the General Government with powers hitherto unknown—under which we shall become, what the miserable proprietors of Jamaica and Barbadoes are to their English mortagees, mere stewards—sentinels—managers of slave labor—we ourselves retaining, on a footing with the slave of the West Indies, just enough of the product of our estates to support life, while all the profits go with the course of the Gulf stream. Sir, this is a state of things that cannot last. If it shall continue with accumulated pressure, we must oppose to it associations, and every other means short of actual insurrection. We must begin to construe the Constitution like those who treat it as a bill of indictment, in which they are anxious to pick a flaw—we shall keep on the windward side of treason—but we must combine to resist, and that effectually, these encroachments, or the little upon which we now barely subsist will be taken from us. With these observations, Mr. R. abandoned the question to its fate.

II. The Worker

The Transportation Revolution provided a major stimulus for economic growth. Inevitably, some members of society benefit more from such changes than others. It may be true, as some argue, that all members benefit in the long run, but as New Dealer Harry Hopkins observed, "People don't eat in the long run, they eat every day." Understandably, few who live through periods of great economic change are willing to suffer patiently for an intangible and impersonal future gain, especially those who feel that they bear all the disadvantages of the progress and reap few if any of the rewards. Such thinking permeated the early labor movement of the nineteenth century. Those best able to take advantage of the new markets opened by the canals and railroads celebrated the quantitative changes made possible by the Transportation Revolution, but their positive impact on the American workers was more difficult to articulate. An expanding market economy threatened the worker's status as a craftsman. Prices ruled in the new marketplace, and the temptation was great to cut prices by lowering workers' wages. Trapped in a seemingly impersonal economic arrangement, the worker could only feel that his economic position in society and his psychological well-being were rapidly declining. Organization offered a way to strike back. Although unsuccessful in their attempts to alter society's basic economic relationships, the efforts of labor unions in this period provide one of the most important modifications of the concept of American individualism.

1. AN EARLY LABOR MANIFESTO

The selection which follows typifies labor attitudes in the Age of Jackson. It stresses the injustice done to the laborers, particularly since they, the "industrious classes," produced society's wealth. The choice of language indi-

31

cates a shift in stock Jeffersonian rhetoric employed on behalf of the many to attack the privileged few, especially in the statement's concern with the problems of the growing urban centers. The statement wavered uncertainly between the acceptance of a working-class concept and the hope for final elimination of this necessity. On a less speculative level, the argument's economic assumptions were essentially realistic. The Whig mentality of this period rested upon the assumption of the interdependence and compatibility among economic groups, but Whigs had no monopoly upon this insight as the following statement indicates. The Mechanics' Union spokesman reminded capitalists that their exalted position ultimately rested upon the laborers' ability to purchase goods, and that production without consumption represented no progress, moral or economic. [John R. Commons et al., ed., A Documentary History of American Industrial Society (10 vols., Cleveland, 1910), V: 84–90.]

PREAMBLE OF THE MECHANICS' UNION OF TRADE ASSOCIATIONS

When the disposition and efforts of one part of mankind to oppress another, have become too manifest to be mistaken and too pernicious in their consequences to be endured, it has often been found necessary for those who feel aggrieved, to associate, for the purpose of affording to each other mutual protection from oppression.

We, the Journeymen Mechanics of the City and County of Philadelphia, conscious that our condition in society is lower than justice demands it should be, and feeling our inability, individually, to ward off from ourselves and families those numerous evils which result from an unequal and very excessive accumulation of wealth and power into the hands of a few, are desirous of forming an Association, which shall avert as much as possible those evils with which poverty and incessant toil have already inflicted, and which threaten ultimately to overwhelm and destroy us. And in order that our views may be properly understood, and the justness of our intention duly appreciated, we offer to the public the following summary of our reasons, principles and objects.

If unceasing toils were actually requisite to supply us with a bare, and in many instances wretched, subsistence; if the products of our industry or an equitable proportion of them, were appropriated to our actual wants and comfort, then would we yield without a murmur to the stern and irrevocable decree of necessity. But this is infinitely wide of the fact. We appeal to the most intelligent of every community, and ask—Do not you, and all society, depend solely for subsistence on the products of human industry? Do not those who labour, while acquiring to themselves thereby only a scanty and penurious support, likewise maintain in affluence and luxury the rich who never labour?

Do not all the streams of wealth which flow in every direction and are emptied into and absorbed by the coffers of the unproductive, exclusively take their rise in the bones, marrow, and muscles of the industrious classes? In return for which, exclusive of a bare subsistence, (which likewise is the product of their own industry,) they receive—not any thing! . . .

As freemen and republicans, we feel it a duty incumbent on us to make known our sentiments fearlessly and faithfully on any subject connected with the general welfare; and we are prepared to maintain, that all who toil have a natural and unalienable right to reap the fruits of their own industry; and that they who by labour (the only source) are the authors of every comfort, convenience and luxury, are in justice entitled to an equal participation, not only in the meanest and the coarsest, but likewise the richest and the choicest of them all.

The principles upon which the institution shall be founded, are principles, alike, of the strictest justice, and the most extended philanthropy. Believing that, whatever is conducive to the real prosperity of the greatest numbers, must in the nature of things conduce to the happiness of all; we cannot desire to injure nor take the smallest unjust advantage, either of that class of the community called employers or of any other portion. It is neither our intention nor desire to extort inequitable prices for our labour; all we may demand for this shall not exceed what can be clearly demonstrated to be a fair and full equivalent. If we demand more we wrong the society of which we are members, and if society require us to receive less, she injures and oppresses us.

With respect to the relation existing between employers and the employed, we are prepared, we think, to demonstrate, that it is only through an extremely limited view of their real interests, that the former can be induced to attempt to depreciate the value of human labour. The workman is not more dependent upon his wages for the support of his family than they are upon the demand for the various articles they fabricate or vend. If the mass of the people were enabled by their labour to procure for themselves and families a full and abundant supply of the comforts and conveniences of life, the consumption of articles, particularly of dwellings, furniture and clothing, would amount to at least twice the quantity it does at present, and of course the demand, by which alone employers are enabled either to subsist or accumulate, would likewise be increased in an equal proportion. Each would be enabled to effect twice the quantity of sales or loans which he can effect at present, and the whole industry of a people, consisting of their entire productive powers, whether manual or scientific, together with all their capital, might be put into a full, healthful, and profitable action. The workman need not languish for want of employment, the vender for sales, nor the capitalist complain for want of profitable modes of investment. It is therefore the real interest (for instance) of the Hatter, that every man in the community should be enabled to clothe his own head and those of his family with an abundant supply of the best articles of that description; because the flourishing demand, thereby created, and which depends altogether on the ability of the multitude to purchase, is that which alone enables him to pay his rent and support his family in comfort.

The same may be said with respect to the Tailor, the Shoemaker, the Carpenter, the Cabinetmaker, the Builder, and indeed of every other individual in society, who depends for subsistence or accumulation upon the employment of his skill, his labour, or his capital. All are dependent on the demand which there is for the use of their skill, service, or capital, and the demand must ever be regulated by the ability or inability of the great mass of the people to purchase and consume. If, therefore, as members of the community, they are desirous to prosper, in vain will they expect to succeed, unless the great body of the community is kept in a healthy, vigorous and prosperous condition.

No greater error exists in the world than the notion that society will be benefited by deprecating the value of human labour. Let this principle (as at this day in England) be carried towards its full extent, and it is in vain that scientific power shall pour forth its inexhaustible treasures of wealth upon the world. Its products will all be amassed to glut the over-flowing storehouses, and useless hoards of its insatiable monopolizers; while the mechanic and productive classes, who constitute the great mass of the population, and who have wielded the power and laboured in the production of this immense abundance, having no other resource for subsistence than what they derive from the miserable pittance, which they are compelled by competition to receive in exchange for their inestimable labour, must first begin to pine, languish, and suffer under its destructive and withering influence. But the evil stops not here. The middling classes next, venders of the products of human industry, will begin to experience its deleterious effects. The demand for their articles must necessarily cease from the forced inability of the people to consume: trade must in consequence languish, and losses and failures become the order of the day. At last the contagion will reach the capitalist, throned as he is, in the midst of his ill gotten abundance, and his capital, from the most evident and certain causes, will become useless, unemployed and stagnant, himself the trembling victim of continual alarms from robberies, burnings, and murder, the unhappy and perhaps ill fated object of innumerable imprecations, insults and implacable hatred from the wronged, impoverished, and despairing multitude. The experience of the most commercial parts of the world sufficiently demonstrates that this is the natural, inevitable, and, shall we not say, righteous consequences of a principle, whose origin is injustice and an unrighteous depreciation of the value and abstraction of the products of human labour—a principle which in its ultimate effects, must be productive of universal ruin and misery, and destroy alike the happiness of every class and individual in society.

The real object, therefore, of this association, is to avert, if possible, the desolating evils which must inevitably arise from a depreciation of the intrinsic value of human labour; to raise the mechanical and productive classes to that condition of true independence and in-equality [sic] which their practical skill and ingenuity, their immense utility to the nation and their growing intelligence are beginning imperiously to demand: to promote, equally, the happiness, prosperity and welfare of the whole community—to aid in conferring a due and full proportion of that invaluable promoter of happiness, leisure, upon all its useful members; and to assist, in conjunction with such other institutions of this nature as shall hereafter be formed through-out the union, in establishing a just balance of power, both mental, moral, political and scientific, between all the various classes and in-dividuals which constitute society at large.

2. THE ANTILABOR MENTALITY

Organized labor had to fight widespread prejudice and hurdle legal barriers in order to gain recognition of its right to exist. In the 1820s and early 1830s, employers seeking to crush union activity got help from courts which branded unions illegal combinations in restraint of trade —conspiracies under common law. In addition to such heavy-handed repression, the employers and their spokes-men argued that unionization would impede progress and the betterment of all.

The following editorial from the New York Journal of Commerce in 1833 briefly stated the general arguments used against union activity. These associations were in-stigated by the most inferior and least ambitious crafts-men and consequently, if successful, they would bring all men in the trade down to the lowest level. By contrast a natural order of things allowed excellence to rise to the top. So ran the argument, and it generally prevailed in an era of nascent unionization, economic expansion, and great social mobility. Big Labor's rise would have to wait many decades until American industrialism dominated the country's entire economic process, but the individualistic arguments, like those of the Journal of Commerce, continued to act as a brake on collective action by labor and still influence American social thought. [Commons et al., A Documentary History of American Industrial Society, V: 209–11.]

THE AMERICAN SYSTEM AMONG THE JOURNEYMEN

We see by notices in the papers, that the Journeymen of various other branches of business are rallying to sustain the Carpenters. Well, their cause is as good and worthy of support as the combinations for the same purpose in any other occupation. Just as good as the combinations, where they exist, among lawyers, or doctors, or merchants, or manufacturers, or newspaper editors, or any body else. Yet we apprehend that many will condemn the combination of Journeymen, who think it very right for employers to combine to keep up the prices of their commodities, or even to keep down the price of labor. But according to our notions of the obligations of society, all combinations to compel others to give a higher price or take a lower one, are not only inexpedient, but at war with the order of things which the Creator has established for the general good, and therefore wicked. . . .

The means resorted to, to cement and sustain the combinations, whether they are simple individual pledges, or legislative enactments, or menaces and violence, are all wrong, and in spirit equally so. The plans of each class have their distinctive evil features. The combinations of journeymen and others whose income is from labor, are characterised with less craft and studied plot, but with more of direct appeals to force or fear. Disguise it as the associates may, no such combination is sustained but by threats at least. There will always be a large number who are indisposed for the combination. These will keep up the operations of the trade, and unless forced into the ranks, render the combination abortive. It is surprising how such persons are deprived of their self possession, and drawn into the general league. The principal threat is, that the combinants will never again permit those who do not join them, to have employment. The expedient to accomplish this, is the same to which the doctors and lawyers resort for the same purpose, viz, that the combinants will never consult—work with one who is not of their number. . . .

Combinations among journeymen are usually set on foot by the dissolute, improvident, and therefore restless; and in the outset chiefly sustained by the second and third rate class of hands. There is one thing about this infatuation at which we confess our astonishment. It is, that prime hands so readily enter into combinations for a general average of price. It is a partnership in which some put in capital and others bankruptcy, yet all are to take out and share alike. Men whose wages would go up to the desired point, if they would but go upon their own merits, consent to stand in the attitude of lifting up the unworthy, though they sink themselves proportionably.

Turn-outs are always miserably profitless jobs. If they are successful they cannot in the long run benefit the class whose wages are raised; for the diminution in the quantity of occupation and the increased number of labourers drawn to the spot, will more than compensate for all the gains. If a day's work receives a higher reward, that advantage will be more than counterbalanced by days spent in idleness for want of occupation. The journeymen carpenters, now, in a harvest time, when all hands were employed, have turned out for an additional shilling. For this, they throw away the certainty of eleven shillings. They have stood out some twenty days, so that their certain loss is is already more than equal to the gain they demand, upon six months labor: and they are in no little danger of being displaced altogether by workmen who are coming in from surrounding places, and who, not being acquaintances of the turn-outs, are effectually beyond the reach of their influence. To the master-carpenters, we repeat what we said some days ago, that it is their duty, and the duty of all good citizens, to set their faces like a flint against all such combinations.

3. A EUROPEAN OBSERVER AND THE LOWELL "MIRACLE"

The "grand tour" of foreign visitors to pre-Civil War America usually included inspections of schools, plantations, legislatures, prisons, and, by Jackson's time, a manufacturing town. The selection below is from Michael Chevalier's 1834 description of Lowell, Massachusetts, an early cotton manufacturing center distinguished for its employment of young women—the famous Lowell girls. Chevalier opened with a near poetic description of the town and admiration for the profit-seeking energies of the merchants who established Lowell. His reveries were cut

short, however, by the fear that American manufacturing
would ultimately produce the same miseries he had witnessed in Europe. These doubts were stilled by Chevalier's
confidence that the wage system could not lead to the degradation of the American worker; the abundance of land
would save America from class war and social revolution.
[Michael Chevalier, Society, Manners and Politics in the
United States (Boston, 1839), 128–29, 131, 133, 140,
142–44.]

The town of Lowell dates its origin eleven years ago, and it now
contains 15,000 inhabitants, inclusive of the suburb of Belvedere.
Twelve years ago it was a barren waste, in which the silence was in-
terrupted only by the murmur of the little river of Concord, and the
noisy dashings of the clear waters of the Merrimac, against the granite
blocks that suddenly obstruct their course. At present, it is a pile of
huge factories, each five, six, or seven stories high, and capped with
a little white belfry, which strongly contrasts with the red masonry of
the building, and is distinctly projected on the dark hills in the horizon.
By the side of these larger structures rise numerous little wooden
houses, painted white, with green blinds, very neat, very snug, very
nicely carpeted, and with a few small trees around them, or brick
houses in the English style, that is to say, simple, but tasteful without
and comfortable within; on one side, fancy-goods shops and milliners'
rooms without number, for the women are the majority in Lowell, and
vast hotels in the American style, very much like barracks (the only
barracks in Lowell); on another, canals, water-wheels, water-falls,
bridges, banks, schools, and libraries, for in Lowell reading is the only
recreation, and there are no less than seven journals printed here. All
around are churches and meeting-houses of every sect, Episcopalian,
Baptist, Congregationalist, Methodist, Universalist, Unitarian, &c., and
there is also a Roman Catholic chapel. Here are all the edifices of a
flourishing town in the Old World, except the prisons, hospitals, and
theatres; everywhere is heard the noise of hammers, of spindles, of
bells calling the hands to their work, or dismissing them from their
tasks, of coaches and six arriving or starting off, of the blowing of
rocks to make a mill-race or to level a road; it is the peaceful hum
of an industrious population, whose movements are regulated like
clockwork; a population not native to the town, and one half of which
at least will die elsewhere, afer having aided in founding three or four
other towns; for the full-blooded American has this in common with
the Tartar, that he is encamped, not established, on the soil he treads
upon. . . .
Such is Lowell. Its name is derived from that of a Boston merchant,

who was one of the first promoters of the cotton-manufacture in the United States. It is not like one of our European towns that was built by some demi-god, a son of Jupiter, or by some hero of the Trojan war, or by the genius of an Alexander or a Cæsar, or by some saint, attracting crowds by his miracles, or by the whim of some great sovereign, like Louis XIV or Frederic, or by an edict of Peter the Great. It was neither a pious foundation, nor an asylum for fugitives, nor a military post; but it is one of the speculations of the merchants of Boston. The same spirit of enterprise, which a year ago suggested the idea of sending a cargo of ice from Boston to Calcutta round Cape Horn, to cool the drink of Lord William Bentinck and the nabobs of the India company, has led them to build up a town here, wholly at their own expense, with all the buildings required by the wants of a civilised community, in order to be able to manufacture white cottons and calicoes; and they have succeeded, as they always succeed in their speculations. The semi-annual dividends of the manufacturing companies in Lowell, are generally from 5 to 6 per cent. . . .

. . . On arriving at Lowell, the first impression of pleasure caused by the sight of the town, new and fresh like an opera scene, fades away before the melancholy reflection, will this become like Lancashire? Does this brilliant glare hide the misery and suffering of operatives, and those degrading vices, engendered by poverty in the manufacturing towns, drunkenness and prostitution, popular sedition hanging over the heads of the rich by a frail thread, which an ordinary accident, and slight imprudence, or a breath of the bad passions, would snap asunder? This question I hasten to answer. . . .

The manufacturing companies exercise the most careful supervision over these girls. I have already said, that, twelve years ago, Lowell did not exist; when, therefore, the manufactories were set up, it also became necessary to provide lodgings for the operatives, and each company has built for this purpose a number of houses within its own limits, to be used exclusively as boarding-houses for them. Here they are under the care of the mistress of the house, who is paid by the company at the rate of one dollar and a quarter a week for each boarder, that sum being stopped out of the weekly wages of the girls. These housekeepers, who are generally widows, are each responsible for the conduct of her boarders, and they are themselves subject to the control and supervision of the company, in the management of their little communities. Each company has its rules and regulations, which are not merely paper-laws, but which are carried into execution with all that spirit of vigilant perseverance that characterises the Yankee. . . .

These regulations, which amongst us would excite a thousand objections and would be in fact impracticable, are here regarded as the most simple and natural thing in the world; they are enforced without opposition or difficulty. Thus in regard to Sunday, for instance, which with us is a holiday, a day of amusement and gaiety, it is here a day of retirement, meditation, silence, and prayer. This is one of the features in which the French type most strongly contrasts with the Anglo-American. In a moral and religious point of view, there prevail among us a laxity and a toleration, which form a counterpart to the American *let-alone* principle in political matters; whilst the principle of political authority, which has always been established in great vigour among us, under all forms of government, monarchy, empire, or republic, corresponds to the austere reserve of American manners, to their rigid habits of life, and to the religious severity which exists here by the side of the great multiplicity of sects. So true is it, that both order and liberty are essential to human nature, and that it is impossible to establish a society on one of these principles alone! If you abandon a portion of the social institutions exclusively to the spirit of liberty, be assured that the principle of order will take no less exclusive possession of some other portion. Yield up to liberty the whole field of politics, and you are compelled to give religion and manners wholly up to order. Leave manners and religion to liberty, and you find yourself obliged to strengthen the principle of order in politics, under pain of suffering society itself to fall into ruins. Such are the general laws of equilibrium which govern the nations and the universe of worlds.

Up to this time, then, the rules of the companies have been observed. Lowell, with its steeple-crowned factories, resembles a Spanish town with its convents; but with this difference, that in Lowell, you meet no rags nor Madonnas, and that the nuns of Lowell, instead of working *sacred hearts*, spin and weave cotton. Lowell is not amusing, but it is neat, decent, peaceable, and sage. Will it always be so? Will it be so long? It would be rash to affirm it; hitherto the life of manufacturing operatives has proved little favorable to the preservation of severe morals. . . . But as there is a close connexion between morality and competence, it may be considered very probable, that while the wages shall continue to be high at Lowell, the influences of a good education, a sense of duty, and the fear of public opinion, will be sufficient to maintain good morals. . . . In Europe, work is often wanting for the hands; here, on the other side, hands are wanting for the work. While the Americans have the vast domain in the West, a common fund, from which, by industry, each may draw for himself and by himself, an ample heritage, an extreme fall of wages is not to be apprehended.

4. AN AMERICAN RADICAL

Despite the enthusiasm and zeal of sympathetic historians, the ranks of accepted American radicals remain remarkably thin. Of course, what may appear radical at an earlier time may seem only quaint to the modern eye, and historians have recently cast doubt upon the credentials of many alleged radicals of the American past. Whether cast as radical or reactionary, Orestes Brownson remains one of the most arresting commentators on the political economy of pre-Civil War America. New England intellectual, Jacksonian partisan and pamphleteer, and finally convert to Roman Catholicism, Brownson searched passionately for a sense of community and attacked many forms of inequality. Selections from one of his most celebrated essays, "The Laboring Classes," published as campaign material in 1840, appear below. The essay is as interesting for what Brownson rejects as for the solutions he offers for the uplifting of the American worker. Decidedly more pessimistic than Chevalier, Brownson dismissed the concept of abundant land as a "safety valve." He also attacked the idea of mobility and progress through hard work, an important item of faith for most Americans, and the belief in individual character regeneration, a favored idea among New England Transcendentalists. Scorning these "remedies," Brownson asserted that unless the government redressed the balance of power in American society all hope of maintaining social order peaceably would vanish. [Boston Quarterly Review, III (July, October, 1840): 372–73, 391–93, 460, 467–68, 477, 480–81, 506–8.]

The actual condition of the workingman to-day, viewed in all its bearings, is not so good as it was fifty years ago. If we have not been altogether misinformed, fifty years ago, health and industrious habits, constituted no mean stock in trade, and with them almost any man might aspire to competence and independence. But it is so no longer. The wilderness has receded, and already the new lands are beyond the reach of the mere laborer, and the employer has him at his mercy. If the present relation subsist, we see nothing better for him in reserve than what he now possesses, but something altogether worse.

We are not ignorant of the fact that men born poor become wealthy, and that men born to wealth become poor; but this fact does not necessarily diminish the numbers of the poor, nor augment the numbers of the rich. The relative numbers of the two classes remain, or may remain, the same. But be this as it may; one fact is certain, no man born poor has ever, by his wages, as a simple operative, risen to the class of the wealthy. Rich he may have become, but it has not been by his own manual labor. He has in some way contrived to tax for his benefit the labor of others. . . .

Now the great work for this age and the coming, is to raise up the laborer, and to realize in our own social arrangements and in the actual condition of all men, that equality between man and man, which God has established between the rights of one and those of another. In other words, our business is to emancipate the proletaries, as the past has emancipated the slaves. This is our work. . . .

Reformers in general . . . would have all men wise, good, and happy; but in order to make them so, they tell us that we want not external changes, but internal; and therefore instead of declaiming against society and seeking to disturb existing social arrangements, we should confine ourselves to the individual reason and conscience; seek merely to lead the individual to repentance, and to reformation of life; make the individual a practical, a truly religious man, and all evils will either disappear, or be sanctified to the spiritual growth of the soul. . . .

Now the evils of which we have complained are of a social nature. That is, they have their root in the constitution of society as it is, and they have attained to their present growth by means of social influences, the action of government, of laws, and of systems and institutions upheld by society, and of which individuals are the slaves. This being the case, it is evident that they are to be removed only by the action of society, that is, by government, for the action of society is government.

. . . We have no faith in those systems of elevating the working classes, which propose to elevate them without calling in the aid of the government. We must have government, and legislation expressly directed to this end.

. . . We want first the legislation which shall free the government, whether State or Federal, from the control of the Banks. The Banks represent the interest of the employer, and therefore of necessity interests adverse to those of the employed; that is, they represent the interests of the business community in opposition to the laboring community. So long as the government remains under the control of the Banks, so long it must be in the hands of the natural enemies of the laboring classes, and may be made, nay, will be made, an instrument of depressing them yet lower. It is obvious then that, if our object be the elevation of the laboring classes, we must destroy the power of the Banks over the government, and place the government in the hands of the laboring classes themselves, or in the hands of those, if such there be, who have an identity of interest with them. . . .

Following the distruction of the Banks, must come that of all monopolies, of all PRIVILEGE. There are many of these. We cannot specify them all; we therefore select only one, the greatest of them all, the privilege which some have of being born rich while others are born poor. It will be seen at once that we allude to the hereditary descent of property, an anomaly in our American system, which must be removed, or the system itself will be destroyed. . . .

We are not ignorant that there is a class of our fellow citizens, who stare at us as if we were out of our wits, or possessed of no ordinary malignancy, when we represent the workingman as still a slave, and demand his enfranchisement. In their estimation he is already enfranchised, already a free man, in the full significance of the term; and no more dependent on the capitalist, than the capitalist is on him. . . .

We have never pretended that the proletary is no advance on the slave; he is in advance of the slave; for his rights as a man are legally recognised, though not in fact enjoyed; for he is nearer the day of his complete enfranchisement, and has a greater moral force and more instruments with which to effect it. It is only on the supposition that one or the other is to be a permanent system, that we have given the preference to the slave system over that of labor at wages. We however oppose with all our might both systems. We would have neither the slave nor the proletary. We would combine labor and capital in the same individual. What we object to, is the division of society into two classes, of which one class owns the capital, and the other performs the labor. If, however, this division must always take place, we prefer the slave system which prevails at the South, to the free labor system which prevails here at the North. . . .

Why is it, we would ask, that so few of the real workingmen here are abolitionists? Why do they interest themselves so little in the freedom of the negro slave? It is because they feel that they themselves are virtually slaves, while mocked with the name of freemen, and that the movements in behalf of freedom should be first directed towards their emancipation. . . .

With this view of the case, it becomes necessary to seek something more ultimate, more radical than our most approved reformers have as yet ventured upon. . . .

The doctrine we have long labored to maintain is, that the work of this country is to emancipate labor, by raising up the laborer from a mere workman, without capital, to be a proprietor, and a workman on his own farm, or in his own shop. Those who have read our writings, or listened to our public lectures and addresses, must have perceived this. In maintaining this doctrine, we have been seconded by not a few. We have been censured for it by no party, and by no individuals, save a few who have never accepted the doctrine, that all men are born with equal rights. . . .

. . . What in one word is this American system? Is it not the abolition of all artificial distinctions, all social advantages founded on birth or any other accident, and leaving every man to stand on his own feet, for precisely what God and nature have made him? Does not this system declare that society should make no distinction between the child of the rich man and the child of the poor man; that she shall neither reward the child for the virtues, nor punish him for the vices of the parent? Is this the American system, yes or no? If it be not, what mean all our boasts of equality, all our Fourth of July oratory, all our patriotic songs and national glorifications? . . .

But property we are told is a sacred institution. Touch it and you throw everything into confusion, cut society loose from all its old fastenings, and send us all back to the savage state, to live by plundering and devouring one another. So said the defenders of hereditary monarchy, of hereditary nobility, of an hereditary priesthood, of primogeniture and entail. Yet society survives, and, for aught we can see, looks as likely for a long life as ever it did. Now, for ourselves, we are not quite so squeamish on this subject as some others are. We believe property should be held subordinate to man, and not man to property; and therefore that it is always lawful to make such modifications of its constitution as the good of Humanity requires. . . .

With regard to physical force, we have not much to say. We see an immense system of wrong everywhere established, and everywhere upheld. This system is the growth of a hundred ages, and is venerable in the eyes of many; but it must be overthrown. Man must be free, and SHALL be free,—free to develop his lofty and deathless nature, and prove himself a child of God. This is in his destiny. But how can he become thus free? How can the huge system of accumulated wrongs, under which he now groans, be overthrown, and a new and better system introduced and established? Peaceably? We would fain hope so; but we fear not. . . .

The Past has always stood in the gate, and forbid the Future to enter; and it has been only in mortal encounter, that the Future has as yet ever been able to force its entrance. It may be different in the future; we hope it will be. We would rather be found, on this subject, a false prophet than a true one. But we fear the age of peace has not yet dawned. Commerce has indeed spread her meshes all over the world, but she cannot hold it quiet. We need but glance at Europe, Asia, Africa, and even our own country, at the present moment, to see that no permanent peace has as yet been established. Everywhere are warlike preparations going on, and our speculators are already beginning to count on their means of turning the coming contest to their own profit. If a general war should now break out, it will involve all quarters of the globe, and it will be in the end more than a war between nations. It will resolve itself into a social war, a war between two social elements; between the aristocracy and the democracy, between the people and their masters. It will be a terrible war! . . . But the war, if it comes, will not be brought about by reformers, but by conservatives, in order to keep the people out of their rights; and on the heads of conservatives, then, must fall the blame.

III. Religion

From the Massachusetts Bay founders of the Puritan "city upon a hill" to more modern crusades, Americans have chosen to interpret their communal efforts in moralistic terms. Nineteenth-century American values still officially emanated from the pulpit, although clerical power had begun to slip to the pew. The religion of the common man of Jackson's day reflected the democratization taking place in all aspects of American life. In 1800 religious orthodoxy was concentrated in sophisticated, aristocratic communities along the eastern seaboard. The religious establishment was overly concerned, many thought, about the doctrine of original sin and emphasis upon man's helplessness and culpability. Other ministers increasingly noticed the indifference of the expanding population to religious practice in America and called for a great crusade to make the church more relevant to American experience. These "liberal" ministers offered a more optimistic and flattering conception of man than strict Calvinist doctrine. Some of them provoked a controversy within American Protestantism by using methods and techniques considered irreligious by their more conservative brethren. But these revivalists, the new-style ministers, pointed to their success in terms of the numbers who came to hear them and avoided any excessive concern with the intelligence or sophistication of church doctrine. What mattered was what appealed to the greatest number. This section indicates the changes in American religion during the Jacksonian era which narrowed the gap between the next world and this and democratized hopes for salvation.

1. THE UNITARIAN SUNRISE: WILLIAM ELLERY CHANNING

A significant break with orthodox Calvinism came with the Unitarian movement. Unitarians wanted to bring

46

more humanity into religion and emphasize man's potential rather than his damnation. The loose organization of American Protestantism allowed new ideas to infiltrate into various congregations, and no man did more to undermine orthodox Calvinism than William Ellery Channing, minister of Boston's Federal Street Church from 1803 until his death in 1842.

The general drift of American Christianity toward modernity revolved around altered perceptions of God and man. The selections below from one of Channing's sermons indicates the nature of these alterations. Unitarians emphasized God's goodness, the perfectibility of man, his free will and individual responsibility. These ideas, of course, were never entirely unknown in the Christian experience, but their emphasis at this time coincided with a changed American experience that made them more realistic and workable. Although charged with all sorts of heresies by their more conservative brethren, the Unitarians did not reject authority but stressed the intuitive knowledge of moral conscience, or what Channing termed the "inward monitor." This emphasis upon the intuitive over the colder, more formalistic reason was developed by George Bancroft, political theoretician of Jacksonianism, into a celebrated defense of the Democratic faith. While Channing avoided party politics, the ideas he expressed formed the basis for the New Politics of Jackson's day. [The Works of William Ellery Channing (*Boston, 1886*), *109–13, 115, 120–21.*]

Among the many and inestimable blessings of Christianity, I regard as not the least the new sentiment with which it teaches man to look upon his fellow beings; the new interest which it awakens in us toward everything human; the new importance which it gives to the soul; the new relation which it establishes between man and man. In this respect it began a mighty revolution, which has been silently spreading itself through society, and which, I believe, is not to stop until new ties shall have taken the place of those which have hitherto, in the main, connected the human race. Christianity has as yet but begun its work of reformation. Under its influences a new order of society is advancing, surely though slowly; and this beneficent change it is to accomplish in no small measure by revealing to men their own nature, and teaching them to "honor all" who partake it.

As yet Christianity has done little, compared with what it is to do, in establishing the true bond of union between man and man. The old bonds of society still continue in a great degree. They are instinct, interest, force. The true tie, which is mutual respect, calling forth mutual, growing, never-failing acts of love, is as yet little known. A new revelation, if I may so speak, remains to be made; or rather, the truths of the old revelation in regard to the greatness of human nature are to be brought out from obscurity and neglect. The soul is to be regarded with a religious reverence hitherto unfelt; and the solemn claims of every being to whom this divine principle is imparted are to be established on the ruins of those pernicious principles, both in church and state, which have so long divided mankind into the classes of the abject many and the self-exalting few.

There is nothing of which men know so little as themselves. They understand incomparably more of the surrounding creation, of matter and of its laws, than of that spiritual principle to which matter was made to be the minister, and without which the outward universe would be worthless. . . . Men have as yet no just respect for themselves, and of consequence no just respect for others. The true bond of society is thus wanting; and accordingly there is a great deficiency of Christian benevolence. There is, indeed, much instinctive, native benevolence, and this is not to be despised; but the benevolence of Jesus Christ, which consists in a calm purpose to suffer and, if need be, to die, for our fellow creatures, the benevolence of Christ on the cross, which is the true pattern to the Christian, this is little known; and what is the cause? It is this. We see nothing in human beings to entitle them to such sacrifices; we do not think them worth suffering for. Why should we be martyrs for beings who awaken in us little more of moral interest than the brutes?

I hold that nothing is to make man a true lover of man but the discovery of something interesting and great in human nature. We must see and feel that a human being is something important, and of immeasurable importance. We must see and feel the broad distance between the spiritual life within us and the vegetable or animal life which acts around us. I cannot love the flower, however beautiful, with a disinterested affection which will make me sacrifice to it my own prosperity. . . .

To show the grounds on which the obligation to honor all men rests, I might take a minute survey of that human nature which is common to all, and set forth its claims to reverence. But, leaving this wide range, I observe that there is one principle of the soul which makes all men essentially equal, which places all on a level as to means of happiness, which may place in the first rank of human beings those who are the most depressed in worldly condition, and which therefore gives the most depressed a title to interest and respect. I refer to the sense of duty, to the power of discerning and doing right, to the moral and religious principle, to the inward monitor which speaks in the name of God, to the capacity of virtue or excellence. This is the great gift of God. We can conceive no greater. In seraph and archangel, we can conceive no higher energy than the power of virtue, or the power of forming themselves after the will and moral perfections of God. This power breaks down all barriers between the seraph and the lowest human being; it makes them brethren. Whoever has derived from God this perception and capacity of rectitude has a bond of union with the spiritual world stronger than all the ties of nature. He possesses a principle which, if he is faithful to it, must carry him forward forever, and insures to him the improvement and happiness of the highest order of beings. . . .

Having shown, in the preceding remarks, that there is a foundation in the human soul for the honor enjoined in our text toward all men, I proceed to observe that, if we look next into Christianity, we shall find this duty enforced by new and still more solemn considerations. This whole religion is a testimony to the worth of man in the sight of God, to the importance of human nature, to the infinite purposes for which we were framed. God is there set forth as sending to the succor of his human family his Beloved Son, the bright image and representative of his own perfections; and sending him, not simply to roll away a burden of pain and punishment (for this, however magnified in systems of theology, is not his highest work), but to create men after that divine image which he himself bears, to purify the soul from every stain, to communicate to it new power over evil, and to open before it immortality as its aim and destination—immortality, by which we are to understand, not merely a perpetual, but an ever-improving and celestial being. Such are the views of Christianity. And these blessings it proffers, not to a few, not to the educated, not to the eminent, but to all human beings, to the poorest and the most fallen; and we know that, through the power of its promises, it has in not a few instances raised the most fallen to true greatness, and given them in their present virtue and peace an earnest of the Heaven which it unfolds. Such is Christianity. Men, viewed in the light of this religion, are beings cared for by God, to whom he has given his Son, on whom he pours forth his Spirit, and whom he has created for the highest good in the universe, for participation in his own perfections and happiness. My friends, such is Christianity. Our skepticism as to our own nature cannot quench the bright light which that religion sheds on the soul and on the prospects of mankind; and just as far as we receive its truth, we shall honor all men. . . .

. . . I would only say, "Honor all men." Honor man, from the beginning to the end of his earthly course. Honor the child. Welcome into being the infant with a feeling of its mysterious grandeur, with the feeling that an immortal existence has begun, that a spirit has been kindled which is never to be quenched. Honor the child. On this principle all good education rests. Never shall we learn to train up the child till we take it in our arms, as Jesus did, and feel distinctly that "of such is the kingdom of heaven." In that short sentence is taught the spirit of the true system of education; and for want of understanding it, little effectual aid, I fear, is yet given to the heavenly principle in the infant soul.—Again. Honor the poor. This sentiment of respect is essential to improving the connection between the more and less prosperous conditions of society. This alone makes beneficence truly godlike. Without it, almsgiving degrades the receiver. We must learn how slight and shadowy are the distinctions between us and the poor; and that the last in outward condition may be first in the best attributes of humanity. . . .

. . . The great revelation which man now needs is a revelation of man to himself. The faith which is most wanted is a faith in what we and our fellow beings may become—a faith in the divine germ or principle in every soul. In regard to most of what are called the mysteries of religion, we may innocently be ignorant. But the mystery within ourselves, the mystery of our spiritual, accountable, immortal nature, it behooves us to explore. Happy are they who have begun to penetrate it, and in whom it has awakened feelings of awe toward themselves, and of deep interest and honor toward their fellow creatures.

2. THE REVIVALIST CAMPFIRE:
CHARLES G. FINNEY

Channing's humanitarianism and disinterested benevolence were most zealously advanced by a group of young ministers, most notably Charles Grandison Finney. Finney directed a crusade which swept through sections of western New York, soon dubbed the Burned-Over District because of the religious excitement. Finney supported the emotionalism of revival meetings, often sustained for days, saying that the excitement brought one closer to God. He defended the excitement of revivalist preaching and other new methods introduced—the protracted meetings, use of young "uneducated" laymen as preachers, and the "anxious Seat" (where the near-converted could move up front directly below the pulpit when he felt ready for conversion). Channing may not have recognized the "inward monitor" under the revivalist tent, but among the multitudes who flocked to hear preachers like Finney were many who were certain of God's presence. [Charles G. Finney, Revivals of Religion (Westwood, N.J., 1962), 201, 204–6, 210–11, 214–15, 308–13.]

Ministers ought to know *what measures* are best calculated to aid in accomplishing the great end of their office, the salvation of souls. Some measures are plainly necessary. . . .

What do politicians do? They get up meetings, circulate handbills and pamphlets, blaze away in the newspapers, send ships about the streets on wheels with flags and sailors, send conveyances all over the town, with handbills, to bring people up to the polls—all to gain attention to their cause, and elect their candidate. . . . The object is to get up an excitement, and bring the people out. They know that unless there can be an excitement it is in vain to push their end. I do not mean to say that their measures are pious, or right, but only that they are wise, in the sense that they are the appropriate application of means to the end. . . .

Take the case of a physician. The greatest quack may now and then stumble upon a remarkable cure, and so get his name up with the the ignorant. But sober and judicious people judge of the skill of a physician by the *uniformity* of his success in overcoming disease, the variety of diseases he can manage, and the number of cases in which he is successful in saving his patients. The most skilful saves the most. . . . And it is just as true in regard to success in saving souls, and true in just the same sense. . . .

Success in saving souls is evidence that a man *understands the Gospel,* and understands human nature; that he knows how to adapt means to his end; that he has common sense, and that kind of tact, that practical discernment, to know how to get at people. And if his success is extensive, it shows that he knows how to deal, in a great variety of circumstances, with a great variety of characters, who are all the enemies of God, and to bring them to Christ. To do this requires great wisdom. And the minister who does it shows that he is wise. . . .

A *want of common sense* often defeats the ends of the Christian ministry. There are many good men in the ministry, who have learning, and talents of a certain sort, but they have no common sense to win souls.

We see one great defect in our theological schools. Young men are confined to books, and shut out from intercourse with the *common people,* or contact with the common mind. Hence they are not familiar with the mode in which common people think. This accounts for the fact that some plain men, who have been brought up to business, and are acquainted with human nature, are ten times better qualified to win souls than those who are educated on the present principle, and are in fact ten times as well acquainted with the proper business of the ministry. These are called "uneducated men." This is a grand mistake. They are not learned in science, but they are learned in the very things which they need to know *as ministers.* They are not ignorant

ministers, for they know exactly how to reach the mind with truth.
They are better furnished *for their work*, than if they had all the
machinery of the schools.

I wish to be understood. I do not say, that I would not have a young
man go to school. Nor would I discourage him from going over the
field of science. The more the better, if together with it he learns also
the things that the minister needs to know, in order to win souls—
if he understands his Bible, and understands human nature, and knows
how to bring the truth to bear, and how to guide and manage minds,
and to lead them away from sin and lead them to God. . . .

I suppose I shall be reproached for saying this. But it is too true
and too painful to be concealed. Those fathers who have the training of
our young ministers are good men, but they are ancient men, men
of another age and stamp from what is needed in these days, when
the Church and world are rising to new thought and action. . . . [U]n-
less our theological professors preach a good deal, mingle much with
the Church, and sympathise with her in all her movements, it is
morally, if not naturally, impossible, that they should succeed in training young men to the spirit of the age. It is a shame and a sin, that
theological professors, who preach but seldom, who are withdrawn
from the active duties of the ministry, should sit in their studies and
write their letters, advisory or dictatorial, to ministers and Churches
who are in the field, and who are in circumstances to judge what
needs to be done. . . .

It is truly astonishing that grave ministers should really feel alarmed
at the new measures of the present day, as if new measures were something new under the sun, and as if the present form and manner of
doing things had descended from the apostles, and were established
by a "Thus saith the Lord"; when the truth is, that every step of the
Church's advance from the gross darkness of Popery, has been through
the introduction of one new measure after another. . . .

Without new measures it is impossible that the Church should succeed in gaining the attention of the world to religion. There are so
many exciting subjects constantly brought before the public mind . . .
that the Church cannot maintain her ground without sufficient novelty
in measures, to get the public ear. The measures of politicians, of in-
fidels, and heretics, the scrambling after wealth, the increase of luxury,
and the ten thousand exciting and counteracting influences that bear
upon the Church and upon the world, will gain men's attention, and
turn them away from the sanctuary and from the altars of the Lord,
unless we increase in wisdom and piety, and wisely adopt such new
measures as are calculated to get the attention of men to the Gospel of
Christ. . . . [N]ew measures we must have. And may God prevent the

Church from settling down in any set of forms, or getting the present or any other edition of her measures *stereotyped*. . . .

We see the importance of having *young ministers obtain right views of revivals*. In a multitude of cases I have seen that great pains are taken to frighten our young men, who are preparing for the ministry, about "the evils of revivals," and the like. Young men in some theological seminaries are taught to look upon new measures as if they were the very inventions of the devil. How can such men have revivals? So when they come out, they look about and watch, and start, as if the devil were there. Some young men in Princeton a few years ago came out with an essay upon the "Evils of Revivals." I should like to know, now, how many of those young men have *enjoyed* revivals among their people, since they have been in the ministry; and if any have, I should like to know whether they have not repented of that piece about "the evils of revivals"? . . .

. . . Must we educate young men for the ministry, and have them come out frightened to death about new measures? They ought to know that new measures are no new thing in the Church. Let them go to work, and keep at work, and not be frightened. I have been pained to see that some men, in giving accounts of revivals, have evidently felt it necessary to be particular in detailing the measures used, to avoid the inference that *new* measures were introduced; evidently feeling that even the Church would undervalue the revival unless it appeared to have been promoted without new measures. . . .

. . . The fact is that God has established, in no Church, any particular *form*, or manner of worship, for promoting the interests of religion. The Scriptures are entirely silent on these subjects, under the Gospel dispensation, and the Church is left to exercise her own discretion in relation to all such matters. . . .

The only thing insisted upon under the Gospel dispensation, in regard to measures, is that there should be *decency and order*. . . . Will it be said that an anxious meeting, or a protracted meeting, or an anxious seat, is inconsistent with decency and order? I should most sincerely deprecate, and most firmly resist, whatever was indecent and disorderly in the worship of God's house. But I do not suppose that by "order," we are to understand any particular set mode, in which any Church may have been accustomed to perform its service.

3. A CONSERVATIVE INDICTMENT: FRANCIS LIEBER

The value of religion to some is that it acts to internalize moral restraints, thereby moderating man's allegedly

antisocial nature. The emphasis upon man's perfectibility
and goodness threatened these restraints, and many conservatives worried over the consequences of the common
man being "churched" in the Finney style. An interesting
description and indictment of a Methodist camp meeting
survives in the form of an 1835 account by Francis Lieber.
German-born, conservative, and a professor of history and
political economy at the University of South Carolina,
Lieber cast a disapproving eye on revivals. Suspicious of
the sincerity of the participants and worried about the
effect of the excitement upon them, Lieber's account is
part of that American tradition which was puzzled, fas-
cinated, and a bit shocked by the deep cultural changes
going on around them. Lieber concludes by attributing the
religious excitement to an excessive American individualism which ignores all authority. [Francis Lieber, The
Stranger in America (Philadelphia, 1835), 310–17, 324.]

We went first to the "camp" at about eight o'clock in the evening,
when the meeting had already lasted five long days and nights. . . .
We entered one of the tents where a "class" was assembled. These
tents, destined for class meetings, are divided lengthwise by a bench
about a foot high, and called the mourners' bench. On one side are the
men, on the other the women; they lie or sit in disorder on the
straw, which is strewn on the ground, and was by this time broken
into small particles, causing in those places where the people moved
much about, dense dust, extremely offensive to the lungs. This dust,
together with the hot atmosphere, poisoned by the breath of so many
people crowded into a narrow space, and the smoke of lamps, rendered
the interior of the tents very obnoxious to a spectator coming from the
fresh and pure air without, and not in such a state of excitement as to
be insensible to its injurious effects upon the human organs. Along
both sides of the mourners' bench kneel "the sinners in a repenting
state" who wish to join the faithful; or, overpowered by their feelings
or by exhaustion, they lie on the ground, or in the arms of others, quiet,
half faint, exclaiming, groaning or weeping, while, from time to time,
the minister or any other "brother" speaks into their ears of impending everlasting damnation, or the bright hope of salvation; and
I saw, repeatedly, men taking the hands of women between their hands,
and patting and striking them, exhorting them, mean while, to trust
in God, or, if they stood at the entrance of the tent as mere spectators,
to join those in the interior and to repent. In these cases, as well as at
several times when the ministers or other "brethren" addressed the
uninitiated, a language was used, the familiarity of which struck our

ears as very strange. "Now come," they would say, "why won't you try?—come my dear brother or sister; God calls upon you—don't you see how powerful his spirit is? just try it, you will see how sweet it is —won't you? Come in, the mourners' bench is open for you, come in, it may soon be too late"; and other expressions of this kind.

One actually indecorous scene we saw, which I have no doubt would be considered so by most methodists themselves, were their attention directed to it. A man stood near the entry of a tent as spectator, and a woman, a friend, perhaps a cousin of his, because she called him James, was very anxious that he should join their service. She tried her best, though, of course, she did not use any kind of argument; but during the whole time she stroked his hand or fingers, taking one after the other between her hands. She succeeded at length in persuading the man to enter the tent, which he did with the words, "I don't care, but you won't catch me." We saw another man ushered into the tent, in a way which really reminded one of a similar kind of seizing on men, adopted by persons of which the methodists would not like to remind the spectator. He half walked, and was half pushed in by one of the ministers, handed over to the minister of the respective tent, and pushed down to the mourners' bench, where he lay for some time, his face resting on the bench, but he soon turned it upward, with convulsive distortions of his eyes and the muscles of his face. As many of the methodists' songs appear undignified, so is their language in speaking of religious subjects not unfrequently offensively quaint and familiar to unaccustomed ears. . . .

In the tent which we visited first there were several persons in a state of blessing, as the methodists call it; I shall say presently more about it. One woman exclaimed, several times, "Five or six sins I have committed, which, I fear, never can be forgiven"; weeping, at the same time, bitterly. Others prayed aloud, or called amen, whenever a passage in the prayer of the loudest seemed to strike them as particularly true; some slept in the corner, others, again, were quiet, but, from time to time, they would ejaculate expressions of sorrow or delight; and the laugh, not the smile, but the loud laugh with which these people greet the assurances of the bliss and happiness of the saved, or the glory in which Christ will appear to his faithful followers, or their familiar exclamations, such as, "God bless my soul," and the like, are as strange to others as many of their expressions of grief and religious fear. The constant and invariable theme of their exhortations was, as long as we were witnesses of these proceedings, "It is yet time to repent, come then and do so; death may suddenly cut you off, when your eternal doom will be pronounced upon you": and it seems to be a decidedly settled opinion with the methodists, that, whenever and however you may happen to die, the state in which you are at the time

of death is the sole testimony for the great judge by which to pronounce his irrevocable sentence for eternity. Not one single time, (I
state this while I am fully aware of the import of my words,) have I
heard a rational advice calculated to lead to the fulfilment of our
duties, to a true elevation of the soul, or to teach forbearance to others;
and I can assure you, that the constant repetition of the words "everlasting flames and eternal damnation," would alone be sickening to
the hearer, leaving their meaning entirely out of consideration. . . .

After having listened to their singing, exhorting, praying and violent
preaching, we entered one of the tents, which distinguished itself by a
greater noise, and wilder devotional exercise, at nearly two o'clock in
the morning. The air was pestilential; the dust from pulverized straw
and particles of dried earth very thick; the general appearance of the
whole was similar to that of a room in an insane hospital, but even more
frightful; the same motions of the limbs, expressions of faces, and
fearful noise. Some were seen rubbing their hands, apparently in great
agony, others clapping them together, others stretching them out toward heaven, and distorting their eyes, some stamping with the feet,
some rubbing their knees, some moving the upper part of the body forward and backward, others screaming, and weeping, surrounded by a
number of friends, who prevented the small current of air, which yet
existed, from reaching them, and sung and spoke into their ears; some
leaping up and down, with staring eyes, their hair dishevelled, others,
lying on the ground, distended as if in a swoon, some sitting in a
state of perfect exhaustion and inanity, with pale cheeks and vacant
eyes, which bore traces of many tears. One before all, was lying on
his knees, apparently in a state of great agony, and uttering the expressions of a desponding soul, addressed to a wrathful God. . . .

We approached two of the girls, extended on the ground in a "state
of blessing," in order to find out their precise condition, determined to
retire immediately, should we be considered as intruders. But I had
not miscalculated; fanatics are invariably pleased with attention being
shown to their proceedings. We touched the pulses of the girls and
found them rather slow, but not more so than can be easily explained
from previous great exhaustion, and the quiet breathing, lying as they
had been, for a long time on the ground. One had her hands cramped
together and her eyes open; the other, the hands extended: the skin
of both had a perfectly natural heat. We attracted, of course, immediate attention, and from some girls near us, a sneer of religious conceit
at the benighted profanity, which endeavored to become acquainted
with this state of blessedness, by the common method of worldly
science. Two girls, I observed, found it amusing, and had a real girlish
giggling at it. I addressed one of the first females and said, "My dear
young woman, you do not seem to have yet learned one very important

lesson from your religion, and that is to be charitable toward those whom you consider ignorant." This was attacking her on her own ground, and she was not unconscious of it; a modest silence showed that she confessed herself guilty.

Another girl, a bright and friendly little person, came up to us, as well as many men, and a long conversation ensued, of which I will give you the substance as accurately as I can remember, and which strikingly illustrates one of the most amiable traits of American character,—namely, the allowing every one to have and state fully his own opinion,—displayed even here, in this scene of violent excitement. I spoke with unreserved freedom, without at all provoking their indignation; on the contrary, they listened calmly to what I had to say. . . .

An elderly man came up to me, one of the very few more aged persons present, and asked me, what we thought of the girls, meaning those extended on the ground. I said, that we thought that many of them were actually endeavoring to deceive the others: an assertion in which we were justified; because one of the females who lay with open and staring eyes, had winked when we passed our hand at some distance from her face, and the other, who had her eyes closed, rolled them instantly up, when we opened the eyelids,—an evident proof, that the light had its full effect upon them; nor were her pupils either unnaturally dilated or contracted, but appeared in their natural extension. Indeed, any physician will tell you whether it be possible, that an individual can lie for two or three hours together in a state of real exhaustion and unconsciousness, deprived of all the power of volition, without laboring under a serious affection of the nervous system and experiencing the evil consequences of such a fit for several weeks. Yet these individuals appear a few hours after, in a comparatively sound state of health. That these simulations cannot but finally bring on disturbances of the various functions of the body, is evident. . . .

At nine o'clock on Saturday morning, a procession was formed, when each member shook hands with each minister. We had then a sight of every individual, and I was horror-struck at the dire expression of many countenances among those who came up. Some continued their distortions and frightful movements even in this procession, some looked down, many girls cried, and looked shockingly worn out. Beware, beware ye who promote this fanaticism, what you are enacting—literally the most revolting physical and mental mischief, to the advancement of ignorance and the depriving your fellow-beings of the choicest blessing—peace of spirit, and an enlightened mind.

There are many reasons, physical, moral and political, by which we must explain the great religious excitement now prevailing in the United States, and extending to more than the methodist sect. . . .

The American is an independent being; his government is founded upon an appeal to the reason of every individual, and as there is nothing in human life—no principle of action, no disposition or custom which forms an isolated part of his being, but must necessarily send its ramifications in every direction through his whole character, so also this spirit of independence, although productive of much good in many respects, induces the American sometimes to act for himself, in circumstances where he cannot have sufficient knowledge or experience to guide him.

IV. The Spirit and Practice of Reform

Although reformers seek change, not all of them fit the stereotype of wild-eyed radicals. Historians have recently recast many reformers in conservative roles, individuals who attempted to contain the forces of social disintegration and reshape a sense of community. Undoubtedly much of this energy stemmed from the religious roots of the American experience—the Christian sense of community and Calvinist zeal to do battle against sin. The reformism outburst in the 1830s and 1840s was linked to the religious changes then sweeping society. The religious message raised the question of why so much evil persisted in society in view of God's omnipotence and man's presumed perfectibility? This heightened awareness of the religiously defined ideal and the sordid social reality gave special urgency to reform activity, and made some reformers moralistic busybodies, prying into their neighbors' private concerns. Reformers divided their energies among a variety of causes from pacifism to temperance, creating a kind of interlocking directorate of benevolent brethren. No attempt has been made here to cover the entire reformist spectrum. Prominence is given to slavery, not only because contemporary events have directed attention to the roots of racial prejudice, but because the enslaved individual became the focal point of reformist concern. Trapped, helpless, often literally in chains, the unfortunate slave represented the antithesis of all American ideals, and abolition became the solemn objective of reformist zeal.

1. THE GOOD SOUL: RALPH WALDO EMERSON

Emerson was more a theoretician of reform than an active participant. Although sympathetic to reformism,

Emerson's critical detachment led him to produce dispassionate analyses of the reform temper. In the following
selections from "Man the Reformer" (1841), Emerson
argued that no one was blameless for society's ills, even
those who claimed to live the simplest and most noncom-
mercial existence, and that all shared the responsibility to
correct the evils of society. At the same time Emerson
pointed to the distinguishing feature of this era—the
tendency of the reformer to reevaluate radically a whole
society. Emerson cautioned that only through the triumph
of love and understanding could man expect to live har-
moniously and justly with his fellows. Though sounding
banal and hypocritical, perhaps, had they come from another source, Emerson voiced these sentiments with forcefulness, intelligence, and sincerity. [Ralph Waldo Emerson, Nature: Addresses and Lectures (Boston, 1903), 228–
31, 233, 247–49, 252–56.]

In the history of the world the doctrine of Reform had never such
scope as at the present hour. Lutherans, Herrnhutters, Jesuits, Monks,
Quakers, Knox, Wesley, Swedenborg, Bentham, in their accusations of
society, all respected something,—church or state, literature or history,
domestic usages, the market town, the dinner table, coined money. But
now all these and all things else hear the trumpet, and must rush to
judgment,—Christianity, the laws, commerce, schools, the farm, the
laboratory; and not a kingdom, town, statute, rite, calling, man, or
woman, but is threatened by the new spirit. . . .

It cannot be wondered at that this general inquest into abuses
should arise in the bosom of society, when one considers the practical
impediments that stand in the way of virtuous young men. The young
man, on entering life, finds the way to lucrative employments blocked
with abuses. The ways of trade are grown selfish to the borders of
theft, and supple to the borders (if not beyond the borders) of fraud.
The employments of commerce are not intrinsically unfit for a man,
or less genial to his faculties; but these are now in their general course
so vitiated by derelictions and abuses at which all connive, that it requires more vigor and resources than can be expected of every young
man, to right himself in them; he is lost in them; he cannot move hand
or foot in them. Has he genius and virtue? the less does he find them
fit for him to grow in, and if he would thrive in them, he must sacrifice
all the brilliant dreams of boyhood and youth as dreams; he must
forget the prayers of his childhood and must take on him the harness
of routine and obsequiousness. If not so minded, nothing is left him

but to begin the world anew, as he does who puts the spade into the ground for food. We are all implicated of course in this charge; it is only necessary to ask a few questions as to the progress of the articles of commerce from the fields where they grew, to our houses, to become aware that we eat and drink and wear perjury and fraud in a hundred commodities. . . . The sins of our trade belong to no class, to no individual. One plucks, one distributes, one eats. Every body partakes, every body confesses,—with cap and knee volunteers his confession, yet none feels himself accountable. He did not create the abuse; he cannot alter it. What is he? an obscure private person who must get his bread. That is the vice,—that no one feels himself called to act for man, but only as a fraction of man. It happens therefore that all such ingenuous souls as feel within themselves the irrepressible strivings of a noble aim, who by the law of their nature must act simply, find these ways of trade unfit for them, and they come forth from it. Such cases are becoming more numerous every year.

But by coming out of trade you have not cleared yourself. The trail of the serpent reaches into all the lucrative professions and practices of man. Each has its own wrongs. . . .

I do not wish to be absurd and pedantic in reform. I do not wish to push my criticism on the state of things around me to that extravagant mark that shall compel me to suicide, or to an absolute isolation from the advantages of civil society. . . . But I think we must clear ourselves each one by the interrogation, whether we have earned our bread to-day by the hearty contribution of our energies to the common benefit; and we must not cease to *tend* to the correction of flagrant wrongs, by laying one stone aright every day.

But the idea which now begins to agitate society has a wider scope than our daily employments, our households, and the institutions of property. We are to revise the whole of our social structure, the State, the school, religion, marriage, trade, science, and explore their foundations in our own nature; we are to see that the world not only fitted the former men, but fits us, and to clear ourselves of every usage which has not its roots in our own mind. What is a man born for but to be a Reformer, a Remaker of what man has made; a renouncer of lies; a restorer of truth and good, imitating that great Nature which embosoms us all, and which sleeps no moment on an old past, but every hour repairs herself, yielding us every morning a new day, and with every pulsation a new life? Let him renounce everything which is not true to him, and put all his practices back on their first thoughts, and do nothing for which he has not the whole world for his reason. . . .

The power which is at once spring and regulator in all efforts of reform is the conviction that there is an infinite worthiness in man, which will appear at the call of worth, and that all particular reforms are the removing of some impediment. Is it not the highest duty that man should be honored in us? I ought not to allow any man, because he has broad lands, to feel that he is rich in my presence. I ought to make him feel that I can do without his riches, that I cannot be bought, —neither by comfort, neither by pride,—and though I be utterly penniless, and receiving bread from him, that he is the poor man beside me. And if, at the same time, a woman or a child discovers a sentiment of piety, or a juster way of thinking than mine, I ought to confess it by my respect and obedience, though it go to alter my whole way of life. . . .

. . . We must be lovers, and at once the impossible becomes possible. Our age and history, for these thousand years, has not been the history of kindness, but of selfishness. Our distrust is very expensive. The money we spend for courts and prisons is very ill laid out. We make, by distrust, the thief, and burglar, and incendiary, and by our, court and jail we keep him so. An acceptance of the sentiment of love throughout Christendom for a season would bring the felon and the outcast to our side in tears, with the devotion of his faculties to our service. . . . In every knot of laborers the rich man does not feel himself among his friends,—and at the polls he finds them arrayed in a mass in distinct opposition to him. We complain that the politics of masses of the people are controlled by designing men, and led in opposition to manifest justice and the common weal, and to their own interest. But the people do not wish to be represented or ruled by the ignorant and base. They only vote for these, because they were asked with the voice and semblance of kindness. They will not vote for them long. They inevitably prefer wit and probity. . . . Let our affection flow out to our fellows; it would operate in a day the greatest of all revolutions. It is better to work on institutions by the sun than by the wind. The State must consider the poor man, and all voices must speak for him. Every child that is born must have a just chance for his bread. Let the amelioration in our laws of property proceed from the concession of the rich, not from the grasping of the poor. Let us begin by habitual imparting. Let us understand that the equitable rule is, that no one should take more than his share, let him be ever so rich. . . . Love would put a new face on this weary old world in which we dwell as pagans and enemies too long, and it would warm the heart to see how fast the vain diplomacy of statesmen, the impotence of armies, and navies, and lines of defence, would be superseded by this unarmed child. Love will creep where it cannot go, will accomplish that by imperceptible methods,—being its own lever, fulcrum, and power,— which force could never achieve.

2. EDUCATION FOR CONSERVATISM: HORACE MANN

From the nineteenth-century Little Red Schoolhouse to the modern university Americans invest a good share of their emotions, hopes, and their dollars in the cause of education. It was not always so. Education beyond the skills of reading and writing necessary for a religious people was considered a special obligation for more aristocratic families. The better classes sent their children on to be "finished," often in Europe, by exposing them to the culture which only gentlemen shared.

The democratization of American social values made universal education inevitable. Horace Mann, the most famous advocate of universal education, argued that proper training of the young was critical for the continued success of the American republican experiment. Adopting a tone similar to James Madison's celebrated Federalist Number Ten, Mann argued that American freedom gave free rein to the vices of human nature as well as its virtues. While these evil propensities could not be totally eradicated, Mann argued that the proper moral instruction of the young would check them and train the good citizens of the future. [The Life and Works of Horace Mann (5 vols., Boston, 1891), II: 143–45, 148–51, 165–66, 183–88.]

The common arguments in favor of Education have been so often repeated, that, in rising to address you on this subject, I feel like appealing to your own judgment and good sense to bear testimony to its worth, rather than attempting to make your convictions firmer, or your feelings stronger, by any attestations of mine.

I hardly need to say, that, by the word *Education*, I mean much more than an ability to read, write, and keep common accounts. I comprehend, under this noble word, such a training of the body as shall build it up with robustness and vigor,—at once protecting it from disease, and enabling it to act, *formatively*, upon the crude substances of Nature,—to turn a wilderness into cultivated fields, forests into ships, or quarries and claypits into villages and cities. I mean, also, to include such a cultivation of the intellect as shall enable it to discover those permanent and mighty laws which pervade all parts of the created universe, whether material or spiritual. This is necessary, because, if we act in obedience to these laws, all the resistless forces of Nature become our auxiliaries, and cheer us on to certain prosperity and triumph;

but, if we act in contravention or defiance of these laws, then Nature resists, thwarts, baffles us; and, in the end, it is just as certain that she will overwhelm us with ruin, as it is that God is stronger than man. And, finally, by the term Education, I mean such a culture of our moral affections and religious susceptibilities, as, in the course of Nature and Providence, shall lead to a subjection or conformity of all our appetites, propensities, and sentiments to the will of Heaven. . . .

Take any individual you please, separate him from the crowd of men, and look at him, apart and alone,—like some Robinson Crusoe in a far-off island of the ocean, without any human being around him, with no prospect of leaving any human being behind him,—and, even in such a solitude, how authoritative over his actions, how decisive of his contemplations and of his condition, are the instructions he received and the habits he formed in early life! But now behold him as one of the tumultuous throng of men; observe the wide influences which he exerts upon others,—in the marts of business, in the resorts of pleasure, in the high places of official trust,—and reflect how many of all these influences, whether beneficent or malign, depend upon the education he has received, and you will have another gauge or standard whereby to estimate the importance of our theme. . . . [L]ook at him as a citizen in a free government, throwing his influence and his vote into one or the other of the scales where peace and war, glory and infamy, are weighed;—look at him in these relations, and consider how a virtuous or a vicious education tends to fit or to unfit him for them all, and you will catch one more glimpse of the importance of the subject now presented to your consideration. . . .

It is a truism, that free institutions multiply human energies. A chained body cannot do much harm; a chained mind can do as little. In a despotic government, the human faculties are benumbed and paralyzed; in a Republic, they glow with an intense life, and burst forth with uncontrollable impetuosity. In the former, they are circumscribed and straitened in their range of action; in the latter, they have "ample room and verge enough," and may rise to glory or plunge into ruin. Amidst universal ignorance, there cannot be such wrong notions about right, as there may be in a community partially enlightened; and false conclusions which have been reasoned out are infinitely worse than blind impulses. . . .

Now it is undeniable that, with the possession of certain higher faculties,—common to all mankind,—whose proper cultivation will bear us upward to hitherto undiscovered regions of prosperity and glory, we possess, also, certain lower faculties or propensities,—equally common,—whose improper indulgence leads, inevitably, to tribulation, and anguish, and ruin. . . . Now despotic and arbitrary governments have dwarfed and crippled the powers of doing evil as much as the powers of doing good; but a republican government, from the very fact of its freedom, unreins their speed, and lets loose their strength. . . .

My proposition, therefore, is simply this:—If republican institutions do wake up unexampled energies in the whole mass of a people, and give them implements of unexampled power wherewith to work out their will, then these same institutions ought also to confer upon that people unexampled wisdom and rectitude. If these institutions give greater scope and impulse to the lower order of faculties belonging to the human mind, then they must also give more authoritative control and more skilful guidance to the higher ones. If they multiply temptations, they must fortify against them. If they quicken the activity and enlarge the sphere of the appetites and passions, they must, at least in an equal ratio, establish the authority and extend the jurisdiction of reason and conscience. In a word, we must not add to the impulsive, without also adding to the regulating forces.

If we maintain institutions, which bring us within the action of new and unheard-of powers, without taking any corresponding measures for the government of those powers, we shall perish by the very instruments prepared for our happiness. . . .

Such, then, are our latent capabilities of evil,—all ready to be evolved, should the restraints of reason, conscience, religion, be removed. Here are millions of men, each with appetites capacious of infinity, and raging to be satisfied out of a supply of means too scanty for any one of them. Millions of coveting eyes are fastened on the same object, —millions of hands thrust out to seize it. What ravening, torturing, destroying, then, must ensue, if these hounds cannot be lashed back into their kennel! They must be governed; they cannot be destroyed. . . .

. . . With us, legislators study the will of the multitude, just as natural philosophers study a volcano,—not with any expectation of doing aught to the volcano, but to see what the volcano is about to do to them. While the law was clothed with majesty and power, and the mind of the multitude was weak, then, as in all cases of a conflict between unequal forces, the law prevailed. But now, when the law is weak, and the passions of the multitude have gathered irresistible strength, it is fallacious and insane to look for security in the moral force of the law. . . .

But, if arms themselves would be beaten in such a contest, if those who should propose the renewal of ancient severities in punishment would themselves be punished, have we not some other resource for the security of moderation and self-denial, and for the supremacy of order and law? . . .

I speak with reverence of the labors of another profession in their sacred calling. No other country in the world has ever been blessed with a body of clergymen, so learned, so faithful, so devout as ours. But by traditionary custom and the ingrained habits of the people, the efforts of the clergy are mainly expended upon those who have passed the forming state;—upon adults, whose characters, as we are accustomed to express it, have become *fixed,* which being interpreted, means, that they have passed from fluid into flint. . . .

But perhaps others may look for security to the public Press, which has now taken its place amongst the organized forces of modern civilization. Probably its political department supplies more than half the reading of the mass of our people. . . . The very existence of the newspaper press, for any useful purpose, presupposes that the people are already supplied with the elements of knowledge and inspired with the love of right; and are therefore prepared to decide; with intelligence and honesty, those complicated and conflicting claims, which the tide of events is constantly presenting, and which, by the myriad messengers of the press, are carried to every man's fireside for his adjudication. . . . Each of two things is equally necessary to our political prosperity; namely, just principles of government and administration, on one side, and a people able to understand and resolute to uphold them, on the other. . . .

. . . Can any Christian man believe, that God has so constituted and so governs the human race, that it is always and necessarily to be suicidal of its earthly welfare? No! the thought is impious. The same Almighty Power which implants in our nature the germs of these terrible propensities, has endowed us also with reason and conscience and a sense of responsibility to Him; and, in his providence, he has opened a way by which these nobler faculties can be elevated into dominion and supremacy over the appetites and passions. But if this is ever done, it must be mainly done during the docile and teachable years of childhood. I repeat it, my friends, *if this is ever done, it must be mainly done during the docile and teachable years of childhood.* Wretched, incorrigible, demoniac, as any human being may ever have become, there was a time when he took the first step in error and in crime; when, for the first time, he just nodded to his fall, on the brink of ruin. Then, ere he was irrecoverably lost, ere he plunged into the abyss of infamy and guilt, he might have been recalled, as it were by the waving of the hand. Fathers, mothers, patriots, Christians! it is this very hour of peril through which our children are now passing. They know it not, but we know it; and where the knowledge is, there rests the responsibility. Society is responsible;—not society considered as an abstraction, but society as it consists of living members, which members we are. Clergymen are responsible;—all men who have enjoyed the opportunities of a higher education in colleges and universities are responsible, for they can convert their means, whether of time or of talent, into instruments for elevating the masses of the people. The conductors of the public press are responsible, for they have daily access to the public ear, and can infuse just notions of this high duty into the public mind. Legislators and rulers are responsible. In our country, and in our times, no man is worthy the honored name of a statesman, who does not include the highest practicable education of the people in all his plans of administration. He may have eloquence, he may have a knowledge of all history, diplomacy, jurisprudence; and by these he might claim, in other countries, the elevated rank of a statesman; but, unless he speaks, plans, labors, at all times and in all places, for the culture and edification of the whole people, he is not, he cannot be, an American statesman.

If this dread responsibility for the fate of our children be disregarded, how, when called upon, in the great eventful day, to give an account of the manner in which our earthly duties have been discharged, can we expect to escape the condemnation: "Inasmuch as ye have not done it to one of the least of these, ye have not done it unto me"?

3. FEMALES, HUMAN RIGHTS, AND REFORM

Despite male incredulity and stubbornness, women also wanted to participate in the religious and secular movements which would redeem America. Females were still less than full citizens; in some matters the law regarded them as children, without full control over their property; nor, of course, could they vote. Nevertheless, many women joined reform organizations and some of them used the opportunity to fight for their own rights. Two of these reformers, Sarah and Angelina Grimké, had abandoned their home state of South Carolina and embraced abolitionism. Soon the causes of the slave and the woman, both victims of involuntary servitude, became one in their minds. Their lecturing in behalf of these causes provoked the Massachusetts General Association of Congregational Ministers to issue a pastoral letter condemning the activities of female preachers. Angelina's cool, hardheaded, and sardonic reply to the protests of two worried colleagues-in-reform illustrated, first, the determination of the women's rights reformers, and, second, the blending of various reforms, one into the other. As for the conservative warning that reformism meant spinsterhood for the female gadflies, Angelina married Theodore Dwight Weld a year later. No one proposed to elder sister Sarah, however. [Gilbert H. Barnes and Dwight L. Dumond, eds., Letters of Theodore Dwight Weld, Angelina Grimké Weld, and

Sarah Grimké, 1822–1844 (2 vols., New York, 1934), I:
427–32.]

TO THEODORE D. WELD AND J. G. WHITTIER

Brookline [Mass.] 8th Mo 20—[1837]

Brethren beloved in the Lord.

As your letters came to hand at the same time and both are devoted mainly to the same subject we have concluded to answer them
on one sheet and jointly. You seem greatly alarmed at the idea of
our advocating the *rights of woman*. Now we will first tell you *how*
we came to begin those letters in the Spectator. Whilst we were at
Newburyport we received a note from Mary Parker telling us that
Wm. S. Porter had requested her to try to obtain some one to write
for his paper in order that it might be better sustained. She asked
him whether *she* might choose the subject and named the *province
of woman:* he said yes, he would be glad to have such pieces to
publish. Just at this time the Pastoral Letter came out, and Mary
requested us to write something every week about *Woman* for the
Spectator. We consulted together and viewed this unexpected opportunity of throwing our views before the public as providential.
As I was writing to C[atherine] E. B[eecher], S[arah] M. G. undertook
it and as this paper was not an abolition paper we could not see any
impropriety in embracing this opening. These letters have not been the
means of *arousing* the public attention to the subject of Womans
rights, it was the Pastoral Letter which did the mischief. The ministers
seemed panic struck at once and commenced a most violent attack
upon us. I do not say *absurd* for in truth if it can be fairly established
that women *can lecture*, then why may they not preach and if *they*
can preach, then woe! woe be unto that Clerical Domination which
now rules the world under the various names of Gen'l Assemblies,
Congregational Associations, etc. *This Letter* then roused the attention of the whole country to enquire what *right* we had to open our
mouths for the dumb; the people were continually told "it is a
shame for a *woman* to speak in the churches." Paul suffered not a
woman to *teach* but commanded *her* to be in silence. The pulpit
is too *sacred a place* for *woman's* foot etc. Now my dear brothers
this invasion of *our rights* was just such an attack upon *us*, as that
made upon Abolitionists generally when they were told a few years
ago that *they had no right* to discuss the subject of Slavery. Did *you*
take no notice of this assertion? Why no! With one heart and one
voice you said, *We* will settle *this right before* we go one step further.
The time to assert a right is *the* time when *that* right is denied.

We must establish this right for if we do not, it will be impossible for *us* to go *on with the work of Emancipation.* But you will say that notwithstand[ing] the denial of your right you still had crowded audiences—*curiosity,* it was a new thing under the sun to see a *woman* occupy the place of a lecturer and the people were very anxious to *hear* and *see* for themselves: but you certainly *must* know that the leaven which the ministers are so assiduously working into the minds of the people *must* take effect in process of time, and *will close every church to us,* if we give the community no reasons to counteract the sophistry of priests and levites. In this State particularly there is an utter ignorance on the subject. Some few noble minds bursting thro' the trammels of educational prejudice FEEL that woman does stand on the same platform of human rights with man, but even these cannot sustain their ground by argument, and as soon as they open their lips to assert her *rights,* their opponents throw perverted scripture into their faces and call O yea, clamor for *proof,* PROOF, PROOF! and this *they cannot* give and are beaten off the field in disgrace. Now we are confident that there are scores of such minds panting after light on this subject: "the children *ask* bread and no MAN giveth it unto them." There is an eagerness to understand our views. Now is it wrong to give those views in a series of letters in a paper NOT devoted to Abolition?

And can you not see that women *could* do, and *would* do a hundred times more for the slave if she were not fettered? Why! we are gravely told that we are out of our sphere even when we circulate petitions; out of our "appropriate sphere" when we speak to women only; and out of them when we *sing* in the churches. Silence is *our* province, submission *our* duty. If then we "give *no reason* for the hope that is in us," that we have *equal rights* with our brethren, how can we expect to be permitted *much longer to exercise those rights?* IF I know my own heart, I am NOT actuated by any selfish considerations (but I do sincerely thank our dear brother J. G. W[hittier] for the suggestion) but we are actuated by the full conviction that if we are to do any good in the Anti Slavery cause, our *right* to labor in it *must* be firmly established; *not* on the ground of Quakerism, but on the only firm bases of human rights, the Bible. Indeed I contend brethren that *this* is not *Quaker* doctrine, it is no more like *their* doctrine on Women than our Anti Slavery is like their Abolition, just about the same difference. I will explain myself. Women are regarded as equal to men on the ground of *spiritual gifts, not* on the broad ground of *humanity.* Woman may *preach;* this is a *gift;* but woman must *not* make the discipline by which *she herself* is to be governed. O that you were here that we might have a good long, *long* talk over matters and things, then I could explain myself far

better. And I think we could convince you that *we* cannot push
Abolitionism forward with all our might *until* we take up the stumbling block out of the road. We cannot see with brother Weld in this
matter. We acknowledge the excellence of his reasons for urging us
to labor in this cause of the Slave, our being Southerners, etc., but
then we say how can we expect to be able to hold meetings much
longer when people are so diligently taught to *despise us* for thus
stepping out of the sphere of woman! Look at this instance: after we
had left Groton the *Abolition* minister there, at a Lyceum meeting
poured out his sarcasm and ridicule upon our heads and among other
things said, he would as soon be caught robbing a hen roost as encouraging a woman to lecture. Now brethren if the leaders of the people
thus speak of our labors, *how long* will we be allowed to prosecute them?
. . . They utterly deny *our right* to interfere with this or any other
moral reform except in the particular way *they* choose to mark out for
us to walk in. If we dare to stand upright and do our duty according
to the dictates of *our own* consciences, why then we are compared to
Fanny Wright and so on. Why, my dear brothers can you not see
the deep laid scheme of the clergy against us as lecturers? They
know full well that if they can persuade the people it is a *shame*
for us to speak in public, and that every time we open our mouths
for the dumb we are breaking a divine command, that even if we
spoke with the tongues of *men* or of angels, we should have *no
hearers*. They are springing a deep mine beneath our feet, and we
shall *very* soon be compelled to retreat for we shall have *no* ground
to stand on. If we surrender the right to *speak* to the public this
year, we must surrender the right to petition next year and the right
to *write* the year after and so on. What *then* can *woman* do for the
slave when she is herself under the feet of man and shamed into
silence? Now we entreat *you* to weigh candidly the *whole subject*,
and then we are sure you will see, this is no more than an abandonment of our first love than the effort made by Anti Slavery men to
establish the *right* of free discussion.

   With regard to brother Welds ultraism on the subject of marriage,
he is quite mistaken if he fancies he has got far *ahead* of *us* in the
human rights reform. We do *not* think his doctrine at all shocking:
it is *altogether right*. But I am afraid I am *too proud* ever to exercise the right. The fact is we are living in such an artificial state
of society that there are some things about which we dare not speak
out, or act out the most natural and best feelings of our hearts. O!
when shall we be "delivered from the *bondage of corruption* into
the glorious liberty of the sons of God"! By the bye it will be very
important to establish this right, for the men of Mass. stoutly declare that women who hold such sentiments of *equality* can never

expect to be courted. They seem to hold out this as a kind of threat to deter us from asserting our rights, not *knowing wherunto this will grow*. But jesting is inconvenient says the Apostle: to business then.

Anti Slavery men are trying very hard to separate what God hath joined together. I fully believe that so far from keeping different moral reformations entirely distinct that no such attempt can ever be successful. They are bound together in a circle like the sciences; they blend with each other like the colors of the rain bow; they are the parts only of our glorious whole and that whole is Christianity, pure *practical* christianity. The fact is I believe—but dont be alarmed, for it is only I—that Men and Women will have to go out on their own responsibility, just like the prophets of old and declare the *whole* counsel of God to the people. The whole Church Government must come down, the clergy stand right in the way of reform, and I do not know but this stumbling block too must be removed *before* Slavery can be abolished, for the system is supported by *them;* it could not exist without the Church as it is called. . . . Is brother Weld frightened at *my ultraism?* Please write to us soon and let us know what you think after reflecting on this letter. We are now at S. Philbricks and will we expect be here two weeks more lecturing in the neighboring towns. May the Lord bless you my dear brothers is the prayer of your sister in Jesus

A.E.G

We never mention women's rights in our *lectures* except so far as is necessary to urge them to meet their responsibilities. We speak of their *responsibilities* and leave *them* to *infer* their *rights*. I could cross this letter all over but must not encroach on your time.

I should not be at all surprized if the public demanded of us "by what authority doest thou this thing," and if we had to lecture on this subject specifically and call upon the men "to show cause if any they had" why *women* should not open their mouths for the dumb.

4. ESTABLISHMENT REFORM:
AFRICAN COLONIZATION

In pre-Civil War America no activity affecting slavery initially appeared more prestigious and capable of success than the American Colonization Society. The Society, formed in 1816, attracted many influential members from both sides of the Mason-Dixon line. They confidently solicited federal aid for their "noble" purpose on the grounds that federal activity would maximize individual

humanitarian efforts, a common theme in the nationalist
spirit which flowered after the War of 1812.

By 1837 Colonizationists had lost enthusiasm and supporters, and had gained a growing number of critics. Two
selections from Henry Clay's speeches to the national and
Kentucky state Society document this transformation.
Under attack by both supporters and opponents of slavery,
Clay defended the Society's efforts against the radical demands of friend and foe, but he could not conceal his disappointment over the federal government's failure to contribute funds. Equally revealing was Clay's address to the
Kentucky chapter of the Society. He vividly portrayed the
nature of racial prejudice in America and nervously predicted a violent future unless the free blacks were removed
from America. Coupling this fear with missionary expan-
sionism, Clay concluded with an appeal for a black empire in Africa to endow the "Dark Continent" with the
light of American civilization. [U.S. House of Representatives, Report No. 283, 27th Cong., 3rd sess., 172–76, 945–
46, 954–56.]

MEMORIAL OF THE AMERICAN COLONIZATION SOCIETY

That in the year 1816 a number of respectable individuals formed
themselves into a society, at the seat of the National Government, for
the purpose of promoting the voluntary colonization of the free people of color of the United States, in Africa or elsewhere; and soon afterwards adopted preparatory measures for the accomplishment of their
purpose. . . .

Notwithstanding the difficulties inseparable from the opening and
first settlement of distant and uncultivated regions, difficulties increased
on the present occasion by the scanty means to be drawn from the only
sources of supply open to the society, the colony has annually increased
in population, and now contains more than twelve hundred individuals.
A government has been established, republican in its principles, (as
far as the unformed character of the colony will permit,) regular and
efficient in its operation, and thus far providing the necessary securities
for life, liberty, and property. One hundred and fifty miles of the coast
are under the colonial jurisdiction; and no less than eighty important
stations, on this line, are occupied by traders from the colony. From
this territory the slave trade is believed to be nearly, if not quite,
banished; and the natives begin to engage in agriculture, and carry
on a valuable commerce with the inhabitants of Liberia. The trade of
the colony has increased with remarkable rapidity, and many of the

settlers have each acquired by it, in the course of three or four years, property to the amount of several thousand dollars.

Many plantations have been cleared and put under cultivation, and so fertile is the soil, that an annual product will soon doubtless be realized, adequate to the supply not only of those who have already emigrated, but of those also who may be induced hereafter to seek for happiness and independence in the land of their fathers, and a home of their own.

Schools have been established, and every child in the colony enjoys their benefits. Fortifications and many public buildings have been erected; a spirit of enterprise prevails; and peace, order, and contentment, are the evidences of general prosperity. . . .

Such is a general outline of the operations of the society, and such the present condition of the colony. In the progress that has been made, your memorialists have found nothing to discourage them, and from the actual state of things which they have thus been enabled to present to the view of your honorable body, they derive the pleasing anticipation of being able to demonstrate to the world, that they are engaged in an enterprise neither unwise nor impracticable. In the course of a few short years, a small number of individuals, actuated only by the most philanthropic motives, possessing no political power, and destitute of all pecuniary resources, except such as were to be found in the charity, the benevolence, and the patriotism of their fellow-citizens, and the efforts of Congress to abolish the African slave trade, have succeeded in exploring a distant coast, in overcoming, in a great measure, the very natural but very powerful prejudices of the community in which they live, and in transporting to the western shores of a remote continent, and maintaining, in a state of perfect security, a colony of several hundred of the free colored population of their country. But a period has at length arrived, when the society would no longer be justified in relying on its own limited resources for accomplishing what yet remains of its patriotic undertaking.

The colony that has been settled, small as it is, is yet too large to be governed by a distant and unincorporated society. The acknowledged imperfections of human nature, and the uniform history of mankind, evince the dangers necessarily connected with the sudden transition of any people from a state of moral and political degradation to one of unqualified freedom. If, with such evidences before it, the society should leave its infant settlement to the inadequate protection to be derived from its own resources, it would be justly chargeable with all the evils that must necessarily result from the defective powers of control with which it is invested, for tranquillity at home, or security from foreign danger.

In reference, too, to the great objects to be accomplished, it is now time to look to other means than such as can be supplied by individual charity. The extent to which reliance may be placed on this resource has been in a great measure ascertained; and if, at the very commencement of the undertaking, aided as it has been by all the charms of novelty, means have been furnished for removing only a few hundred out of the many thousand that are annually added to the free colored population of the country, it is obvious that a further dependence on this resource would be little less than an abandonment of the enterprise. The evil to be removed is continually increasing; and with every exertion on the part of the Colonization Society, unless access can be had to other resources, each succeeding year must find it more remote from the object of its pursuit. Under these circumstances, the society has felt itself justified in asking the immediate and effectual interposition of the Government of the country. The object it proposes to accomplish is the removal to Africa, with their own consent, of such people of color within the United States as are already free, and of such others as the humanity of individuals and the laws of the different States may hereafter liberate.

Such an object, connected as it is with the justice, the humanity, and the welfare of our country, and calculated to elevate the character and to improve the condition of a degraded portion of the human race, cannot fail to be considered as one of deep and general interest; and the wisdom of the National Legislature may be safely relied on for suggesting and applying the necessary means for its accomplishment. Your memorialists confidently trust that in this explicit avowal of the real and only design of the American Colonization Society will be found its best vindication from the contradictory imputations cast upon it, of attempting, at the same moment, and by the same process, to interfere, on the one hand, with the legal obligations of slavery, and, on the other, to rivet the chains more firmly on its present subjects. The society has at all times recognised the constitutional and legitimate existence of slavery; and, whatever may have been thought of its unhappy influence on the general interests of the country, the Government of the Union has never been looked to as the proper or authorized instrument for effecting its removal.

But to that Government it has been thought that resort might be had for furnishing the means of voluntary emigration to another description of population, exercising a confessedly injurious influence on every portion of our country, but especially so on those parts of it in which slavery still exists.

And if, in relation to the latter, the effects of such a measure should be to afford to individual humanity a wider field for action, and to the State authorities an opportunity and an inducement to encourage rather than to forbid emancipation within their respective limits, your memorialists have hoped that this consideration alone, instead of prejudicing their present application, would operate as one of its most powerful recommendations. And that such would be the case with the nation, they have every reason to believe. . . .

The reception which the Colonization Society has met, in almost every instance, from the people, bespeaks a deep and general interest in its success.

And the resolutions which have been adopted by a very large proportion of the Legislatures of the States, in favor of the plan of colonizing the free people of color, indicate it as an object entitled, in every respect, to the aid and patronage of a Government, whose peculiar province it is, in the exercise of its legitimate powers, as the exclusive Legislature of the District of Columbia, to promote the welfare of the people subject to its sole authority, by legislation as unrestricted and discretionary as can be exercised by any State Government over its citizens; and, in its capacity of a General Government, under the limitations of the Constitution, to suppress the African slave trade, by all the means, direct or auxiliary, conducive to that great end of general policy and public morality—a power claimed and practically exercised by the Government, in a spirit manifesting a sense of duty as high and imperative as the power is unquestionable. To that Government the question is now fairly submitted, in the fullest confidence that it will receive the consideration due to its importance, and a decision worthy of the Legislature of a free, a great, and an enlightened nation.

ADDRESS OF MR. CLAY AT THE 21st ANNUAL MEETING OF THE SOCIETY, DECEMBER 12, 1837, ON THE OCCASION OF HIS TAKING THE CHAIR AS PRESIDENT OF THE SOCIETY

The society was formed to demonstrate the practicability of colonization in Africa; and if it were unhappily dissolved to-morrow, that great purpose of its founders will have been completely accomplished. No one can now doubt that, with the application of adequate means, such as the Governments of the several States of the Union could supply, almost without an effort, the colonization of the descendants of the African race may be effected to any desirable extent. The founders of the society never imagined that, depending as it does upon spontaneous contributions from the good and the benevolent, irregularly made, without an established revenue, and without power, the society alone was competent to colonize all the free persons of color in the United States. They hoped, and the society still hopes, that, seeing what has been done, and can be done, Governments may think fit to take hold of the principle, and carry it out as far as they may deem right, with their ample powers and abundant resources. . . .

It has been objected against the society, that its aim and tendency have been to perpetuate slavery, and to draw still tighter the bonds of the slave. It has, on the other hand, been proclaimed that its purpose is to abolish slavery forthwith, and to let loose the untutored and unprepared slaves upon society. Both objections cannot be founded in truth. Neither is. The society does not meddle with slavery, either to prolong or to discontinue its existence. Its abstract opinion, or rather the abstract opinions of its members, is well known. They believe it a deplorable evil; but here it is to be touched, if touched at all, with the greatest caution and delicacy, and only with authorized hands. . . .

But the society attacks no person and no association. It neither assails those who believe slavery a blessing, nor those who believe it a great curse, and seek its immediate extirpation. It pursues the even tenor of its way, appealing to the understanding, to the humanity, and to the religion of an enlightened community. . . . The roads of colonization and abolition lead in different directions, but they do not cross each other. We deal only with free persons of color; their efforts are directed towards the slave. We seek to better the condition of the free person of color; they the slave. Why should our humane design be impeded, or derided, or thwarted, by those who profess to be in the prosecution of another but distinct design, which they profess to consider also humane? No, gentlemen; we are no ultraists. We neither seek to perpetuate nor to abolish slavery. Our object is totally different from either, and has been proclaimed and clung to from the beginning of the society to this hour. . . .

Those who thus assail us seek to try us by an imaginary standard of their own creation. They argue that the whole of the African portion of our population amounts to some two or three millions; that in a period of twenty years we have been able to colonize only a few thousand, and hence they infer that colonization cannot exercise any sensible influence upon the mass of the African element of the American population. Now, all that we ask is to be tried by the standard of our own promises and pledges. . . .

Those who complain of the tardy operations of the society should recollect that great national enterprises are not to be speedily executed like those of individuals, in the short span of the life of one person. Many years, sometimes more than a century, may be necessary to their completion; and this is emphatically the case when we reflect upon the magnitude and the duration of the wrongs inflicted upon Africa. Near two centuries elapsed, during which her sons were constantly transported to the shores of the New World, doomed to a state of bondage. A period of similar extent may possibly be necessary to restore their descendants to the parent country, with all the blessings of law and liberty, religion and civilization. A sudden and instantaneous separation of the two races, if it were possible, would be good for neither, nor for either country. We should be greatly affected by an immediate abstraction to such a vast extent from the labor and industry of our country: and Africa could not be prepared, morally or physically, to receive and sustain such a vast multitude of emigrants. For both parties, and for all interests, the process of separation, like the original unnatural union, had perhaps better be slow and gradual. And the consoling reflection may be entertained, that during every step in its progress good will have been done. . . .

CLAY'S ADDRESS TO THE COLONIZATION SOCIETY OF KENTUCKY

When we consider the cruelty of the origin of negro slavery, its nature, the character of the free institutions of the whites, and the irresistible progress of public opinion, throughout America as well as in Europe, it is impossible not to anticipate frequent insurrections among the blacks in the United States. They are rational beings like ourselves, capable of feeling, of reflection, and of judging of what naturally belongs to them as a portion of the human race. By the very condition of the relation which subsists between us, we are enemies of each other. . . .

Happily for us, no such insurrection can ever be attended with permanent success, as long as our Union endures. It would be speedily suppressed by the all-powerful means of the United States; and it would be the madness of despair in the blacks that should attempt it. But if attempted in some parts of the United States, what shocking scenes of carnage, rapine, and lawless violence, might not be perpetrated before the arrival at the theatre of action of a competent force to quell it! And after it was put down, what other scenes of military rigor and bloody executions would not be indispensably necessary to punish the insurgents, and impress their whole race with the influence of a terrible example!

Of all the descriptions of our population, and of either portion of the African race, the free people of color are by far, as a class, the most corrupt, depraved, and abandoned. There are many honorable exceptions among them, and I take pleasure in bearing testimony to some I know. It is not so much their fault as the consequence of their anomalous condition. Place ourselves, place any men in the like predicament, and similar effects would follow. They are not slaves, and yet they are not free. The laws, it is true, proclaim them free; but prejudices, more powerful than any laws, deny them the privileges of freemen. They occupy a middle station between the free white population and the slaves of the United States, and the tendency of their habits is to corrupt both. . . .

Is there no remedy, I again ask, for the evils of which I have sketched a faint and imperfect picture? Is our posterity doomed to endure forever not only all the ills flowing from the state of slavery, but all which arise from incongruous elements of population, separated from each other by invincible prejudices and by natural causes? Whatever may be the character of the remedy proposed, we may confidently pronounce it inadequate, unless it provides efficaciously for the total and absolute separation, by an extensive space of water or of land, at least, of the white portion of our population from that which is free of the colored. . . .

We may boldly challenge the annals of human nature for the record of any human plan, for the melioration of the condition or advancement of the happiness of our race, which promised more unmixed good, or more comprehensive beneficence, than that of African colonization, if carried into full execution. Its benevolent purpose is not limited by the confines of one continent, nor to the prosperity of a solitary race, but embraces two of the largest quarters of the earth, and the peace and happiness of both of the descriptions of their present inhabitants, with the countless millions of their posterity who are to succeed. It appeals for aid and support to the friends of liberty here and every where. . . .

. . . Africa, although a portion of it was among the first to emerge from barbarism, is now greatly in the rear of all the continents, in knowledge, and in the arts and sciences. America owes to the old world a debt of gratitude for the possession of them. Can she discharge it in any more suitable manner than that of transplanting them on a part of its own soil, by means of its own sons, whose ancestors were torn by fraud and violence from their native home, and thrown here into bondage? . . . Who, if this promiscuous residence of whites and blacks, of freemen and slaves, is forever to continue, can imagine the servile wars, the carnage and the crimes, which will be its probable consequences, without shuddering with horror? . . . Almost all Africa is in a state of the deepest ignorance and barbarism, and addicted to idolatry and superstition. It is destitute of the blessings both of Christianity and civilization. . . . The society proposes to send not on or two pious members of Christianity into a foreign land, among a different and perhaps a suspicious race, of another complexion, but to transport annually, for an indefinite number of years, in one view of its scheme, six thousand—in another, fifty-six thousand missionaries, of the descendants of Africa itself, with the same interests, sympathies, and constitutions of the natives, to communicate the benefits of our religion and of the arts. And this colony of missionaries is to operate not alone by preaching the doctrines of truth and of revelation, which, however delightful to the ears of the faithful and intelligent, are not always comprehended by untutored savages, but also by works of ocular demonstration. It will open forests, build towns, erect temples of public worship, and practically exhibit to the native sons of Africa the beautiful moral spectacle and the superior advantages of our religious and social systems. . . .

. . . And when we shall, as soon we must, be translated from this into another form of existence, is the hope presumptuous that we shall there behold the common Father of whites and of blacks, the great Ruler of the Universe, cast His all-seeing eye upon civilized and regenerated Africa, its cultivated fields, its coast studded with numerous cities, adorned with towering temples, dedicated to the pure religion of His redeeming Son, its far-famed Niger, and other great rivers, lined with flourishing villages, and navigated with that wonderful power which American genius first successfully applied; and that, after dwelling with satisfaction upon the glorious spectacle, He will deign to look with approbation upon us, His humble instruments, who have contributed to produce it?

5. COLONIZATION UNDER FIRE: THE ABOLITIONIST TEMPER

The most outspoken foe of colonization was William Lloyd Garrison. Garrison attacked the assumptions, activities, and meager accomplishments of the Colonization Society. The importance of Garrison's attack, however, was not the "exposé" of the Colonizationists itself but what it revealed about the abolitionist mind. Abolitionists have been criticized by some historians as irresponsible agitators, men who stirred up a complex, sensitive issue which should have been approached moderately. Garrison dismissed any hope of cooperation with southerners, the basis for colonization, by branding slaveholders as criminals. The charge that abolitionists regarded slavery abstractly and called only for the slave's freedom is not borne out in this selection. Note that Garrison calls for a "remuneration for years of unrequited toil," as well as schooling and useful employment for the former slave. But it is primarily Garrison's refusal to compromise with evil which characterized the hard-line abolitionist attitude developed in the 1830s. [William Lloyd Garrison, Thoughts on African Colonization (reprinted, New York, 1968), 19–21, 78–80, 85–86, 90, 93–94.]

I should oppose this Society, even were its doctrines harmless. It imperatively and effectually seals up the lips of a vast number of influential and pious men, who, for fear of giving offence to those slaveholders with whom they associate, and thereby leading to a dissolution of the compact, dare not expose the flagrant enormities of the system of slavery, nor denounce the crime of holding human beings in bondage. They dare not lead to the onset against the forces of tyranny; and if *they* shrink from the conflict, how shall the victory be won? I do not mean to aver, that, in their sermons, or addresses, or private conversations, they never allude to the subject of slavery; for they do so frequently, or at least every Fourth of July. But my complaint is, that they content themselves with representing slavery as an evil,—a misfortune,—a calamity which has been entailed upon us by former generations,—*and not as an individual* CRIME, embracing in its folds robbery, cruelty, oppression and piracy. *They do not identify the criminals;* they make no direct, pungent, earnest appeal to the consciences of men-stealers; by consenting to walk arm-in-arm with them, they virtually agree to abstain from all offensive remarks, and to aim entirely at the expulsion of the free people of color; their lugubrious exclamations, and solemn animadversions, and reproachful reflections, are altogether indefinite; they "go about, and about, and all the way round to nothing"; they generalize, they shoot into the air, they do not disturb the repose nor wound the complacency of the sinner; "they have put no difference between the holy and profane, neither have they shewed difference between the unclean and the clean." Thus has free inquiry been suppressed, and a universal fear created, and the tongue of the boldest silenced, and the sleep of death fastened upon the nation. . . .

Were the American Colonization Society bending its energies directly to the immediate abolition of slavery; seeking to enlighten and consolidate public opinion, on this momentous subject; faithfully exposing the awful guilt of the owners of slaves; manfully contending for the bestowal of equal rights upon our free colored population in this their native land; assiduously endeavoring to uproot the prejudices of society; and holding no fellowship with oppressors; my opposition to it would cease. It might continue to bestow its charities upon those who should desire to seek another country, and at the same time launch its thunders against the system of oppression. But, alas! it looks to the banishment of the free people of color as the only means to abolish slavery, and conciliate the feelings of the planters.

The popularity of the Society is not attributable to its merits, but exclusively to its congeniality with those unchristian prejudices which have so long been cherished against a sable complexion. It is agreeable to slaveholders, because it is striving to remove a class of persons who they fear may stir up their slaves to rebellion; all who avow undying hostility to the people of color are in favor of it; all who shrink from acknowledging them as brethren and friends, or who make them a distinct and inferior caste, or who deny the possibility of elevating them in the scale of improvement here, most heartily embrace it. Having ample funds, it has been able to circulate its specious appeals in every part of the country; and to employ active and eloquent agents, who have glowingly described to the people the immense advantages to be reaped from the accomplishment of its designs. With this entire preoccupancy of the ground, and these common though unworthy dispositions in its favor, the wonder is, that it is not more popular. . . .

It follows, as a necessary consequence, that a Society which is not hostile to slavery, which apologises for the system and for slaveholders, which recognises slaves as rightful property, and which confessedly increases their value, is *the enemy of immediate abolition.* This, I am aware, in the present corrupt state of public sentiment, will not generally be deemed an objectionable feature; but I regard it with inexpressible abhorrence and dismay.

Since the deception practised upon our first parents by the old serpent, there has not been a more fatal delusion in the minds of men than that of the gradual abolition of slavery. *Gradual* abolition! do its supporters really know what they talk about? Gradually abstaining from what? From sins the most flagrant, from conduct the most cruel, from acts the most oppressive! Do colonizationists mean, that slave-dealers shall purchase or sell a few victims less this year than they did the last? that slave-owners shall liberate one, two or three out of every hundred slaves during the same period? that slave-drivers shall apply the lash to the scarred and bleeding backs of their victims somewhat less frequently? . . . Do colonizationists mean that the practice of separating the husband from the wife, the wife from the husband, or children from their parents, shall come to an end by an almost imperceptible process? or that the slaves shall be defrauded of their just remuneration, less and less every month or every year? or that they shall be under the absolute, irresponsible control of their masters? . . .

I utterly reject, as delusive and dangerous in the extreme, every plea which justifies a procrastinated and an indefinite emancipation, or which concedes to a slave owner the right to hold his slaves as *property* for any limited period, or which contends for the gradual preparation of the slaves for freedom; believing all such pretexts to be a fatal departure from the high road of justice into the bogs of expediency, a surrender of the great principles of equity, an indefensible prolongation of the curse of slavery, a concession which places the guilt upon upon any but those who incur it, and directly calculated to perpetuate the thraldom of our species.

Immediate abolition does not mean that the slaves shall immediately exercise the right of suffrage, or be eligible to any office, or be emancipated from law, or be free from the benevolent restraints of guardianship. We contend for the immediate personal freedom of the slaves, for their exemption from punishment except where law has been violated, for their employment and reward as free laborers, for their exclusive right to their own bodies and those of their own children, for their instruction and subsequent admission to all the trusts, offices, honors and emoluments of intelligent freemen. . . . The slaves, if freed, will come under the watchful cognizance of law; they will not be idle, but *avariciously* industrious; they will not rush through the country, firing dwellings and murdering the inhabitants; for freedom is all they ask—all they desire—the obtainment of which will transform them from enemies into friends, from nuisances into blessings, from a corrupt, suffering and degraded, into a comparatively virtuous, happy and elevated population. . . .

. . . The . . . *gradualists* . . . talk as if the friends of abolition contended only for the emancipation of the slaves, without specifying or caring what should be done with or for them! as if the planters were invoked to cease from one kind of villany, only to practise another! as if the manumitted slaves must necessarily be driven out from society into the wilderness, like wild beasts! This is talking nonsense: it is a gross perversion of reason and common sense. Abolitionists have never said, that mere manumission would be doing justice to the slaves: they insist upon a remuneration for years of unrequited toil, upon their employment as free laborers, upon their immediate and coefficient instruction, and upon the exercise of a benevolent supervision over them on the part of their employers. . . . The very ground which they assume for their opposition to slavery,—that it necessarily prevents the improvement of its victims,—shows that they contemplate the establishment of schools for the education of the slaves, and the furnishing of productive employment, immediately upon their liberation. If this were done, none of the horrors which are now so feelingly depicted, as the attendants of a sudden abolition, would ensue. . . .

It is said, by way of extenuation, that the present owners of slaves are not responsible for the origin of this system. I do not arraign them for the crimes *of their ancestors*, but for the constant perpetration and extension of similar crimes. The plea that the evil of slavery was entailed upon them, shall avail them nothing: in its length and breadth it means that the robberies of one generation justify the robberies of another! . . . Scarcely any one denies that blame attaches somewhere:

the present generation throws it upon the past—the past, upon its predecessor—and thus it is cast, like a ball, from one to another, down to the first importers of the Africans! . . . Sixty thousand infants, the offspring of slave-parents, are annually born in this country, and doomed to remediless bondage. Is it not as atrocious a crime to kidnap these, as to kidnap a similar number on the coast of Africa? . . .

Those who prophesy evil, and only evil, concerning immediate abolition, absolutely disregard the nature and constitution of man, as also his inalienable rights, and annihilate or reverse the causes and effects of human action. They are continually fearful lest the slaves, in consequence of their grievous wrongs and intolerable sufferings, should attempt to gain their freedom by revolution; and yet they affect to be equally fearful lest a general emancipation should produce the same disastrous consequences. How absurd! They *know* that oppression must cause rebellion; and yet they pretend that a removal of the cause will produce a bloody effect! This is to suppose an effect without a cause, and, of course, is a contradiction in terms. Bestow upon the slaves personal freedom, and all motives for insurrection are destroyed. Treat them like rational beings, and you may surely expect rational treatment in return: treat them like beasts, and they will behave in a beastly manner.

Part Two

THE NEW POLITICS

V. The New Rules

The sluggishness of national politics during the Era of Good Feelings (1815–24) only partly obscured political transformations then underway reflecting basic changes in society itself. One-party, Republican rule had dampened popular interest and reduced voter participation. This "clubby" atmosphere in which the Republican representatives ran things without frequent reference to their constituents (and chose the presidential candidate within their party caucus in Congress) first fell apart in the states. The aftermath of the Panic of 1819 revived interest in politics, shattering many long-standing factional arrangements. Elections were again contested, and since the depression lasted half-a-dozen years, voter interest did not flag. Inevitably, the newer, more volatile, and definitely more popular politics reached the national scene too. Andrew Jackson of Tennessee did not call the new currents into being, but in 1824 he ignored the decision of the congressional caucus (as did John Quincy Adams and Henry Clay) and almost won the Presidency. The New Politics took many forms, all of them helping to usher in revisions in style and content that still dominate American politics.

1. UNIVERSAL SUFFRAGE: DIVERGENT VIEWS

Revolutionary America may have been a Land of Liberty, but it was not yet a land of mass participation in representative government. By European standards and practice, of course, America of the late eighteenth century had already entered the egalitarian age, since a relatively high level of political participation prevailed. But property qualifications for voting remained on the books, poorly enforced though they sometimes were, barring some from the polls

with their economic hurdle and discouraging many more
with their psychological barrier. In the first quarter of the
nineteenth century, however, universal suffrage not only
became a popular idea but it became the practice in most
states. At the many conventions assembled to draft or
modify state constitutions, the suffrage issue revealed basic
conflicts among politicians concerning the advantages
and/or perils of mass participation. Selections below are
from speeches at the New York and Virginia constitutional conventions and cover both sides of the argument.
Finally, the Frenchman Alexis DeTocqueville, the most
perceptive foreign observer of Jacksonian America, eval-
uated some of the side effects and perils of extended suffrage. [Nathaniel H. Carter and William L. Stone, comps.,
Reports of the Proceedings and Debates of the Convention of 1821 . . . (Albany, 1821), 225–59, 261–65; Proceedings and Debates of the Virginia State Convention of
1829–30 . . . (Richmond, 1830), 362–68; Alexis De-
Tocqueville, Democracy in America (2 vols., New York,
1900), I: 200–207.]

MARTIN VAN BUREN ADDRESSES THE NEW YORK CONVENTION

. . . The committee had been entertained with the most frightful
conjectures, on subjects, if not wholly, certainly in a great degree, un-
connected with the object of the amendment. They had been told of
the present bad character, and worse propensities of a great portion of
their present population—the demoralizing effects of great manufacturing establishments, which might, or might not, hereafter grow up
among us, had been pourtrayed in the darkest colours—the dissolute
and abandoned character of a large portion of the inhabitants of the
old cities of Europe, and the probability of similar degeneracy in this
happy land, had been represented in hideous deformity—And all the
powers of eloquence, and the inventions of imagination, had been
enlisted, to present to our view, a long train of evils, which would
follow, from extending the right of suffrage to such a description of
people. . . .

There were two words, continued Mr. V. B., which had come into
common use with our revolutionary struggle; words which contained
an abridgment of our political rights; words which, at that day, had
a talismanic effect; which led our fathers from the bosoms of their
families to the tented field; which, for seven long years of toil and
suffering, had kept them to their arms; and which finally conducted
them to a glorious triumph. They were "TAXATION and REPRESENTA-
TION"; nor did they lose their influence with the close of that struggle.

They were never heard in our halls of legislation, without bringing to our recollections the consecrated feelings of those who won our liberties, or without reminding us of every thing that was sacred in principle. . . .

In whose name, and for whose benefit, he inquired, were they called upon to disappoint the just expectations of their constituents, and to persevere in what he could not but regard as a violation of principle? It was in the name, and for the security of '*farmers,*' that they were called upon to adopt this measure. . . .

But let us, said he, consider this subject in another and different point of view; it was their duty, and he had no doubt it was their wish, to satisfy all, so that their proceedings might meet with the approbation of the whole community; it was his desire to respect the wishes and consult the interest of all; he would not hamper the rich nor tread upon the poor, but would respect each alike. He would, he said, submit a few considerations to the men of property, who think this provision necessary for its security, and in doing so, he would speak of property in general, dropping the important distinction made by the amendment offered between real and personal estate. Admitting, for the sake of argument, that the distinction was just, and wise, and necessary, for the security of property, was the object effected by the present regulation? He thought not; property was not now represented in the senate on the extent it was erroneously supposed to be. To represent *individual property,* it would be necessary that each individual should have a number of votes in some degree at least, in proportion to the amount of his property; this was the manner in which property was represented, in various corporations and in monied institutions. Suppose in any such institution one man had one hundred shares, another, one share, could you gravely tell the man who held one hundred shares, that his property was represented in the direction, if their votes were equal. To say that because a man worth millions, as is the case of one in this committee, has one vote, and another citizen worth only two hundred and fifty dollars in real estate, has one vote for senators, that therefore their property is equally represented in the senate, is, to say the least, speaking very incorrectly; it is literally substituting a shadow for a reality; and though the case he had stated by way of illustration, would not be a common one, still the disparity which pervaded the whole community, was sufficiently great to render his argument correct.

If to this it was answered, as it had been by the gentleman from Albany, (Mr. Van Vechten) that the amount was not material; that the idea of their representing freeholders would be sufficient; his reply was, that this purpose was already effected by the constitution as it stands. It now provides that the senators shall be freeholders; and that part of the constitution it was not proposed to alter. There was no objection to fixing the amount of the freehold required in the elected, and to place it on a respectable, but not extravagant footing. If, therefore, an ideal representation of property was of any value, that object was fully obtained without the amendment. But the preservation of individual property, is not the great object of having it represented in the senate.

When the people of this state shall have so far degenerated; when the principles of order or of good government which now characterize our people, and afford security to our institutions, shall have so far given way to those of anarchy and violence, as to lead to an attack on private property, or an agrarian law; to which allusion had been made by the gentleman from Albany, (Mr. Kent); or by an attempt to throw all the public burthens on any particular class of men; then all constitutional provisions will be idle and unavailing, because they will have lost all their force and influence. In answer to the apprehension so frequently expressed, that unless this amendment prevails, there is nothing to prevent all the taxes being laid on the real estate, it is only necessary to state, that there is no more in the constitution of the United States, than there will be in ours, if the amendment fails, to prevent all the revenues of the union from being raised by direct taxation. And was such a fear ever entertained for the general government? How is it possible for gentlemen to suppose, that in a constitutional regulation, under which all the states are enjoying the most ample security for property, an individual state would be exposed to danger?

He had no doubt but the honourable gentlemen who had spoken in favour of the amendment, had suffered from the fearful forebodings which they had expressed. That ever to be revered band of patriots who made our constitution, entertained them also, and therefore they engrafted in it the clause which is now contended for. But a full and perfect experience had proved the fallacy of their speculations, and they were now called upon again to adopt the exploded notion; and on that ground, to disfranchise, if not a majority, nearly a moiety, of our citizens. He said he was an unbeliever in the speculations and mere theories on the subject of government, of the best and wisest men, when unsupported by, and especially when opposed to, experience. He believed with a sensible and elegant modern writer, "That constitutions are the work of time, not the invention of ingenuity; and that to frame a complete system of government, depending on habits of reverence and experience, was an attempt as absurd as to build a tree, or manufacture an opinion."

All our observation, he said, united to justify this assertion—when they looked at the proceedings of the Convention which adopted the constitution of the United States, they could not fail to be struck by the extravagance, and, as experience had proved, the futility of the fears and hopes that were entertained and expressed, from the different provisions of that constitution, by the members. The venerable and enlightened Franklin, had no hope if the president had the qualified negative, that it would be possible to keep him honest; that the extensive power of objecting to laws, would inevitably lead to the bestowment of doucers to prevent the exercise of the power; and many, very many of the members, believed that the general government, framed as it was, would, in a few years, prostrate the state governments. While, on the other hand, the lamented Hamilton, Mr. Madison, and others, distressed themselves with the apprehension, that unless they could infuse more vigour into the constitution they were about to adopt, the work of their hands could not be expected to survive its framers. Experience, the only unerring touchstone, had proved the fallacy of all those speculations, as it had also those of the framers of our state constitution, in the particular now under consideration; and having her records before them, he was for being governed by them. . . .

If, then, it was true that the present representation of property in the senate was ideal, and purely ideal, did not, continued Mr. V. B. sound policy dictate an abandonment of it, by the possessors of property? He thought it did; he thought so because he held it to be at all times, and under all circumstances, and for all interests, unwise to struggle against the wishes of any portion of the people—to subject yourselves to a wanton exposure to public prejudice to struggle for an object, which, if attained, was of no avail. He thought so, because the retaining of this qualification in the present state of public opinion, would have a tendency to excite jealousy in the minds of those who had no freehold property, and because more mischief was to be apprehended from that source than any other. . . .

But, said Mr. V. B. we have been referred to the opinions of General Hamilton, as expressed in his writings in favour of the constitution of the United States, as supporting this amendment. He should not detain the committee by adding any thing to what had been said of his great worth, and splendid talents. . . . But there was nothing in the Federalist to support the amendment:—Without troubling the committee by reading the number which had been referred to, it would be sufficient for him to say, that it could not be supposed, that the distinguished men who had done a lasting benefit to their country, and had earned for themselves the highest honours, by the work in question, could have urged the propriety, of a property representation, in one branch of the legislature, in favour of a constitution, which contained no such provision. They had not done so. . . .

The next consideration which had been pressed upon the committee by the honourable mover of the amendment, was, the apprehension that the persons employed in the manufactories which now were, or which, in the progress of time, might be established amongst us, would be influenced by their employers. So far as it respected the question before the committee, said Mr. V. B. it was a sufficient answer to the argument, that if they were so influenced, they would be enlisted on the same side, which it was the object of the amendment to promote, on the side of property. If not—if they were independent of the influence of their employers, they would be safe depositories of the right. For no man, surely, would contend that they should be deprived of the right of voting on account of their poverty, except so far as it might be supposed to impair their independence, and the consequent purity of the exercise of that invaluable right. . . .

. . . What, sir, said he, was the cause of the corruptions which confessedly prevail in that portion of the representation in the parliament of Great Britain? Was it the lowness of the qualification of the electors, in comparison with the residue of the country? No. . . . I will tell you, sir, said Mr. V. B. what is the cause—it is because the representation in question, is a representation of things, and not of men—it is because that it is attached to territory, to a village or town, without regard to the population; as by the amendment under consideration, it is attempted here to be attached to territory, and to territory only. . . .

If he could possibly believe, added Mr. V. B. that any portion of the calamitous consequences could result from the rejection of the amendment, which had been so feelingly pourtrayed by the honourable gentleman from Albany, (Mr. Kent,) and for whom he would repeat the acknowledgment of his respect and regard, he would be the last man in society who would vote for it. But, believing, as he conscientiously did, that those fears were altogether unfounded; hoping and expecting that the happiest results would follow from the abolition of the freehold qualification, and hoping too, that caution and circumspection would preside over the settlement of the general right of suffrage, which was hereafter to be made, and knowing, besides, that this state, in abolishing the freehold qualifications, would but be uniting herself in the march of principle, which had already prevailed in every state of the union, except two or three, including the royal charter of Rhode-Island, he would cheerfully record his vote against the amendment.

PHILIP N. NICHOLAS ADDRESSES THE VIRGINIA CONVENTION

The amendment has certainly the merit of advancing boldly to the question, and proposes, what I conceive, amounts essentially to Universal Suffrage. There cannot be a more fit occasion to enquire, what ought to be the basis of Suffrage, than when it is proposed to extend that right to almost every man in the country. . . .

. . . This subject has received from me, Mr. Chairman, my anxious consideration; not only since it has been agitated in this Convention, but whilst during the canvass, which preceded the elections, it was discussed in the public prints, in speeches to the people, and in the addresses of various gentlemen who were called on to declare their sentiments. Amongst the arguments relied upon by the advocates of a very extended Suffrage, one of the most fallacious, is, that which attempts to found the right upon principles of natural equality. This pre-supposes that Suffrage is derived from nature. Now, nothing can be clearer, than that Suffrage is a conventional, and not a natural right. In a state of nature, (if such state ever existed except in the imagination of the poets,) every man acts for himself, and is the sole judge of what will contribute to his happiness. When he enters into the social state, which he is compelled to do, to guard himself against violence, and to protect him in the enjoyment of the fruits of his industry, he gives up to the society the powers of Government, and surrenders to it, so much of his natural rights as are essential to secure to him such portion of those rights which he retains, or such other rights as grow out of the new relations in which he is placed. . . .

. . . This plain exposition of the origin and formation of society, incontestibly shows that both Representation and Suffrage are social institutions. It proves that it is a solecism to insist, that it is proper to refer back to a state of nature, for principles to regulate rights which never existed in it—which could only exist after mankind abandoned it, rather than by a correct estimate of those relations, which are to be found in a state of society, of which, both Representation and Suffrage are the offspring. It has been attempted to sustain almost unlimited suffrage, (I know not whether in the Committee, as I did not come in until after the gentleman from Loudoun had been speaking some time, but certainly elsewhere,) by reference to those general phrases in the Bill of Rights, which declare, "that all men are by nature equally free and independent." But the same section of the Bill of Rights plainly discriminates between the state of nature, and the social state, and admits the modification which natural rights may receive by entering into society. . . . What then, is the rule laid down by the authors of our Constitution on this subject? It is, "that all men having sufficient evidence of permanent, common interest with, and attachment to, the community, have the Right of Suffrage." Every part of this definition, Mr. Chairman, is highly important. First, there must be "sufficient evidence," and next, it must be the evidence "of permanent, common interest with, and attachment to, the community." Now, I contend that this sufficient evidence of common, permanent interest, is only to be found in a lasting ownership of the soil of the country.

This kind of property is durable, it is indestructible; and the man who acquires, or is the proprietor of it, connects his fate by the strongest of all ties, with the destiny of the country. No other species of property has the same qualities, or affords the same evidence. Personal property is fluctuating—it is frequently invisible, as well as intangible—it can be removed, and can be enjoyed as well in one society as another. What evidence of permanent interest and attachment, is afforded by the ownership of horses, cattle, or slaves? Can it retard or impede the removal from the State, in times of difficulty or danger impending over it? What security is the ownership of Bank or other stocks, or in the funded debt? None. A man may transfer this kind of property in a few moments, take his seat in the stage, or embark in the steamboat, and be out of the State in one day, carrying with him all he possesses.

The same objection applies to admitting persons who have only a temporary interest in the soil: besides, that these temporary interests give a control to others, over the votes of the holder, just as certainly, as that "a control over a man's subsistence, is always a control over his will." In vain do gentlemen refer to the example of other States. Here we have a safe rule laid down, by the wisdom of our ancestors, whom gentlemen unite in canonizing, and tested and approved by the experience of more than half a century. Sir, I always thought I was a republican, but gentlemen would argue me out of my belief. I have always supposed, that our Right of Suffrage was so constructed, as to protect both persons and property. God forbid that I should wish to exclude any, who I can be convinced ought to be admitted, or that I would oppress any portion of my fellow-citizens. My principles would lead me to admit all I could, consistently with what I believe the welfare of society requires. I am no enemy to the non-freeholder; but I must vote for that rule, which by securing the tranquillity and happiness of society, secures those inestimable blessings to every member of it. I do not deny to the advocates of greatly extended suffrage, either in this House or out of it, perfect rectitude and sincerity of motive. Enthusiasm is always sincere—but that truth does not at all mitigate the evils and desolations, which it has often inflicted on mankind. . . .

. . . Gentlemen argue this question as if it was one between the Satraps, (the existence of whom they choose to suppose) and the poor of the land. Instead of making war upon the middling or even the poorer classes, we believe we are defending their best interests. We go not for the interests of wealth, when we say, that we are of opinion that an interest in the soil is the best evidence of permanent attachment. This idea of an aristocracy of freeholders, is not only incorrect but ludicrous. Are we contending for giving wealth in the distribution of suffrage, a weight in proportion to its extent? The answer is, that a freeholder, whose farm is worth fifty dollars, has as available a suffrage as one who has land worth two hundred thousand dollars. Are we for fixing a high property qualification? We reply, that it appears from this debate, that a man can get a freehold in almost any county in the State for fifty dollars, and in some (indeed many) for twenty-five dollars, or for a smaller sum. And yet we are gravely told, that these freeholds, accessible as they are to the industry and exertions of all, constitute an odious aristocracy. Sir, we do not even require that these freeholds should be productive, (as many of them are not) of one cent of revenue. Sir, the beauty of this system, its republican feature, is that the humblest freeholder is put on a footing with the richest man in the State. . . .

The gentleman from Loudoun has stated, that he knows of no particular virtue attached to the soil, that we should select the owners as the sole depositories of political power. All professions are on a par in his estimation. I do not pretend that great virtues may not be found in all the professions and walks of life. But I do believe, if there are any chosen people of God, they are the cultivators of the soil. If there be virtue to be found any where, it would be amongst the middling farmers, who constitute the yeomanry, the bone and sinew of our country. Sir, they are men of moderate desires, they have to labor for their subsistence, and the support of their families; their wishes are bounded by the limits of their small possessions; they are not harassed by envy, by the love of show and splendor, nor agitated by the restless and insatiable passion of ambition. When they lay their heads at night upon their pillows under the consciousness of having spent the day in the discharge of their duties to their families, they enjoy a sweeter sleep under their humble roofs, than frequently do those who repose in gilded palaces. Amid the same description of persons, I should look for independence of character. It is a fact, that our voters are less exposed to influence and intrigue, than any, I believe, in the United States. . . .

There is one consideration which shows the propriety of making land the basis of political power. It is, that the land, has always been, and will ever continue to be, the principal source from which all your taxes are derived. The freeholders, if they are an aristocracy, are the most lenient aristocrats who ever existed. . . . So far from being aristocratic, it is the best safeguard against aristocracy. It places the power in the hands of those who are interested to guard both property and persons against oppression. The idea of aristocracy is absurd. Did you ever hear of an aristocracy of fifty dollar, or twenty-five dollar freeholders? In the hands of these freeholders, personal rights are just as secure as the rights of property. Many of the non-freeholders are the sons of freeholders. Would they support measures which would oppress their own sons? Besides, have not the great body of the freeholders such perfect identity of condition with the non-freeholders, that they could pass no law for the regulation of personal rights which would not equally affect them as well as the non-freeholders. To those who take a superficial view of things, it might appear that placing the power in the hands of men, without regard to their condition, would advance the cause of liberty. Many will tell you, Sir, that they would do this to counteract the influence of wealth in society.

But these men, many of whom are ardent friends of liberty, are unconsciously laboring to undermine the cause of which they mean to be the strenuous advocates. As long as political power is placed as it now is in Virginia, in the hands of the middling classes, who, though not rich, are yet sufficiently so, to secure their independence, you have nothing to fear from wealth. But place power in the hands of those who have none, or a very trivial stake in the community, and you expose the poor and dependent to the influence and seductions of wealth. The extreme rich, and the extreme poor, if not natural allies, will become so in fact. The rich will relieve the necessities of the poor, and the latter will become subservient to the ambition of the rich. You hear nothing of the bribery and corruption of freeholders. No man is hardy enough to attempt it. But extend the Right of Suffrage to every man dependent, as well as independent, and you immediately open the flood-gates of corruption.

Our lot in this Commonwealth is a happy one, if we would but be content with it. Our institutions are free, no man is oppressed, and every man is secure in the enjoyment of the fruits of honest industry. Our Government has no taint of monarchy, or aristocracy, and power is in the hands of the great body of the yeomanry of the country. What can a people want more!

DE TOCQUEVILLE ON DEMOCRACY IN AMERICA

Many people in Europe are apt to believe without saying it, or to say without believing it, that one of the great advantages of universal suffrage is, that it entrusts the direction of public affairs to men who are worthy of the public confidence. They admit that the people is unable to govern for itself, but they aver that it is always sincerely disposed to promote the welfare of the State, and that it instinctively designates those persons who are animated by the same good wishes, and who are the most fit to wield the supreme authority. I confess that the observations I made in America by no means coincide with these opinions. On my arrival in the United States I was surprised to find so much distinguished talent among the subjects, and so little among the heads of the Government. It is a well-authenticated fact, that at the present day the most able men in the United States are very rarely placed at the head of affairs; and it must be acknowledged that such has been the result in proportion as democracy has outstepped all its former limits. The race of American statesmen has evidently dwindled most remarkably in the course of the last fifty years.

Several causes may be assigned to this phenomenon. It is impossible, notwithstanding the most strenuous exertions, to raise the intelligence of the people above a certain level. Whatever may be the facilities of acquiring information, whatever may be the profusion of easy methods and of cheap science, the human mind can never be instructed and educated without devoting a considerable space of time to those objects.

The greater or the lesser possibility of subsisting without labor is therefore the necessary boundary of intellectual improvement. This boundary is more remote in some countries and more restricted in others; but it must exist somewhere as long as the people is constrained to work in order to procure the means of physical subsistence, that is to say, as long as it retains its popular character. It is therefore quite as difficult to imagine a State in which all the citizens should be very well informed as a State in which they should all be wealthy; these two difficulties may be looked upon as correlative. It may very readily be admitted that the mass of the citizens are sincerely disposed to promote the welfare of their country; nay more, it may even be allowed that the lower classes are less apt to be swayed by considerations of personal interest than the higher orders: but it is always more or less impossible for them to discern the best means of attaining the end which they desire with sincerity. Long and patient observation, joined to a multitude of different notions, is required to form a just estimate of the character of a single individual; and can it be supposed that the vulgar have the power of succeeding in an inquiry which misleads the penetration of genius itself? The people has neither the time nor the means which are essential to the prosecution of an investigation of this kind: its conclusions are hastily formed from a superficial inspection of the more prominent features of a question. Hence it often assents to the clamor of a mountebank who knows the secret of stimulating its tastes, while its truest friends frequently fail in their exertions.

Moreover, the democracy is not only deficient in that soundness of judgment which is necessary to select men really deserving of its confidence, but it has neither the desire nor the inclination to find them out. It cannot be denied that democratic institutions have a very strong tendency to promote the feeling of envy in the human heart; not so much because they afford to every one the means of rising to the level of any of his fellow-citizens, as because those means perpetually disappoint the persons who employ them. Democratic institutions awaken and foster a passion for equality which they can never entirely satisfy. This complete equality eludes the grasp of the people at the very moment at which it thinks to hold it fast, and "flies," as Pascal says, "with eternal flight"; the people is excited in the pursuit of an advantage, which is more precious because it is not sufficiently remote to be unknown, or sufficiently near to be enjoyed. The lower orders are agitated by the chance of success, they are irritated by its uncertainty; and they pass from the enthusiasm of pursuit to the exhaustion of ill-success, and lastly to the acrimony of disappointment. Whatever transcends their own limits appears to be an obstacle to their desires, and there is no kind of superiority, however legitimate it may be, which is not irksome in their sight. . . .

In the United States the people is not disposed to hate the superior classes of society; but it is not very favorably inclined towards them, and it carefully excludes them from the exercise of authority. It does not entertain any dread of distinguished talents, but it is rarely captivated by them; and it awards its approbation very sparingly to such as have risen without the popular support.

Whilst the natural propensities of democracy induce the people to reject the most distinguished citizens as its rulers, these individuals are no less apt to retire from a political career in which it is almost impossible to retain their independence, or to advance without degrading themselves. This opinion has been very candidly set forth by Chancellor Kent, who says, in speaking with great eulogiums of that part of the Constitution which empowers the Executive to nominate the judges: "It is indeed probable that the men who are best fitted to discharge the duties of this high office would have too much reserve in their manners, and too much austerity in their principles, for them to be returned by the majority at an election where universal suffrage is adopted." Such were the opinions which were printed without contradiction in America in the year 1830!

I hold it to be sufficiently demonstrated that universal suffrage is by no means a guarantee of the wisdom of the popular choice, and that, whatever its advantages may be, this is not one of them. . . .

Causes Which May Partly Correct These Tendencies of the Democracy

In New England the education and the liberties of the communities were engendered by the moral and religious principles of their founders. Where society has acquired a sufficient degree of stability to enable it to hold certain maxims and to retain fixed habits, the lower orders are accustomed to respect intellectual superiority and to submit to it without complaint, although they set at naught all those privileges which wealth and birth have introduced among mankind. The democracy in New England consequently makes a more judicious choice than it does elsewhere.

But as we descend towards the South, to those States in which the constitution of society is more modern and less strong, where instruction is less general, and where the principles of morality, of religion, and of liberty are less happily combined, we perceive that the talents and the virtues of those who are in authority become more and more rare.

Lastly, when we arrive at the new South-western States, in which the constitution of society dates but from yesterday, and presents an agglomeration of adventurers and speculators, we are amazed at the persons who are invested with public authority, and we are led to ask by what force, independent of the legislation and of the men who direct it, the State can be protected, and society be made to flourish.

There are certain laws of a democratic nature which contribute, nevertheless, to correct, in some measure, the dangerous tendencies of democracy. On entering the House of Representatives of Washington one is struck by the vulgar demeanor of that great assembly. The eye frequently does not discover a man of celebrity within its walls. Its members are almost all obscure individuals whose names present no associations to the mind: they are mostly village lawyers, men in trade, or even persons belonging to the lower classes of society. In a country in which education is very general, it is said that the representatives of the people do not always know how to write correctly.

At a few yards' distance from this spot is the door of the Senate, which contains within a small space a large proportion of the celebrated men of America. Scarcely an individual is to be perceived in it who does not recall the idea of an active and illustrious career: the Senate is composed of eloquent advocates, distinguished generals, wise magistrates, and statesmen of note, whose language would at all times do honor to the most remarkable parliamentary debates of Europe. . . .

. . . The only reason which appears to me adequately to account for it is, that the House of Representatives is elected by the populace directly, and that the Senate is elected by elected bodies. . . .

The time may be already anticipated at which the American Republics will be obliged to introduce the plan of election by an elected body more frequently into their system of representation, or they will incur no small risk of perishing miserably amongst the shoals of democracy.

2. THE LAWMAKERS

Americans have always been proud of their republican institutions, especially so in the Jacksonian era. Representative government seemed best exemplified at the time by the two dozen state legislatures, the governing units closest

to the people and, some historians have argued, the era's
real centers of power. Many European travelers visited one
or more of these legislatures, or special state conventions,
and most came away with reactions much less euphoric
than the boastings of American republican defenders. Basil
Hall visited the New York legislature on the eve of Jackson's election and penned a frank report stressing the untutored rambling of the debate. Charles Joseph Latrobe,
another sharp-eyed and tough-minded British observer,
happened upon a state constitutional convention in Georgia. Again, the American politicians' gush of rhetoric
created negative impressions, and prompted Latrobe to
speculate about America's coming rendezvous with the
future. [Basil Hall, Travels in North America in the Years
1827 and 1828 (3 vols., Edinburgh, 1829), II: 33–39;
Charles Joseph Latrobe, The Rambler in North America:
1832–1833 (2 vols., London, 1835), II: 66–70.]

BASIL HALL ON THE NEW YORK STATE LEGISLATURE

. . . During this excursion among the clouds, he referred frequently
to the History of England, gave us an account of the manner in which
Magna Charta was wrested from "that monster King John," and detailed
the whole history of the Bill of Rights. In process of time, he brought
his history down to the commencement of the American Revolution,
then to the period of the Declaration of Independence—the Articles
of Confederation—and so on, till my patience, if not that of the House,
was pretty well worn out by the difficulty of following these threadbare
commonplaces.

The next member who spoke declared his ignorance of Latin, and
his consequent inability to study Magna Charta—which, I presume,
was a good joke—but thought that, if these occasional opportunities
were lost, of impressing upon the minds of the people a sense of their
rights, their immediate descendants, who were not so familiar, of course,
as they themselves were, with the history of their country, to say nothing of posterity, would gradually forget their own privileges; "and then,"
said he, "the Americans will cease to be the great, the happy, and the
high-minded people they are at the present day!"

At length a man of sense, and habits of business, got up, and instantly
commanded the closest attention of the House. He had been one of the
committee, he said, appointed to revise the laws, and as such, had voted
for the insertion of the particular clause, not from any great or immediate good which it was likely to produce, but simply because it was
consistent with other parts of the American Government, and because

it was suitable to the present genius of the people, to make these frequent references to their rights. "Here," he observed, "is a fair opportunity to enumerate some of these rights, and I trust the committee will see the propriety of embodying these few but important precepts in the Revised Code of Laws which is to become the standard authority of the State."

I imagined this clear explanation would put an end to the debate; but the same invincible speaker who had so frequently addressed them before, rose again, and I don't know when the discussion would have ended, had not the hand of the clock approached the hour of two, the time for dinner. A motion to rise and report progress was then cheerfully agreed to, and the House adjourned.

I do not pretend to have done justice to this debate; in truth the arguments seemed to me so shallow, and were all so ambitiously, or rather wordily, expressed, that I was frequently at a loss for some minutes to think what the orators really meant, or if they meant any thing. The whole discussion, indeed, struck me as being rather juvenile. The matter was in the highest degree commonplace, and the manner of treating it still more so. The speeches, accordingly, were full of set phrases and rhetorical flourishes about their "ancestors having come out of the contest full of glory, and covered with scars—and their ears ringing with the din of battle." This false taste, waste of time—conclusions in which nothing was concluded—splitting of straws, and ingeniously elaborate objections, all about any thing or nothing in the world, appeared to me to arise from the entire absence of those habits of public business, which can be acquired only by long-continued and exclusive practice.

These gentlemen were described to me as being chiefly farmers, shopkeepers, and country lawyers, and other persons quite unaccustomed to abstract reasoning, and therefore apt to be led away by the sound of their own voices, farther than their heads could follow. It is probable too, that part of this wasteful, rambling kind of argumentation may be ascribed to the circumstance of most of the speakers being men, who, from not having made public business a regular profession or study, were ignorant of what had been done before—and had come to the legislature, straight from the plough—or from behind the counter— from chopping down trees—or from the bar, under the impression that they were at once to be converted into statesmen.

Such were my opinions at this early stage of the journey, and I never afterwards saw much occasion to alter them; indeed, the more I became acquainted with the practical operation of the democratical system, the more I became satisfied that the ends which it proposed to accomplish, could not be obtained by such means. By bringing into these popular assemblies men who—disguise it as they may—cannot but feel themselves ignorant of public business, an ascendency is given to a few abler and more intriguing heads, which enables them to manage matters to suit their own purposes. And just as the members begin to get a slight degree of useful familiarity with the routine of affairs, a fresh election comes on, and out they all go; or at least a great majority go out, and thus, in each fresh legislature, there must be found a preponderance of unqualified, or, at all events, of ill-informed men, however patriotic or well-intentioned they may chance to be.

On the same distrustful principle, all men in office are jealously kept out of Congress, and the State legislatures; which seems altogether the most ingenious device ever hit upon for excluding from the national councils, all those persons best fitted by their education, habits of business, knowledge, and advantageous situation of whatever sort, for performing, efficiently, the duties of statesmen: while, by the same device, the very best, because the most immediate and the most responsible sources of information are removed to a distance; and the men who possess the knowledge required for the purposes of deliberation, are placed out of sight, and on their guard, instead of being always at hand, and liable to sudden scrutiny, face to face, with the representatives of the nation. . . .

. . . I was much struck with one peculiarity in these debates—the absence of all cheering, coughing, or other methods by which, in England, public bodies take the liberty of communicating to the person who is speaking a full knowledge of the impression made upon the audience. In America there is nothing to supply the endless variety of tones in which the word Hear! Hear! is uttered in the House of Commons, by which the member who is speaking ascertains, with the utmost distinctness and precision, whether the House are pleased or displeased with him, bored or delighted, or whether what he says is granted or denied—lessons eminently useful in the conduct of public debate.

In America, in every legislative assembly, the speakers are listened to with the most perfect silence and forbearance. This practice, while it must be particularly discouraging to good speakers, cannot fail to protract the wearisome prosings of the dullest and longest-winded orators, to the great loss of good time, and the mystification of business. It was not till long after the period I am now describing, however, that I came to any satisfactory explanation of this curious anomaly, which at first sight appeared inconsistent with the general state of things out of doors. But I found I was quite mistaken, in supposing this decorous silence could be safely dispensed with; and eventually became satisfied, not only of the policy, but of the absolute necessity, of the rule, so long as the deliberative bodies in question are framed on the principles of universal suffrage, and annual changes.

During the debate,—if the desultory discussion which has led me into this digression can be so called,—and while I was standing near the door, the member who had spoken so often came up to me, and said, with a chuckling air of confident superiority, but in perfect good humour,—

"Well, sir, what do you think of us? Don't we tread very close on the heels of the Mother Country?"

I evaded the question as well as I might, by saying, that I did not think there was any race between us, or any danger of treading on one another's heels—that the countries were so differently circumstanced, it was hardly discreet to make comparisons.

CHARLES JOSEPH LATROBE VISITS GEORGIA

The soil throughout Georgia, and indeed through the whole range of country from Maryland southward, is of a deep red. Towards Milledgeville, the plantations became more numerous, and appeared well cultivated, producing maize, wheat, cotton, and barley. The seat of Government above-named, is pleasantly situated in an undulating country, on the upper branch of the Alatamaha river, and considerable taste reigns in the style of architecture adopted, and in the interspersion of fine trees among the dwellings. A State Convention summoned for the purpose of revising the Constitution, was just in the act of opening its sessions. With regard to these Conventions, we found that there were very diverse opinions held by different individuals; many urging, that, as an assembly of men elected with carelessness, acting without check, superseding all law, and in fact taking the place of the original framers of the Constitution of the State,—they were more likely to do harm than good, and that it was always a matter of thankfulness when they dispersed without having done any great mischief. Others would say—that besides the acknowledged necessity of an occasional revision of the Constitution, the Conventions have this advantage, that many eminent men and servants of the State, whom distaste to a life of constant political warfare had sent into retirement, are induced on such occasions to come forward, and give the country the aid of their matured experience.

The proceedings of the Convention I am unable to detail, as we resumed our route the following morning.

In peeping in upon the proceedings of retired courts of justice, or listening to the harangues delivered right and left for political purposes, by the public men of the United States, whether on the stump or in the senate, the Englishman cannot but be struck with the general diffusion throughout the United States of that gift usually called the "gift of the gab." Nothing can be more provoking than the fluency of the country lawyers in spite of their shabby coats: and to one who would be inclined to consider quantity rather than quality, their unhesitating delivery, command of language, and long-windedness, might indeed be a subject of envy. But a little attention will show him, that sound and sense are not always companions. He will detect innumerable expletives —sentences without legitimate beginning or end—deductions from nothing—big words meaning little, and out of place, leading to the most astounding examples of bathos—digressions without end—and, after all, that to extract sense and facts from that wholesale production of words, he must patiently sit down like a searcher after gold dust, and sift bushel after bushel of sand to find the ore. He will find even in the style of eloquence in vogue among the majority of the members of the supreme courts of the country, the same sacrifice of dignity and simplicity evident.

That the people of the United States should be sanguine about the durability of their institutions, is not to be wondered at. They do not allow the justice of an appeal to the history of the past in Europe, to prove the probable mutability of their governments—because they are in their youth, and have, they believe, set out on a more excellent principle and under more favourable circumstances than any people since the world began.

They conceive the doubts which pass the lips of a foreigner to originate in prejudice and jealousy. As to the apparent, and I believe real aptitude of their form of government to the present circumstances of the country and the people, that appears evident; and attached as I may well be to the monarchical form of my own country, finding a great deal in both my Bible and in the book of the world's history, that would incline me to doubt their wisdom or ultimate success; and thinking it their misfortune that circumstances have deprived them and their children of that class of noble feelings and impulses which unite a people to its prince; I am far from expecting or wishing to see the day when they may have a king among them, however some might whisper the probability. By the bye, even among themselves I have seen those who considered the conduct of the honest-hearted and straight-forward officer at present at the head of their executive, as little better than despotism, and it appeared that not a few among them expected to hear of the worthy General doffing his beaver for a kingly crown, or perhaps that he had even begun to exercise the right divine, and touch for the king's evil.

It is not merely because their government is a democratic republic, that I think it liable to change, or to pass away—but because it is one of human institution, and as such the seeds of mutability are within its bosom. It is but an experiment, and that it is such will be seen more and more. . . .

If a government formed upon a Republican model does not succeed there—surely, the question of its suitableness to the state of mankind as they are, should be considered as determined for ever. But it must occur to every one, that the United States of America have not only to combat the difficulties which may arise within their own bosom, of which there will be many before the lapse of many years,—but also those that menace them from without. Will they not, more or less, be influenced by the spirit of the times. They are separated from the Old World by the vast ocean, but they are not without the influence of the vortex; every thing, their language, literature, necessities, increasing facility of communication with Europe, all render them intimately connected with us. We whirl, they whirl too. Do we feel the revolution which is taking place in every thing—politics—religious opinion—science—so must they. There may be this difference, that as yet they have more room, the sweep is a wider one than our's, but they still obey the same law as ourselves.

3. THE ACCEPTANCE OF PARTY

In the early days of the Republic, American politicians agreed that political parties were evil. Scored as "factions," they were supposedly lethal to republicanism. This view, usually maintained with most vehemence by politicians in office, began to break down early in the nineteenth century. Political machines sprang up in several states, machines which not only practiced a different doctrine but whose spokesmen openly defended the necessity and morality of party organization. In New York, in the 1820s, one of these machines, the Albany Regency, fought a long and successful war for domination of the state's politics. The Regency's chief opponent was DeWitt Clinton, organizer of the Erie Canal, and very much a personalist politico who scorned the discipline of party organization. While Governor, Clinton lashed out at party politics several times. He had nothing to lose, and probably would have been defeated by the Regency even if he had not died in 1828. In 1829 a Regency Governor, Enos T. Throop, defended the New Politics and wrote a political epitaph for the older, negative ideas about parties. [Charles Z. Lincoln, comp., Messages of the Governors of the State of New York . . . (10 vols., Albany, 1909), III: 54–55, 198–99, 274–78.]

DeWitt Clinton, 1825

The excitements and animosities which have hitherto rent us asunder, degraded our character, and impaired our ability for doing good, are yielding to a spirit of moderation and conciliation: and it is to be hoped, that in future, the great subject of competition, and the great prize of ambition, will be confined to a distinguished career of public spirit, unalloyed by the debasing influence of faction, which, in seeking its own gratification, by the elevation of a part, generally overlooks the prosperity of the whole. Our civil and political institutions are derived from the wisdom, and exist in the will of the people, the source of all rightful authority, and of all legitimate sovereignty. Conceiving it to be the sacred duty of public servants, entrusted with power and authority by the people, to consult the wishes, as well as the interests of their constituents, it is my earnest desire, and shall be my favorite object, to recommend that course, and to pursue that policy, which may prove the most gratifying to the community, and the most auspicious to the great interests of the state. And in selecting persons for offices of power, trust and emolument, it will be my aim to look for capacity, integrity, patriotic zeal, and public services. The times are auspicious to the healing of those dissensions which have so long interfered with our general happiness, and so greatly diminished the just consideration of the state in the councils of the nation. As far as in my power, I shall be happy to embrace this auspicious occasion, and make every proper effort to promote internal peace and tranquillity. Having been elected to office, not by a party, but by the people, it is my ardent wish to cast myself upon their candor and judgment, to meet their scrutiny, to consult their will, and to promote their happiness. And I shall always be solicitous to cultivate a good understanding with the co-ordinate authorities, and to produce an harmonious union of effort for the public good. . . .

But it cannot, nor ought it to be concealed, that our country has been more or less exposed to agitations and commotions, for the last seven years. Party spirit has entered the recesses of retirement, violated the sanctity of female character, invaded the tranquillity of private life, and visited with severe inflictions the peace of families; neither elevation nor humility has been spared; nor the charities of life, nor distinguished public services, nor the fireside, nor the altar, been left free from attack; but a licentious and destroying spirit has gone forth, regardless of everything but the gratification of malignant feelings, and unworthy aspirations. The causes of this alarming and portentous evil, must be found in a great measure in the incompetent and injudicious provisions relative to the office of Chief Magistrate of the Union.

A continuance in office but for one term, would diminish, if not disarm, opposition, and divert the incumbent from the pursuits of personal ambition, to the acquisition of that fame which rests for its support upon the public good. The mode of choice is also highly exceptionable. Instead of a uniform system, there are various rules, some of which are calculated to secure unanimity in the electoral colleges, and others to diminish the legitimate power, if not to annihilate the real force of the states, and there is every facility to bring the final determination into the House of Representatives—an ample field for the operations of management and intrigue, and for the production of suspicions, and imputations, which ought never to stain the character of our country. Nor are the claims of the national government in derogation of the constitutional authorities of the states calculated to quiet the agitations of the times, nor to tranquilize the apprehensions of the community.

Although rash innovation ought ever to be discountenanced, yet salutary improvement ought to be unhesitatingly cultivated. And until some adequate preventives, and efficacious remedies are engrafted into the constitution, we must rarely expect a recurrence of the same tranquillity which formerly shed its benign influence over our country.

Enos T. Throop, 1829

I trust that you will not think it amiss, that I should be explicit with you in regard to another matter, to which direct reference is not usually made on occasions like the present. I allude to those political divisions which exist now, and have heretofore existed among us. Desiring to be fully understood by my fellow-citizens upon all points, and willing to abide by their decisions, I can see no reason why I should avoid an explanation of my sentiments upon a subject, which, every one knows, has a controlling influence over the conduct and deliberations of all our public functionaries.

However public opinion may be divided on the question, whether political parties are or are not desirable or beneficial in a government like ours, all sensible men must be convinced, and the experience of the world has shown, that they will prevail where there is the least degree of liberty of action on the part of public agents, or their constituents; and that they are more especially inseparable from a free government. The history of this republic demonstrates the truth of this position, and it is not desirable, in my opinion, that it should be otherwise.

Those party divisions which are based upon conflicting opinions in regard to the constitution of the government, or the measures of the administration of it, interest every citizen, and tend, inevitably, in the spirit of emulation and proselytism, to reduce many shades of opinion into two opposing parties. By the mutual concession of opinion, within the ranks of a party, acerbity of spirit is softened. Thus, organized parties watch and scan each other's doings, the public mind is instructed by ample discussions of public measures, and acts of violence are restrained by the convictions of the people, that the prevailing measures are the results of enlightened reason.

Diversity of opinion results from the infirmity of human judgment; and party spirit is but the passion with which opposing opinions are urged in the strife for the possession of power. As yet, our free institutions have not suffered from an indulgence in feelings of this character. We have, it is true, witnessed, in times past, a degree of party spirit, so highly excited as to alarm the fears of patriotic men for the integrity of the Union: but, at those periods, the compactness and harmony of our admirable system of government were not thoroughly understood, nor had the attachment of the people to it been fairly tested. Experience has proved, that its foundations are laid so deep in the affections of our citizens, and that its complicated machinery is so nicely adjusted, and so well adapted to its design, that it has an energy sufficient for its own preservation. The universal consciousness of these truths has tamed the spirit of party, and stationed it, as the vigilant watchman, over the conduct of those in power. No stronger proof of this position can be desired, than is furnished by the incidents of the election, through which we have just now passed. The excesses which characterized that struggle, were rebuked by the calm, orderly and dispassionate manner which marked the conduct of the people at the polls, in the discharge of their sacred functions as electors—a rebuke which, I have no doubt, will, at future elections, chasten the conduct of meretricious partizans, and bring down the temper of the paper contest to the manners of the times, and the sense of propriety manifested by the people themselves.

Of the political parties known to our history, there has been one, and but one, which, from the adoption of the federal constitution to the present day, has maintained an unvaried character, and has constantly had the public good for its object. Drawing its principles from the whiggism of the revolution, and looking steadfastly to the maintenance of the federal constitution, and the enlargement of the privileges of the people as its results, it triumphed in 1798, supported the government through the perils of the late war, and has recently again triumphed in this state, and throughout the nation. This party has, at times, lost its power by disunion, and by those, often healthful, fluctuations of the will of the people, incident to popular government, and has as often regained it, when an opportunity for reflection and fuller information was afforded. But, through all its fortunes, it has evinced a vital energy, sufficient, in due time, to vindicate its claims to supremacy, and a magnanimity to correct its own errors. It has employed its corrective power upon the measures of government and heterodox political opinions, until it has received the assent of nearly all parties to the purity and fitness of its principles, and the justness of its rule. It stands now upon its original foundation; and for whatever of true political principle or public prosperity we enjoy, we are indebted to its uniformity of character and its undaunted perseverance. I have lived in a reverence of its principles, and am not too fastidious to avow my determination to labor for its continued ascendancy, by the plenary exercise of all the proper means that may be placed at my disposal; with it, I am content to stand or fall.

I have said, and now repeat, that as yet, our invaluable institutions have suffered but little, if any thing, from the spirit of party, fiery and excited as at times it has been. Political parties, at the present day, sobered by past experience, leave scope for the exercise of all the charities and courtesies of life, between opposing members. Their spirit does not enter into families to engender hate, nor into social and religious societies to create dissensions, and to produce bitter and destructive enmities. These are the offices of personal parties, whose spirit is overwrought passion, whose object of pursuit is vengeance, and whose ultimate end is civil disorders and cruel persecution. It is one of the peculiar benefits of a well regulated party spirit in a commonwealth, that it employs the passions actively in a milder mood, and thus shuts the door against faction.

Parties of this description, oftentimes arise from the best of feelings, and for the most honest purposes: to redress the wrongs of an individual, to inflict punishment on public transgressors, to suppress what may be deemed dangerous classes in the community, or to enforce opinions, which its votaries may suppose essential to the comfort or to the temporal and spiritual peace of others. In the full pursuit of their objects, when in the minority, they too often disregard law—when in the majority, they proceed through violent laws, and in disregard of the dictates of humanity and justice, to the end proposed; and they seldom cease when they obtain the mastery, until the heart is wrung by the spectacle of widespread ruin, which has marked their desolating career.

It is not thus, that human passions act by their own impulse. Although they are easily roused by individual suffering, or are strenuous in the effort to proselyte to individual dogmas, they are prone, without extraneous excitement, to return to their duty under the empire of reason. But, while heated, they are exposed to the subtle excitations of selfish, heartless and unprincipled men. Honest men and honest causes are thus made to minister to the unhallowed enterprises of the dissolute intriguer, the discarded partisan, the prurient malcontent, and the unsuccessful politician.

It was through the frenzy of feeling from kindred causes, that non-conforming Quakers were hung in our own country, by unjustifiable laws; the most worthy of Protestants and Catholics were burnt at the stake in Europe, by the instigation of hypocrites, who feigned a zeal for the God of mercy; and Europe, in the middle ages, was drained of its people and treasures by the arts and ambition of popes and priests, and princes and nobles, to force, by the sword, the tenets of Christianity upon the deluded Mahometans. And finally, should a spirit of religious or civil persecution be kindled in this country against the Methodists, the Baptists, the Presbyterians, or any other sect; or against the lawyers, the doctors, or any other profession, or class of citizens; there would not be wanting men of capacious minds, but desperate characters, to fan the flame, and endeavor to lead their honest and fanatic fellows, in the wild tumult of passion, to sacrifice their victims to the Moloch faction.

I still flatter myself that we are not destined, in this happy country to such excesses. Knowledge abounds, to moderate the passions; just laws, enacted by the people themselves, and faithfully administered, afford protection against outrage; and opinion, exercising its moral power over the conduct of partizans, applies correctives, through regular party discipline, to such abuses in individual conduct as cannot be reached by the ordinary operation of the laws.

4. LOOKING FOR VOTES

Before the triumph of democratic politics general agreement existed that candidates should not openly solicit votes. In a deferential society this would have been more than unseemly, it would have been unnecessary. The prejudice against "electioneering" faded in the Jackson period. Politicians, of all parties and principles, had to go to the electors. In the first selection below, Harriet Martineau, a British traveler, describes a meeting in which a candidate for Governor in Massachusetts, Edward Everett, talked down to the crowd in order to ingratiate himself. In the second, Thurlow Weed of New York recalls the details (probably a bit embellished since they were written years after the event) of swinging the election of three state senators. Gentlemanly aloofness, or a candidate's mere declaration and expectation of automatic support, clearly were out of date by the 1830s. [Harriet Martineau, Society in America, 4th ed. (2 vols., New York, 1837), I: 95–99; Harriet A. Weed, ed., Autobiography of Thurlow Weed (Boston, 1889), 476–79.]

HARRIET MARTINEAU ATTENDS A POLITICAL RALLY

One of the then candidates for the highest office in the State, is renowned for his oratory. He is one of the most accomplished scholars and gentlemen that the country possesses. It was thought, "by his friends," that his interest wanted strengthening in the western part of the State. The people were pleased when any occasion procured them the *éclat* of bringing a celebrated orator over to address them. The commemoration of an Indian catastrophe was thought of as an occasion capable of being turned to good electioneering purposes.—Mr. Webster was invited to be the orator, it being known that he would refuse. "Not I," said he. "I won't go and rake up old bloody Indian stories." The candidate was next invited, and, of course, took the opportunity of "strengthening his interest in the western part of the State." I was not aware of this till I sometime after heard it, on indisputable authority. I should have enjoyed it much less than I did, if I had known that the whole thing was got up, or its time and manner chosen, for electioneering objects; that advantage was taken of the best feelings of the people for the political interest of one.

The afternoon of the 29th we went to Bloody Brook, the fearfully-named place of disaster. We climbed the Sugar-loaf; a high, steep hill, from whose precipitous sides is obtained a view of the valley which pleases me more than the celebrated one from Mount Holyoke, a few miles off. Each, however, is perfect in its way; and both so like heaven, when one looks down upon the valley in the light of an autumn afternoon,—such a light as never yet burnished an English scene,—that no inclination is left to make comparisons. The ox team was in the fields, the fishers on the banks of the grey river,—banks and fishers reflected to the life,—all as tranquil as if there was to be no stir the next day.

On descending, we went to the Bloody Brook Inn, and saw the strange and horrible picture of the slaughter of Lothrop's troop; a picture so bad as to be laughable; but too horrible to be laughed at. Every man of the eighty exactly alike, and all looking scared at being about to be scalped. We saw, also, the long tables spread for the feast of to-morrow. Lengths of unbleached cotton for table cloths, plates and glasses, were already provided. Some young men were bringing in long trails of the wild vine, clustered with purple grapes, to hang about the young maple trees which overshadowed the tables; others were trying the cannon. We returned home in a state of high expectation.

The morning of the 30th was bright, but rather cold. It was doubtful how far prudence would warrant our sitting in an orchard for several hours, in such a breeze as was blowing. It was evident, however, that persons at a distance had no scruples on the subject, so thickly did they throng to the place of meeting. The wagon belonging to the band passed my windows, filled with young ladies from the High School at Greenfield. They looked as gay as if they had been going to a fair. By half-past eight, our party set off, accompanied by a few, and passing a great number of strangers from distant villages.

After having accomplished our drive of three or four miles, we warmed ourselves in a friendly house, and repaired to the orchard to choose our seats, while the ceremony of laying the first stone of the monument was proceeding at some distance. The platform from which the orator was to address the assemblage was erected under a rather shabby walnut-tree, which was rendered less picturesque by its lower branches being lopped off, for the sake of convenience. Several men had perched themselves on the tree; and I was beginning to wonder how they would endure their uncomfortable seat, in the cold wind, for three hours, when I saw them called down, and dismissed to find places among the rest of the assemblage, as they sent down bark and dust upon the heads of those who sat on the platform. Long and deep ranges of benches were provided; and on these, with carriage cushions and warm cloaks, we found ourselves perfectly well accommodated. Nothing could be better. It was a pretty sight. The wind rustled fitfully in the old walnut-tree. The audience gathered around it were sober, quiet; some would have said dull. The girls appeared to me to be all pretty, after the fashion of American girls. Every body was well-dressed; and such a thing as ill-behaviour in any village assemblage in New England, is, I believe, unheard of. The soldiers were my great amusement; as they were on the few other occasions when I had the good fortune to see any. Their chief business, on the present occasion, was to keep clear the seats which were reserved for the band, now absent with the procession. These seats were advantageously placed; and newcomers were every moment taking possession of them, and had to be sent, disappointed, into the rear. It was moving to behold the loving entreaties of the soldiers that these seats might be vacated. I saw one, who had shrunk away from his uniform, (probably from the use of tobacco, of which his mouth was full,) actually put his arm round the neck of a gentleman, and smile imploringly in his face. It was irresistible, and the gentleman moved away. It is a perfect treat to the philanthropist to observe the pacific appearance of the militia throughout the United States. It is well known how they can fight, when the necessity arises: but they assuredly look, at present, as if it was the last thing in their intentions:—as I hope it may long be.

The band next arrived, leading the procession of gentlemen, and were soon called into action by the first hymn. They did their best; and, if no one of their instruments could reach the second note of the

German Hymn, (the second note of three lines out of four,) it was not for want of trying.

The oration followed. I strove, as I always did, not to allow difference of taste, whether in oratory, or in anything else, to render me insensible to the merit, in its kind, of what was presented to me: but, upon this occasion, all my sympathies were baffled, and I was deeply disgusted. It mattered little what the oration was in itself, if it had only belonged in character to the speaker. If a Greenfield farmer or mechanic had spoken as he believed orators to speak, and if the failure had been complete, I might have been sorry or amused, or disappointed; but not disgusted. But here was one of the most learned and accomplished gentlemen in the country, a candidate for the highest office in the State, grimacing like a mountebank before the assemblage whose votes he desired to have, and delivering an address, which he supposed level to their taste and capacity. He spoke of the "stately tree," (the poor walnut,) and the "mighty assemblage," (a little flock in the middle of an orchard,) and offered them shreds of tawdry sentiment, without the intermixture of one sound thought, or simple and natural feeling, simply and naturally expressed. It was equally an under estimate of his hearers, and a degradation of himself.

The effect was very plain. Many, I know, were not interested, but were unwilling to say so of so renowned an orator. All were dull; and it was easy to see that none of the proper results of public speaking followed. These very people are highly imaginative. Speak to them of what interests them, and they are moved with a word. Speak to those whose children are at school, of the progress and diffusion of knowledge, and they will hang upon the lips of the speaker. Speak to the unsophisticated among them of the case of the slave, and they are ready to brave Lynch-law on his behalf. Appeal to them on any religious or charitable enterprise, and the good deed is done, almost as soon as indicated. But they have been taught to consider the oratory of set persons on set occasions as a matter of business or of pastime. They listen to it, make their remarks upon it, vote, perhaps, that it shall be printed, and go home, without having been so much moved as by a dozen casual remarks, overheard upon the road.

All this would be of little importance, if these orations consisted of narrative,—or of any mere matter of fact. The grievance lies in the prostitution of moral sentiment, the clap-trap of praise and pathos, which is thus criminally adventured. This is one great evil. Another, as great, both to orators and listeners, is the mis-estimate of the people. No insolence and meanness can surpass those of the man of sense and taste who talks beneath himself to the people, because he thinks its suits them.

Thurlow Weed Influences an Election

The State election this year was only important in its bearing upon the Senate, where a Democratic majority not only refused to confirm Governor Seward's nominations for State officers, but obstructed the passage of bills deemed essential to the public welfare. By reason of two unexpected vacancies, three senators were to be chosen in the third (Albany) district. The political complexion of the Senate depended, therefore, upon the result in that district.

The district had heretofore been Democratic, but we had for two or three years been diminishing the majority against us and on this occasion had determined to make a very spirited canvass. A week before the election I became satisfied that the chances of success were against us, and so reported to my political friends in New York. This stimulated them to renewed efforts. On the Saturday morning previous to the election some Whig merchants and bankers met hastily, and appointed a committee to visit Albany. On Sunday morning early, while dressing, I was summoned to the Eagle Tavern, where I found in the parlor Messrs. Robert B. Minturn, Moses H. Grinnell, Simeon Draper, R. M. Blatchford, and James Bowen. They had arrived about daylight in the steamboat Columbia, especially chartered by them. They took a large bandana handkerchief from a trunk, which they opened and spread upon a centre-table. It contained packages of bank notes of various denominations, amounting to $8,000. My friends remarked that no possible effort must be spared to carry the district, and desired me to take as much of this fund as could be advantageously disbursed, adding that if more were needed they would draw checks for it.

The election was to commence on Monday morning and to terminate on Wednesday evening. I informed them that it would be quite impossible in so short a time to use any such amount of money, and, after explaining what I thought might be accomplished in the brief interval before the election, took $3,000, $1,500 of which was immediately dispatched by messengers to Columbia, Greene, Delaware, and Rensselaer counties; $1,500 was reserved for Albany.

A question of much embarrassment occurred to us, namely, how the unusual circumstance of the arrival of a strange steamer could be explained without exciting suspicions as to the real object of its visit. Governor Seward was sent for, and joined in the consultation. It was decided that all the New York gentlemen named, with one exception, should remain incog. at the hotel. Mr. Minturn, whose father-in-law, Judge Wendell, resided in Albany, went to his relatives' house, and from thence to church. Still, we were very apprehensive that the "Argus" might get some inkling or clew to the business in hand, and this, we knew, would have been fatal to our plans. So it was arranged that G. W. Daly, then known as an efficient fighting Whig at the polls, should see "Abe Vanderzee," a journeyman in the "Argus" office and a Democratic pugilist. Except when excited at the polls these two men were friends, though one was a zealous Whig and the other an equally enthusiastic Democrat. Daly took Vanderzee a stroll along the docks, and said to him with apparent surprise, "Here is a strange steamer. What can she have come for?" They made inquiry, and found that she had arrived there at daylight, without passengers and without apparent object. Daly said, "Well, never mind; I'll find out in the course of the day what this means. . . . After dropping in a grocery or two, and "smiling" once or twice, they separated. Early in the evening Daly went to the "Argus" office, accidentally fell in with Abe, and told him he had found out the whole story of the steamer, adding that, on Saturday evening after the mails had left New York (this being before telegraphs), a steamer had arrived from England, bringing information that the crops had been destroyed, and some flour speculators had chartered the boat to come to Albany, and had immediately upon their arrival started off in different directions to buy up flour, so as to secure a monopoly.

Meanwhile, the steamer dropped down to Van Wie's Point. At sundown the New York gentlemen were driven to that place in close carriages, taken on board, and returned to New York in safety.

That day and most of the night were spent in active preparations for the next three days' battle. Springsted, Beardsley, and Van Schaick were hastily dispatched to the county towns with additional material aid. G. W. Daly, H. Y. Webb, Sam Strong, Bob Chesebro, John Ross, etc., were to organize a physical force sufficient to clear a passage to the polls. Chauncey Dexter, Stillman Witt (then an employee of the People's Line of steamboats, now an Ohio millionaire), Rans Van Valkenburg, James Weldon, Tom Hillson (now in the custom house), Provost Vesey, the brothers Young, etc., were to look after the canal boatmen. The brothers Benedict, I. N. Comstock (now in the appraiser's office), Drs. Kane and Grant, the Fredenrichs, etc., were to look after the "drift" voters in the Texas portion of the ninth and tenth wards. George Cuyler, and others of his tact and vigilance, were to act as challengers. Captain L. W. Brainard (now in the custom house), Rufus Rhoades, and Tommy Cowell were to bring all the Whig steamboat and sloop hands from New York and alongshore between New York and Albany. David Nelligan, Mike Clark, Pat. Murphy, and Michael O'Sullivan (then a Catholic schoolteacher, afterwards a Union officer through the Rebellion) were to look after the "few and far between" Irish voters. Tom Kirkpatrick and Hugh J. Hastings were to swing around the various polls and ascertain where screws were loose or machinery required oiling.

The flour "blind" served to bridge over the danger for one day, Monday morning's "Argus" appearing, to our great relief, without any reference to the arrival of the steamer. The mail of that day brought news from England by the Great Western, announcing among other things the arrival, late on Saturday night, of over $2,000,000 "for British service in Canada." In this circumstance the "Argus" was convinced that it had discovered the whole secret of the sudden appearance of the Columbia, and on Tuesday morning it contained the following editorial:—

A MYSTERY, AND ITS EXPLANATION

Our city was not a little excited on Sunday by the mysterious arrival, about noon, of the steamboat Columbia from New York, which place she left at twelve the previous night, with only four or five persons on board, one of whom started express to the north, and the others returned in the Columbia at two P.M. All the afternoon groups were inquiring, "What's in the wind?" Numerous were the conjectures, and rumors, and surmises which the quidnuncs started to solve the mystery.

The explanation doubtless is, that as the Great Western brought over $2,000,000 for Canada, preparatory to the resumption of specie payments by the provincial banks, an agent was dispatched express to advise of its arrival; and as there is no day boat on Sunday, and as the loss of a day would have ensued by waiting until the afternoon of that day, the Columbia was dispatched specially for the purpose.

The election occupied three days of extraordinary interest and excitement, each party doing its utmost. A great deal of bitter feeling was necessarily provoked on the other side by our boldness and confidence. The result was a signal triumph, our three senators, Erastus Root, Friend Humphrey, and Mitchell Sanford, being chosen by an average majority of one hundred and thirty-three. General Root, however, had a narrow escape, obnoxious as he was to the extreme abolitionists. He was elected by a majority of only two. This victory changed, as was anticipated, the political character of the Senate, giving effect to the nominations of Governor Seward, sustaining the general banking law, and upholding the canal policy of the Whig party.

Thus a memorable *coup d'état*, completely revolutionizing the State, was effected, on the very verge of the election, by the thoughtfulness and liberality of a few zealous politicians in the city of New York. The secret was well kept, for until now no whisper of it has ever been heard.

VI. The Jacksonians Take Over

By the time the Jacksonians assumed office in March 1829 the new political currents were already in motion, and in some cases they had already replaced older forms. Jackson and his supporters did not invent them (anti-Jacksonians, for example, had led in the use of state and later national conventions); but the Jackson men, or Democrats, became the most adept in utilizing the innovations to their advantage. They began with an enormous advantage, the commanding and popular figure of Jackson himself. To this personalism they added the power of refurbished Republican state machines. In the process they modernized national politics, bringing it into a working relationship with the egalitarianism of the age, and with the political reactions that egalitarian spirit had produced.

1. THE BARBARIANS AT THE GATES

For some Americans Jackson's election signaled the end of political civilization as they knew it—or thought they knew it. Earlier, the reaction of the urban rich and "well-born" to Jefferson's election in 1800–01 had demonstrated how self-deluded the upper crust can become when it believes its interests and life-style are threatened. President Jefferson did not inaugurate a Jacobin tyranny; neither was President Jackson to impose a western barbarism, despite such apprehensions during the campaign. Nevertheless, the anticipations of his inauguration and the events of the dreaded day itself combined to confirm the fears of those who devoutly wished to be frightened. Washington had been the last to feel the effects of political egalitarianism, the symbolic arrival of "the people." From the start of government under the Constitution, Virginia planter-statesmen (and a pair of Adamses)

had run the federal government, decorously and safely.
Many of Jefferson's appointees had become by 1829 part
of the entrenched Republican establishment. The response
of one of their wives, Margaret Bayard Smith, to inauguration day festivities reflects the apprehensions of that group
over an uncertain future. In the second selection, Frances
Trollope, an acerbic and unsympathetic Englishwoman,
comments on national politics of the day. Her views,
especially on how Americans made political commitments,
need not be taken literally. Rather, they epitomize upper-
class reaction to American electioneering, as viewed by
British travelers. [Gaillard Hunt, ed., The First Forty
Years of Washington Society, Portrayed by the Family
Letters of Mrs. Samuel Harrison Smith . . . (New York,
1906), 290–97; Frances Trollope, Domestic Manners of
the Americans, 2nd ed. (2 vols., London, 1832), II: 65–
67.]

MRS. SMITH TO MRS. KIRKPATRICK

[Washington] March 11th, Sunday [1829.]
Thursday morning. I left the rest of this sheet for an account of the
inauguration. It was not a thing of detail of a succession of small incidents. No, it was one grand whole, an imposing and majestic spectacle
and to a reflective mind one of moral sublimity. Thousands and thousands of people, without distinction of rank, collected in an immense
mass round the Capitol, silent, orderly and tranquil, with their eyes fixed
on the front of that edifice, waiting the appearance of the President in
the portico. The door from the Rotunda opens, preceded by the mar-
shals, surrounded by the Judges of the Supreme Court, the old man
with his grey locks, that crown of glory, advances, bows to the people,
who greet him with a shout that rends the air, the Cannons, from the
heights around, from Alexandria and Fort Warburton proclaim the
oath he has taken and all the hills reverberate the sound. It was grand,
—it was sublime! An almost breathless silence, succeeded and the multitude was still,—listening to catch the sound of his voice, tho' it was
so low, as to be heard only by those nearest to him. After reading his
speech, the oath was administered to him by the Chief Justice. The
Marshal presented the Bible. The President took it from his hands,
pressed his lips to it, laid it reverently down, then bowed again to the
people—Yes, to the people in all their majesty. And had the spectacle
closed here, even Europeans must have acknowledged that a free people, collected in their might, silent and tranquil, restrained solely by a
moral power, without a shadow around of military force, was majesty,
rising to sublimity, and far surpassing the majesty of Kings and Princes,

surrounded with armies and glittering in gold. But I will not anticipate, but will give you an account of the inauguration in mere detail. The whole of the preceding day, immense crowds were coming into the city from all parts, lodgings could not be obtained, and the newcomers had to go to George Town, which soon overflowed and others had to go to Alexandria. I was told the Avenue and adjoining streets were so crowded on Tuesday afternoon that it was difficult to pass.

A national salute was fired early in the morning, and ushered in the 4th of March. By ten oclock the Avenue was crowded with carriages of every description, from the splendid Barronet and coach, down to waggons and carts, filled with women and children, some in finery and some in rags, for it was the peoples President, and all would see him; the men all walked. Julia, Anna Maria and I, (the other girls would not adventure) accompanied by Mr. Wood, set off before 11, and followed the living stream that was pouring along to the Capitol. The terraces, the Balconies, the Porticos, seemed as we approached already filled. We rode round the whole square, taking a view of the animated scene. Then leaving the carriage outside the palisades, we entered the enclosed grounds, where we were soon joined by John Cranet and another gentleman, which offered each of us a protector. We walked round the terrace several times, every turn meeting new groups of ladies and gentlemen whom we knew. All with smiling faces. The day was warm and delightful, from the South Terrace we had a view of Pennsylvania and Louisiana Avenues, crowded with people hurrying towards the Capitol. It was a most exhilirating scene! Most of the ladies preferred being inside of the Capitol and the eastern portico, damp and cold as it was, had been filled from 9 in the morning by ladies who wished to be near the General when he spoke. Every room was filled and the windows crowded. But as so confined a situation allowed no general view, we would not coop ourselves up, and certainly enjoyed a much finer view of the spectacle, both in its whole and in its details, than those within the walls. We stood on the South steps of the terrace; when the appointed hour came saw the General and his company advancing up the Avenue, slow, very slow, so impeded was his march by the crowds thronging around him. Even from a distance, he could be discerned from those who accompanied him, for he only was uncovered, (the Servant in presence of his Sovereign, the People). The south side of the Capitol hill was literally alive with the multitude, who stood ready to receive the hero and the multitude who attended him. "There, there, that is he," exclaimed different voices. "Which?" asked others. "He with the white head," was the reply. "Ah," exclaimed others, "there is the old man and his gray hair, there is the old veteran, there is Jackson." At last he enters the gate at the foot of the hill and turns to the road that leads round to the front of the Capitol. In a moment every one who until then had stood like statues gazing on the scene below them, rushed onward, to right, to left, to be ready to receive him in the front. Our party, of course, were more deliberate, we waited until the multitude had rushed past us and then left the terrace and walked round to the furthest side of the square, where there were no carriages to impede us, and entered it by the gate fronting the Capitol. Here was a clear space, and stationing ourselves on the central gravel walk we stood so as to have a clear, full view of the whole scene. The Capitol in all its grandeur and beauty. The Portico and grand steps leading to it, were filled with ladies. Scarlet, purple, blue, yellow, white draperies and waving plumes of every kind and colour, among the white marble pillars, had a fine effect. In the centre of the portico was a table covered with scarlet, behind it the closed door leading into the rotunda, below the Capitol and all around, a mass of living beings, not a ragged mob, but well dressed and well behaved respectable and worthy citizens. Mr. Frank Key, whose arm I had, and an old and frequent witness of great spectacles, often exclaimed, as well as myself, a mere novice, "It is beautiful, it is sublime!" The sun had been obscured through the morning by a mist, or haziness. But the concussion in the air, produced by the discharge of the cannon, dispersed it and the sun shone forth in all his brightness. At the moment the General entered the Portico and advanced to the table, the shout that rent the air, still resounds in my ears. When the speech was over, and the President made his parting bow, the barrier that had separated the people from him was broken down and they rushed up the steps all eager to shake hands with him. It was with difficulty he made his way through the Capitol and down the hill to the gateway that opens on the avenue. Here for a moment he was stopped. The living mass was impenetrable. After a while a passage was opened, and he mounted his horse which had been provided for his return (for he had walked to the Capitol) then such a cortege as followed him! Country men, farmers, gentlemen, mounted and dismounted, boys, women and children, black and white. Carriages, wagons and carts all pursuing him to the President's house,—this I only heard of for our party went out at the opposite side of the square and went to Col. Benton's lodgings, to visit Mrs. Benton and Mrs. Gilmore. Here was a perfect levee, at least a hundred ladies and gentlemen, all happy and rejoicing,—wine and cake was handed in profusion. We sat with this company and stopped on the summit of the hill until the avenue was comparatively clear, tho' at any other time we should have thought it terribly crowded. Streams of people on foot and of carriages of all kinds, still pouring towards the President's house. We went Home, found your papa and sisters at the Bank, standing at the upper windows, where they had been seen by the President, who took off his hat to them, which they insisted was better than all we had seen. From the Bank to the President's house for a long while, the crowd rendered a passage for us impossible. Some went into the Cashier's parlour, where we found a number of ladies and gentlemen and had cake and wine in abundance. In about an hour, the pavement was clear enough for us to walk. Your father, Mr. Wood, Mr. Ward, Mr. Lyon, with us, we set off to the President's House, but on a nearer approach found an entrance impossible, the yard and avenue was compact with living matter. The day was delightful, the scene animating, so we walked backward and forward at every turn meeting some new acquaintance and stopping to talk and shake hands. Among others we met Zavr. Dickinson with Mr. Frelinghuysen and Dr. Elmendorf, and Mr. Saml Bradford. We continued promenading here, until near three, returned home unable to stand and threw ourselves on the sopha. Some one came and informed us the crowd before the President's house, was so far lessen'd, that they thought we might enter. This time we effected our purpose. But what a scene did we witness! The *Majesty of the People* had disappeared, and a rabble, a mob, of boys, negros, women, children, scrambling, fighting, romping. What a pity what a pity! No arrangements had been made, no police officers placed on duty, and the whole house had been inundated by the rabble mob. We came too late. The President, after having been *literally* nearly pressed to death and almost suffocated and torn to pieces by the people in their eagerness to shake hands with Old Hickory, had retreated through the back way or south front and had escaped to his lodgings at Gadsby's. Cut glass and china to the amount of several thousand dollars had been broken in the struggle to get the refreshments, punch and other articles had been carried out in tubs and buckets, but had it been in hogsheads it would have been insufficient, ice-creams, and cake and lemonade, for 20,000 people, for it is said that number were there, tho' I think the estimate exaggerated. Ladies fainted, men were seen with bloody noses and such a scene of confusion took place as is impossible to describe,—those who got in could not get out by the door again, but had to scramble out of windows. At one time, the President who had retreated and retreated until he was pressed against the wall, could only be secured by a number of gentlemen forming round him and making a kind of barrier of their own bodies, and the pressure was so great that Col Bomford who was one said that at one time he was afraid they should have been pushed down, or on the President. It was then the windows were thrown open, and the torrent found an outlet, which otherwise might have proved fatal.

This concourse had not been anticipated and therefore not provided against. Ladies and gentlemen, only had been expected at this Levee, not the people en masse. But it was the People's day, and the People's President and the People would rule. God grant that one day or other, the People, do not put down all rule and rulers. I fear, enlightened

Freemen as they are, they will be found, as they have been found in all ages and countries where they get the Power in their hands, that of all tyrants, they are the most ferocious, cruel and despotic. The noisy and disorderly rabble in the President's House brought to my mind descriptions I had read, of the mobs in the Tuileries and at Versailles, I expect to hear the carpets and furniture are ruined, the streets were muddy, and these guests all went thither on foot.

The rest of the day, overcome with fatigue I lay upon the sopha.

Frances Trollope on American Manners

Even in the retirement in which we passed this summer, we were not beyond reach of the election fever which is constantly raging through the land. Had America every attraction under heaven that nature and social enjoyment can offer, this electioneering madness would make me fly it in disgust. It engrosses every conversation, it irritates every temper, it substitutes party spirit for personal esteem; and, in fact, vitiates the whole system of society.

When a candidate for any office starts, his party endow him with every virtue, and with all the talents. They are all ready to peck out the eyes of those who oppose him, and in the warm and mettlesome southwestern states, do literally often perform this operation: but as soon as he succeeds, his virtues and his talents vanish, and, excepting those holding office under his appointment, every man Jonathan of them sets off again full gallop to elect his successor. When I first arrived in America Mr. John Quincy Adams was President, and it was impossible to doubt, even from the statement of his enemies, that he was every way calculated to do honour to the office. All I ever heard against him was, that "he was too much of a gentleman"; but a new candidate must be set up, and Mr. Adams was out-voted for no other reason, that I could learn, but because it was "best to change." "Jackson for ever!" was, therefore, screamed from the majority of mouths, both drunk and sober, till he was elected; but no sooner in his place, than the same ceaseless operation went on again, with "Clay for ever" for its warwhoop.

I was one morning paying a visit, when a party of gentlemen arrived at the same house on horseback. The one whose air proclaimed him the chief of his party, left us not long in doubt as to his business, for he said, almost in entering,

"Mr. P———, I come to ask for your vote."

"Who are you for, sir?" was the reply.

"Clay for ever!" the rejoinder; and the vote was promised.

This gentleman was candidate for a place in the state representation, whose members have a vote in the presidential election.

I was introduced to him as an English woman: he addressed me with,

"Well, madam, you see we do these things openly and above-board here; you mince such matters more, I expect."

After his departure, his history and standing were discussed. "Mr. M. is highly respectable, and of very good standing; there can be no doubt of his election if he is a thorough-going Clay-man," said my host.

2. THE SCOURGE OF PATRONAGE

A major arguing point in the indictment of Jacksonianism was the claim that good government had been prostituted by the political appointment of public officers. Much of this, though not all, was the mock outrage of the recently dispossessed. The openly political use of patronage was neither new nor grossly immoral. It was widely practiced in all states, some more than others, depending on the maturity of the state's party system. What Jackson did after 1829 was to nationalize the practice, far more than previous Presidents, and to tie it firmly to the interests of his party. One Jacksonian politician, Senator William L. Marcy of New York, had no qualms in making an open declaration that to the victorious party belonged the spoils of office. Jackson, as befits a President, spoke more circumspectly. In a message to Congress he defended the spoils system, preferring to call it "rotation in office," as a guarantee against bureaucratic tyranny. And he bowed to the egalitarian spirit by rejecting the notion of bureaucratic expertise and arguing that all intelligent men could serve the public. (He surely did not forget that the Adams forces had called him a nonexpert in government, unfit to govern.) The Whigs delivered tirades against spoils; but the Jacksonians got the offices. One of the sharpest critics from the opposition side was Daniel Webster of Massachusetts, who outlined in 1834 the dangers of an unchecked spoils system. [James D. Richardson, comp., A Compilation of the Messages and Papers of the Presidents, 1789–1897 (10 vols., Washington, 1896–97), II: 448–49; Writings and Speeches of Daniel Webster, National Edition (18 vols., Boston, 1903), VII: 180–83.]

JACKSON DEFENDS THE SPOILS SYSTEM

While members of Congress can be constitutionally appointed to offices of trust and profit it will be the practice, even under the most conscientious adherence to duty, to select them for such stations as they are believed to be better qualified to fill than other citizens; but the purity of our Government would doubtless be promoted by their exclusion from all appointments in the gift of the President, in whose election they may have been officially concerned. The nature of the judicial office and the necessity of securing in the Cabinet and in diplomatic stations of the highest rank the best talents and political experience should, perhaps, except these from the exclusion.

There are, perhaps, few men who can for any great length of time enjoy office and power without being more or less under the influence of feelings unfavorable to the faithful discharge of their public duties. Their integrity may be proof against improper considerations immediately addressed to themselves, but they are apt to acquire a habit of looking with indifference upon the public interests and of tolerating conduct from which an unpracticed man would revolt. Office is considered as a species of property, and government rather as a means of promoting individual interests than as an instrument created solely for the service of the people. Corruption in some and in others a perversion of correct feelings and principles divert government from its legitimate ends and make it an engine for the support of the few at the expense of the many. The duties of all public officers are, or at least admit of being made, so plain and simple that men of intelligence may readily qualify themselves for their performance; and I can not but believe that more is lost by the long continuance of men in office than is generally to be gained by their experience. I submit, therefore, to your consideration whether the efficiency of the Government would not be promoted and official industry and integrity better secured by a general extension of the law which limits appointments to four years.

In a country where offices are created solely for the benefit of the people no one man has any more intrinsic right to official station than another. Offices were not established to give support to particular men at the public expense. No individual wrong is, therefore, done by removal, since neither appointment to nor continuance in office is matter of right. The incumbent became an officer with a view to public benefits, and when these require his removal they are not to be sacrificed to private interests. It is the people, and they alone, who have a right to complain when a bad officer is substituted for a good one. He who is removed has the same means of obtaining a living that are enjoyed by the millions who never held office. The proposed limitation would destroy the idea of property now so generally connected with official station, and although individual distress may be sometimes produced, it would, by promoting that rotation which constitutes a leading principle in the republican creed, give healthful action to the system.

WEBSTER ATTACKS THE SYSTEM

I concur with those who think, that, looking to the present, and looking also to the future, and regarding all the probabilities that await us in reference to the character and qualities of those who may fill the executive chair, it is important to the stability of government and the welfare of the people that there should be a check to the progress of official influence and patronage. The unlimited power to grant office, and to take it away, gives a command over the hopes and fears of a vast multitude of men. It is generally true, that he who controls another man's means of living controls his will. Where there are favors to be granted, there are usually enough to solicit for them; and when favors once granted may be withdrawn at pleasure, there is ordinarily little security for personal independence of character. The power of giving office thus affects the fears of all who are in, and the hopes of all who are out. Those who are *out* endeavor to distinguish themselves by active political friendship, by warm personal devotion, by clamorous support of men in whose hands is the power of reward; while those who are *in* ordinarily take care that others shall not surpass them in such qualities or such conduct as are most likely to secure favor. They resolve not to be outdone in any of the works of partisanship. The consequence of all this is obvious. A competition ensues, not of patriotic labors; not of rough and severe toils for the public good; not of manliness, independence, and public spirit; but of complaisance, of indiscriminate support of executive measures, of pliant subserviency and gross adulation. All throng and rush together to the altar of man-worship; and there they offer sacrifices, and pour out libations, till the thick fumes of their incense turn their own heads, and turn, also, the head of him who is the object of their idolatry.

The existence of parties in popular governments is not to be avoided; and if they are formed on constitutional questions or in regard to great measures of public policy, and do not run to excessive length, it may be admitted that, on the whole, they do no great harm. But the patronage of office, the power of bestowing place and emoluments, creates parties, not upon any principle or any measure, but upon the single ground of personal interest. Under the direct influence of this motive, they form round a leader, and they go for "the spoils of victory." And if the party chieftain becomes the national chieftain, he is still but too apt to consider all who have opposed him as enemies to be punished, and all who have supported him as friends to be rewarded. Blind devotion to party, and to the head of a party, thus takes place of the sentiment of generous patriotism and a high and exalted sense of public duty.

Let it not be said, Sir, that the danger from executive patronage cannot be great, since the persons who hold office, or can hold office, constitute so small a portion of the whole people.

In the first place, it is to be remembered that patronage acts, not only on those who actually possess office, but on those also who expect it, or hope for it; and in the next place, office-holders, by their very situation, their public station, their connection with the business of individuals, their activity, their ability to help or to hurt according to their pleasure, their acquaintance with public affairs, and their zeal and devotion, exercise a degree of influence out of all proportion to their numbers.

Sir, we cannot disregard our own experience. We cannot shut our eyes to what is around us and upon us. No candid man can deny that a great, a very great change has taken place, within a few years, in the practice of the executive government, which has produced a corresponding change in our political condition. No one can deny that office, of every kind, is now sought with extraordinary avidity, and that the condition, well understood to be attached to every officer, high or low, is indiscriminate support of executive measures and implicit obedience to executive will. For these reasons, Sir, I am for arresting the further progress of this executive patronage, if we can arrest it. I am for staying the further contagion of this plague.

The bill proposes two measures. One is to alter the duration of certain offices, now limited absolutely to four years; so that the limitation shall be qualified or conditional. If the officer is in default, if his accounts are not settled, if he retains or misapplies the public money, information is to be given thereof, and thereupon his commission is to cease. But if his accounts are all regularly settled, if he collects and disburses the public money faithfully, then he is to remain in office, unless, for some other cause, the President sees fit to remove him. This is the provision of the bill. It applies only to certain enumerated officers, who may be called accounting officers; that is to say, officers who receive and disburse the public money. Formerly, all these officers held their places at the pleasure of the President. If he saw no just cause for removing them, they continued in their situations, no fixed period being assigned for the expiration of their commissions. But the act of 1820 limited the commissions of these officers to four years. At the end of four years, they were to go out, without any removal, however well they might have conducted themselves, or however useful to the public their further continuance in office might be. They might be nominated again, or might not; but their commissions expired.

Now, Sir, I freely admit that considerable benefit has arisen from this law. I agree that it has, in some instances, secured promptitude, diligence, and a sense of responsibility. These were the benefits which those who passed the law expected from it; and these benefits have, in some measure, been realized. But I think that this change in the tenure of office, together with some good, has brought along a far more than equivalent amount of evil. By the operation of this law, the President can deprive a man of office without taking the responsibility of removing him. The law itself vacates the office, and gives the means of rewarding a friend without the exercise of the power of removal at all. Here is increased power, with diminished responsibility. Here is a still greater dependence, for the means of living, on executive favor, and, of course, a new dominion acquired over opinion and over conduct. The power of removal is, or at least formerly was, a suspected and odious power. Public opinion would not always tolerate it; and still less frequently did it approve it. Something of character, something of the respect of the intelligent and patriotic part of the community, was lost by every instance of its unnecessary exercise. This was some restraint. But the law of 1820 took it all away. It vacated offices periodically, by its own operation, and thus added to the power of removal, which is left still existing in full force, a new and extraordinary facility for the extension of patronage, influence, and favoritism.

I would ask every member of the Senate if he does not perceive, daily, effects which may be fairly traced to this cause. Does he not see a union of purpose, a devotion to power, a cooperation in action, among all who hold office, quite unknown in the earlier periods of the government? Does he not behold, every hour, a stronger development of the principle of personal attachment, and a corresponding diminution of genuine and generous public feeling? Was indiscriminate support of party measures, was unwavering fealty, was regular suit and service, ever before esteemed such important and essential parts of official duty?

Sir, the theory of our institutions is plain; it is, that government is an agency created for the good of the people, and that every person in office is the agent and servant of the people. Offices are created, not for the benefit of those who are to fill them, but for the public convenience; and they ought to be no more in number, nor should higher salaries be attached to them, than the public service requires. This is the theory. But the difficulty in practice is, to prevent a direct reversal of all this; to prevent public offices from being considered as intended for the use and emolument of those who can obtain them. There is a headlong tendency to this, and it is necessary to restrain it by wise and effective legislation. There is still another, and perhaps a greatly more mischievous result, of extensive patronage in the hands of a single magistrate, to which I have already incidentally alluded; and that is, that men in office have begun to think themselves mere agents and servants of the appointing power, and not agents of the government or the country. It is, in an especial manner, important, if it be practicable, to apply some corrective to this kind of feeling and opinion.

3. STRENGTHENING THE PRESIDENCY

Direct Representative of the People: *Jackson vitalized
the Presidency, leaving the office institutionally strengthened far beyond the practice of previous administrations.
Both Washington and Jefferson had been strong execu-
tives, but presidential power after Jefferson was eroded
by powerful congressional factions in the absence of consistent national policies. Jackson was temperamentally unfit for such a subordinate position, and the second American party system with its popularized presidential contests
imposed demands for active leadership. He did not shirk
the responsibilities nor the opportunities which were his
as President. A symbolic yet extremely important aspect
of Jackson's presidential leadership emerged from his
claim to be the direct representative of all the people, the
only man (except for the Vice-President, the President's
shadow) elected by all the people. This novel and significant concept obviously ignored the Founding Fathers'
desire to keep the Presidency several steps removed from
the instability of mass politics. President Jackson immediately called for direct election of the President; later, during the Bank War, he defended his actions, enunciating
the theory of direct, collective representation in a state
paper known as The Protest. As usual, the Counter-Pro-
test came from Daniel Webster. [Richardson, Messages
of the Presidents, II: 447–48, III: 72, 90–93; Writings
and Speeches of Webster, VII: 116, 135–39.]*

THE PROTEST

I consider it one of the most urgent of my duties to bring to your
attention the propriety of amending that part of our Constitution which
relates to the election of President and Vice-President. Our system of
government was by its framers deemed an experiment, and they therefore consistently provided a mode of remedying its defects.

To the people belongs the right of electing their Chief Magistrate;
it was never designed that their choice should in any case be defeated,
either by the intervention of electoral colleges or by the agency confided, under certain contingencies, to the House of Representatives. Experience proves that in proportion as agents to execute the will of the
people are multiplied there is danger of their wishes being frustrated.
Some may be unfaithful; all are liable to err. So far, therefore, as the
people can with convenience speak, it is safer for them to express their
own will.

The number of aspirants to the Presidency and the diversity of the interests which may influence their claims leave little reason to expect a choice in the first instance, and in that event the election must devolve on the House of Representatives, where it is obvious the will of the people may not be always ascertained, or, if ascertained, may not be regarded. From the mode of voting by States the choice is to be made by 24 votes, and it may often occur that one of these will be controlled by an individual Representative. Honors and offices are at the disposal of the successful candidate. Repeated ballotings may make it apparent that a single individual holds the cast in his hand. May he not be tempted to name his reward? But even without corruption, supposing the probity of the Representative to be proof against the powerful motives by which it may be assailed, the will of the people is still constantly liable to be misrepresented. One may err from ignorance of the wishes of his constituents; another from a conviction that it is his duty to be governed by his own judgment of the fitness of the candidates; finally, although all were inflexibly honest, all accurately informed of the wishes of their constituents, yet under the present mode of election a minority may often elect a President, and when this happens it may reasonably be expected that efforts will be made on the part of the majority to rectify this injurious operation of their institutions. But although no evil of this character should result from such a perversion of the first principle of our system—*that the majority is to govern*—it must be very certain that a President elected by a minority can not enjoy the confidence necessary to the successful discharge of his duties.

In this as in all other matters of public concern policy requires that as few impediments as possible should exist to the free operation of the public will. Let us, then, endeavor so to amend our system that the office of Chief Magistrate may not be conferred upon any citizen but in pursuance of a fair expression of the will of the majority.

I would therefore recommend such an amendment of the Constitution as may remove all intermediate agency in the election of the President and Vice-President. The mode may be so regulated as to preserve to each State its present relative weight in the election, and a failure in the first attempt may be provided for by confining the second to a choice between the two highest candidates. In connection with such an amendment it would seem advisable to limit the service of the Chief Magistrate to a single term of either four or six years. If, however, it should not be adopted, it is worthy of consideration whether a provision disqualifying for office the Representatives in Congress on whom such an election may have devolved would not be proper.

. . . the resolution of the Senate is wholly unauthorized by the Constitution, and in derogation of its entire spirit. It assumes that a single branch of the legislative department may for the purposes of a public censure, and without any view to legislation or impeachment, take up, consider, and decide upon the official acts of the Executive. But in no part of the Constitution is the President subjected to any such responsibility, and in no part of that instrument is any such power conferred on either branch of the Legislature. . . .

The high functions assigned by the Constitution to the Senate are in their nature either legislative, executive, or judicial. It is only in the exercise of its judicial powers, when sitting as a court for the trial of impeachments, that the Senate is expressly authorized and necessarily required to consider and decide upon the conduct of the President or any other public officer. Indirectly, however, as has already been suggested, it may frequently be called on to perform that office. Cases may occur in the course of its legislative or executive proceedings in which it may be indispensable to the proper exercise of its powers that it should inquire into and decide upon the conduct of the President or other public officers, and in every such case its constitutional right to do so is cheerfully conceded. But to authorize the Senate to enter on such a task in its legislative or executive capacity the inquiry must actually grow out of and tend to some legislative or executive action, and the decision, when expressed, must take the form of some appropriate legislative or executive act.

The resolution in question was introduced, discussed, and passed not as a joint but as a separate resolution. It asserts no legislative power, proposes no legislative action, and neither possesses the form nor any of the attributes of a legislative measure. It does not appear to have been entertained or passed with any view or expectation of its issuing in a law or joint resolution, or in the repeal of any law or joint resolution, or in any other legislative action.

Whilst wanting both the form and substance of a legislative measure, it is equally manifest that the resolution was not justified by any of the executive powers conferred on the Senate. These powers relate exclusively to the consideration of treaties and nominations to office, and they are exercised in secret session and with closed doors. This resolution does not apply to any treaty or nomination, and was passed in a public session. . . .

The dangerous tendency of the doctrine which denies to the President the power of supervising, directing, and controlling the Secretary of the Treasury in like manner with the other executive officers would soon be manifest in practice were the doctrine to be established. The President is the direct representative of the American people, but the Secretaries are not. If the Secretary of the Treasury be independent of the President in the execution of the laws, then is there no direct responsibility to the people in that important branch of this Government to which is committed the care of the national finances. And it is in the power of the Bank of the United States, or any other corporation, body of men, or individuals, if a Secretary shall be found to accord with them in opinion or can be induced in practice to promote their views, to control through him the whole action of the Government (so far as it is exercised by his Department) in defiance of the Chief Magistrate elected by the people and responsible to them.

But the evil tendency of the particular doctrine adverted to, though sufficiently serious, would be as nothing in comparison with the pernicious consequences which would inevitably flow from the approbation and allowance by the people and the practice by the Senate of the unconstitutional power of arraigning and censuring the official conduct of the Executive in the manner recently pursued. Such proceedings are eminently calculated to unsettle the foundations of the Government, to disturb the harmonious action of its different departments, and to break down the checks and balances by which the wisdom of its framers sought to insure its stability and usefulness.

The honest differences of opinion which occasionally exist between the Senate and the President in regard to matters in which both are obliged to participate are sufficiently embarrassing; but if the course recently adopted by the Senate shall hereafter be frequently pursued, it is not only obvious that the harmony of the relations between the President and the Senate will be destroyed, but that other and graver effects will ultimately ensue. If the censures of the Senate be submitted to by the President, the confidence of the people in his ability and virtue and the character and usefulness of his Administration will soon be at an end, and the real power of the Government will fall into the hands of a body holding their offices for long terms, not elected by the people and not to them directly responsible. If, on the other hand, the illegal censures of the Senate should be resisted by the President, collisions and angry controversies might ensue, discreditable in their progress and in the end compelling the people to adopt the conclusion either that their Chief Magistrate was unworthy of their respect or that the Senate was chargeable with calumny and injustice. Either of these results would impair public confidence in the perfection of the system and lead to serious alterations of its framework or to the practical abandonment of some of its provisions. . . .

Far be it from me to charge or to insinuate that the present Senate of the United States intend in the most distant way to encourage such a result. It is not of their motives or designs, but only of the tendency of their acts, that it is my duty to speak. It is, if possible, to make Senators themselves sensible of the danger which lurks under the precedent set in their resolution, and at any rate to perform my duty as the responsible head of one of the coequal departments of the Government, that I have been compelled to point out the consequences to which the discussion and passage of the resolution may lead if the tendency of the measure be not checked in its inception. . . . I do hereby *solemnly protest* against the aforementioned proceedings of the Senate as unauthorized by the Constitution, contrary to its spirit and to several of its express provisions, subversive of that distribution of the powers of government which it has ordained and established, destructive of the checks and safeguards by which those powers were intended on the one hand to be controlled and on the other to be protected, and calculated by their immediate and collateral effects, by their character and tendency, to concentrate in the hands of a body not directly amenable to the people a degree of influence and power dangerous to their liberties and fatal to the Constitution of their choice.

The resolution of the Senate contains an imputation upon my private as well as upon my public character, and as it must stand forever on their journals, I can not close this substitute for that defense which I have not been allowed to present in the ordinary form without remarking that I have lived in vain if it be necessary to enter into a formal vindication of my character and purposes from such an imputation. In vain do I bear upon my person enduring memorials of that contest in which American liberty was purchased; in vain have I since periled property, fame, and life in defense of the rights and privileges so dearly bought; in vain am I now, without a personal aspiration or the hope of individual advantage, encountering responsibilities and dangers from which by mere inactivity in relation to a single point I might have been exempt, if any serious doubts can be entertained as to the purity of my purposes and motives. If I had been ambitious, I should have sought an alliance with that powerful institution which even now aspires to no divided empire. If I had been venal, I should have sold myself to its designs. Had I preferred personal comfort and official ease to the performance of my arduous duty, I should have ceased to molest it. In the history of conquerors and usurpers, never in the fire of youth nor in the vigor of manhood could I find an attraction to lure me from the path of duty, and now I shall scarcely find an inducement to commence their career of ambition when gray hairs and a decaying frame, instead of inviting to toil and battle, call me to the contemplation of other worlds, where conquerors cease to be honored and usurpers expiate their crimes. The only ambition I can feel is to acquit myself to Him to whom I must soon render an account of my stewardship, to serve my fellowmen, and live respected and honored in the history of my country. No; the ambition which leads me on is an anxious desire and a fixed determination to return to the people unimpaired the sacred trust they have confided to my charge; to heal the wounds of the Constitution and preserve it from further violation; to persuade my countrymen, so far as I may, that it is not in a splendid government supported by powerful monopolies and aristocratical establishments that they will find happiness or their liberties protection, but in a plain system, void of pomp, protecting all and granting favors to none, dispensing its blessings, like the dews of Heaven, unseen and unfelt save in the freshness and beauty they contribute to produce. It is such a government that the genius of our people requires; such an one only under which our States may remain for ages to come united, prosperous, and free.

WEBSTER'S COUNTER-PROTEST

Mr. President, I know not who wrote this Protest, but I confess I am astonished, truly astonished, as well at the want of knowledge which it displays of constitutional law, as at the high and dangerous pretensions which it puts forth. Neither branch of the legislature can express censure upon the President's conduct! Suppose, Sir, that we should see him enlisting troops and raising an army, can we say nothing, and do nothing? Suppose he were to declare war against a foreign power, and put the army and the fleet in action; are we still to be silent? Suppose we should see him borrowing money on the credit of the United States; are we yet to wait for impeachment? Indeed, Sir, in regard to this borrowing money on the credit of the United States, I wish to call the attention of the Senate, not only to what might happen, but to what has actually happened. We are informed that the Post-Office Department, a department over which the President claims the same control as over the rest, *has actually borrowed near half a million of money on the credit of the United States.* . . .

I do not wish, Sir, to impair the power of the President, as it stands written down in the Constitution, and as great and good men have hitherto exercised it. In this, as in other respects, I am for the Constitution as it is. But I will not acquiesce in the reversal of all just ideas of government; I will not degrade the character of popular representation; I will not blindly confide, where all experience admonishes me to be jealous; I will not trust executive power, vested in the hands of a single magistrate, to be the guardian of liberty.

Having claimed for the executive the especial guardianship of the Constitution, the Protest proceeds to present a summary view of the powers which are supposed to be conferred on the executive by that instrument. And it is to this part of the message, Sir, that I would, more than to all others, call the particular attention of the Senate. I confess that it was only upon careful reperusal of the paper that I perceived the extent to which its assertions of power reach. I do not speak now of the President's claims of power as opposed to legislative authority, but of his opinions as to his own authority, duty, and responsibility, as connected with all other officers under the government. He is of opinion that the whole executive power is vested in him, and that he is responsible for its entire exercise; that among the duties imposed on him is that of "taking care that the laws be faithfully executed"; and that, "being thus made responsible for the entire action of the executive department, it is but reasonable that the power of appointing, overseeing, and controlling those who execute the laws, a power in its nature executive, should remain in his hands. It is, therefore, not only his right, but the Constitution makes it his duty, to 'nominate, and, by and with the advice and consent of the Senate, appoint,' all 'officers of the United States whose appointments are not in the Constitution otherwise provided for,' with a proviso that the appointment of inferior officers may be vested in the President alone, in the courts of justice, or in the heads of departments."

The first proposition, then, which the Protest asserts, in regard to the President's powers as executive magistrate, is, that, the general duty being imposed on him by the Constitution, of taking care that the laws be faithfully executed, *he thereby becomes himself responsible for the conduct of every person employed in the government;* "for the entire action," as the paper expresses it, "of the executive department." This, Sir, is very dangerous logic. I reject the inference altogether. No such responsibility, nor any thing like it, follows from the general provision of the Constitution, making it his duty to see the laws executed. If it did, we should have, in fact, but one officer in the whole government. The President would be every body. . . .

According to the Protest, the very duties which every officer under the government performs are the duties of the President himself. It says that the President has a right to employ *agents* of his *own choice,* to aid HIM in the performance of HIS duties.

Mr. President, if these doctrines be true, it is idle for us any longer to talk about any such thing as a government of laws. We have no government of laws, not even the semblance or shadow of it; we have no legal responsibility. We have an executive, consisting of one person, wielding all official power, and which is, to every effectual purpose, completely *irresponsible.* The President declares that he is "responsible for the entire action of the executive department." Responsible? What does he mean by being "responsible"? Does he mean legal responsibility? Certainly not. No such thing. Legal responsibility signifies liability to punishment for misconduct or maladministration. But the Protest does not mean that the President is liable to be impeached and punished if a secretary of state should commit treason, if a collector of the customs should be guilty of bribery, or if a treasurer should embezzle the public money. It does not mean, and cannot mean, that he should be answerable for any such crime or such delinquency. What, then, is its notion of that *responsibility* which it says the President is under for all officers, and which authorizes him to consider all officers as his own personal agents? Sir, it is merely responsibility to public opinion. It is a liability to be blamed; it is the chance of becoming unpopular, the danger of losing a reëlection. Nothing else is meant in the world. It is the hazard of failing in any attempt or enterprise of ambition. This is all the responsibility to which the doctrines of the Protest hold the President subject. . . .

. . . And it is under this view of his own authority that the President calls the Secretaries *his* Secretaries, not once only, but repeatedly. After half a century's administration of this government, Sir;—after we have endeavored, by statute upon statute, and by provision following provision, to define and limit official authority; to assign particular duties to particular public servants; to define those duties; to create penalties for their violation; to adjust accurately the responsibility of each agent with his own powers and his own duties; to establish the prevalence of equal rule; to make the law, as far as possible, every thing, and individual will, as far as possible, nothing;—after all this, the astounding assertion rings in our ears, that, throughout the whole range of official agency, in its smallest ramifications as well as in its larger masses, there is but ONE RESPONSIBILITY, ONE DISCRETION, ONE WILL! True indeed is it, Sir, if these sentiments be maintained,—true indeed is it that a President of the United States may well repeat from Napoleon what he repeated from Louis the Fourteenth. "I am the state!"

The Paradox of the Jacksonian Presidency: *Whatever else the Jacksonian Presidency may have been, it was not boring. During the Jackson years the White House remained the focal point of American politics and public controversy. From this springs a basic irony of Jackson's politics: he used presidential power to counter the threat of centralizing national power (and disruptive state rights, too) at the same time that he was building models for effective use of the machinery of national government. He, more than any previous President, nationalized key political institutions and issues, although (as in the case of the Bank War) he sought to curb the exercise of specific nationwide powers. Many of the foreign visitors of that day called on Jackson, some no doubt to see the alleged western "wild man," and all came away impressed by the man's forcefulness and dignified composure. Two such accounts are printed below. [Thomas Hamilton, Men and Manners in America (Philadelphia, 1833), 275–79; Harriet Martineau, Society in America, I: 60–63.]*

Thomas Hamilton Visits the White House

A few days after the interview already mentioned, I received the honour of an invitation to dine with the President. It unfortunately happened, that, on the day indicated, I was already engaged to a party at Mr. Van Buren's; and on inquiring the etiquette on such occasions, I was informed that an invitation from the President was not held to authorize any breach of engagement to the leading member of the cabinet. The President, however, having politely intimated that he received company every evening, I ventured, along with a distinguished member of the House of Representatives, to present myself, on one occasion, at the "White House."

We found the President had retired with a headache, but in a few minutes he appeared, though from the heaviness of his eye, evidently in a state of considerable pain. This, however, had no influence on his conversation, which was spirited, and full of vivacity. He informed us that he had been unwell for several days, and having the fatigues of a levee to encounter on the following evening, he had retired early, in order to recruit for an occasion which required the presence of all his bodily powers. When this subject was dismissed, the conversation turned on native politics, the Indian question, the powers of the Supreme Court, and a recent debate in the Senate, which had excited considerable attention.

Of the opinions expressed by this distinguished person, it would be unpardonable were I to say any thing; but I heard them with deep interest, and certainly considered them to be marked by that union of boldness and sagacity, which is generally supposed to form a prominent feature of his character. General Jackson spoke like a man so thoroughly convinced of the justice of his views, that he announced them unhesitatingly and without reserve. This openness might be increased, perhaps, by the knowledge of my companion being a decided supporter of his government; but sincerity is so legible both in his countenance and manner, that I feel convinced that nothing but the strongest motives of state policy could make him hesitate, under any circumstances, to express boldly what he felt strongly.

On the following evening I attended the levee. The apartments were already full before I arrived, and the crowd extended even into the hall. Three—I am not sure that there were not four—large saloons were thrown open on the occasion, and were literally crammed with the most singular and miscellaneous assemblage I had ever seen.

The numerical majority of the company seemed of the class of tradesmen or farmers, respectable men, fresh from the plough or the counter, who, accompanied by their wives and daughters, came forth to greet their President, and enjoy the splendours of the gala. There were also generals, and commodores, and public officers of every description, and foreign ministers and members of Congress, and ladies of all ages and degrees of beauty, from the fair and laughing girl of fifteen, to the haggard dowager of seventy. There were majors in broad cloth and corduroys, redolent of gin and tobacco, and majors' ladies in chintz or russet, with huge Paris ear-rings, and tawny necks, profusely decorated with beads of coloured glass. There were tailors from the board, and judges from the bench; lawyers who opened their mouths at one bar, and the tapster who closed them at another;—in short, every trade, craft, calling, and profession, appeared to have sent its delegates to this extraordinary convention.

For myself, I had seen too much of the United States to expect any thing very different, and certainly anticipated that the mixture would contain all the ingredients I have ventured to describe. Yet, after all, I was taken by surprise. There were present at this levee, men begrimed with all the sweat and filth accumulated in their day's—perhaps their week's—labour. There were sooty artificers, evidently fresh from the forge or the workshop; and one individual, I remember—either a miller or a baker—who, wherever he passed, left marks of contact on the garments of the company. The most prominent group, however, in the assemblage, was a party of Irish labourers, employed on some neighbouring canal, who had evidently been apt scholars in the doctrine of liberty and equality, and were determined, on the present occasion, to assert the full privileges of "the great unwashed." I remarked these men pushing aside the more respectable portion of the company with a certain jocular audacity, which put one in mind of the humours of Donnybrook.

A party, composed of the materials I have described, could possess but few attractions. The heat of the apartment was very great, and the odours—certainly not Sabæan—which occasionally affected the nostrils, were more pungent than agreeable. I, therefore, pushed on in search of the President, in order that, having paid my respects in acknowledgment of a kindness for which I really felt grateful, I might be at liberty to depart. My progress, however, was slow, for the company in the exterior saloons were wedged together in a dense mass, penetrable only at occasional intervals. I looked every where for the President as I passed, but without success, but, at length, a friend, against whom I happened to be jostled, informed me that I should find him at the extremity of the most distant apartment.

The information was correct. There stood the President, whose looks still indicated indisposition, paying one of the severest penalties of greatness; compelled to talk when he had nothing to say, and shake hands with men whose very appearance suggested the precaution of a glove. I must say, however, that under these unpleasant circumstances, he bore himself well and gracefully. His countenance expressed perfect good-humour; and his manner to the ladies was so full of well-bred gallantry, that having, as I make no doubt, the great majority of the fair sex on his side, the chance of his being unseated at the next election must be very small.

I did not, however, remain long a spectator of the scene. Having gone through the ordinary ceremonial, I scrambled out of the crowd the best way I could, and bade farewell to the most extraordinary scene it had ever been my fortune to witness. It is only fair to state, however that during my stay in Washington, I never heard the President's levee mentioned in company without an expression of indignant feeling on the part of the ladies, at the circumstances I have narrated. To the better order of Americans, indeed, it cannot but be painful that their wives and daughters should thus be compelled to mingle with the very lowest of the people. Yet the evil, whatever may be its extent, is, in truth, the necessary result of a form of government essentially democratic. Whereever universal suffrage prevails, the people are, and must be, the sole depository of political power. The American President well knows that his only chance of continuance in office, consists in his conciliating the favour of the lowest—and, therefore, most numerous—order of his constituents. The rich and intelligent are a small minority, and their opinion he may despise. The poor, the uneducated, are, in every country, *the people*. It is to them alone that a public man in America can look for the gratification of his ambition. They are the ladder by which he must mount, or be content to stand on a level with his fellowmen.

Under such circumstances, it is impossible there should be any exclusion of the real governors of the country wherever they may think proper to intrude. General Jackson is quite aware, that the smallest demonstration of disrespect even to the meanest mechanic, might incur the loss of his popularity in a whole neighbourhood. It is evident, too, that the class in actual possession of the political patronage of a community is, in effect, whatever be their designation, the *first* class in the state. In America, this influence belongs to the poorest and least educated. Wealth and intelligence are compelled to bend to poverty and ignorance, to adopt their prejudices, to copy their manners, to submit to their government. In short, the order of reason and common sense is precisely inverted; and while the roots of the political tree are waving in the air, its branches are buried in the ground.

Harriet Martineau Assesses Jackson

General Jackson was brought into office by an overpowering majority, and after a series of strong party excitements. If ever there was a possibility of a President marking his age, for good or for evil, it would have been done during Jackson's administration. He is a man made to impress a very distinct idea of himself on all minds. He has great personal courage, much sagacity, though frequently impaired by the strength of his prejudices, violent passions, an indomitable will, and that devotion to public affairs in which no President has ever failed. He had done deeds of war which flattered the pride of the people; and in doing them, he had acquired a knowledge of the people, which has served him instead of much other knowledge in which he is deficient. He has known, however, how to obtain the use, though not the reputation, of the knowledge which he does not possess. Notwithstanding the strength of his passions, and the awkward positions in which he has placed himself by the indulgence of his private resentments, his sagacity has served him well in keeping him a little way a-head of the popular convictions. No physician in the world ever understood feeling the pulse, and ordering his practice accordingly, better than President Jackson. Here are all the requisites for success in a tyrannical administration. Even in England, we heard rumours in 1828, and again in 1832, about the perils of the United States, under the rule of a despotic soldier. The cry revived with every one of his high-handed deeds; with every exercise of the veto,—which he has used oftener than all the other Presidents put together,—with every appointment made in defiance of the Senate; with the removal of the deposites; with his messages of menace to the French government. Yet to what amounts the power now, at the close of his administration, of this idol of the people, this man strong in war, and subtle in council, this soldier and statesman of indomitable will, of insatiable ambition, with the resources of a huge majority at his disposal? The deeds of his administration remain to be justified in as far as they are sound, and undone if they are faulty. Meantime, he has been able to obtain only the barest majority in the Senate, the great object of his wrath: he has been unable to keep the slavery question out of Congress,—the introduction of which is by far the most remarkable event of his administration. One of the most desponding complaints I heard of his administration was, not that he had strengthened the general government—not that his government had tended to centralisation—not that he had settled any matters to his own satisfaction, and left the people to reconcile themselves to his pleasure as they best might,—but that every great question is left unsettled; that it is difficult now to tell any party by its principles; that the principles of such affairs as the currency, land, slavery, internal improvements, &c. remain to be all argued over again. Doubtless, this will be tiresome to such public men as have entirely and finally made up their minds on these subjects. To such, nothing can well be more wearisome than discussion and action, renewed from year to year. But the very fact that these affairs remain unsettled, that the people remain unsatisfied about them, proves that the people have more to learn, and that they mean to learn it. No true friend of his country would wish that the questions of slavery and currency should remain in any position that they have ever yet occupied in the United States; and towards the settlement of the latter of the two, as far as light depends on collision of opinions, it is certain that no man has done so much, whether he meant it or not, as President Jackson. The occasional breaking up and mingling of parties is a necessary circumstance, whether it be considered an evil or a good. It may be an evil, in as far as it affords a vantage-ground to unprincipled adventurers, it is a good, in as far as it leads to mutual understanding, and improves the candour of partisans. For the rest, there is no fear but that parties will soon draw asunder, with each a set of distinctive principles as its badge. Meantime, men will have reason to smile at their fears of the formidable personage, who is now descending from the presidential chair; and their enthusiasm will have cooled down to the temperature fixed by what the event will prove to have been his merits. They will discuss him by their firesides with the calmness with which men speak of things that are past; while they keep their hopes and fears to be chafed up at public meetings, while the orator points to some rising star, or to some cloud no bigger than a man's hand. Irish emigrants occasionally fight out the battle of the Boyne in the streets of Philadelphia; but native Americans bestow their apprehensions and their wrath upon things future; and their philosophy upon things past. While they do this, it will not be in the power of any President to harm them much or long.

VII. The Bank War

The new politics of the 1830s, both in ideology and in practice, affected all aspects of public life but found its most meaningful application in the struggle between President Jackson and the Second Bank of the United States. Jackson's election in 1828 vaguely promised "reform," but the Bank had not been an issue in the campaign of that year. However, once in office the new President announced his opposition to a national Bank and slowly but effectively revived a latent anti-Bank prejudice among the people.

Prosecution of the Bank War involved the marshaling of new techniques, some of them borrowed by the Jacksonians from earlier political assaults upon special privileges and alleged monopolies and from other parties. Building upon the solid foundations of Republican state political machines, Jacksonians effectively incorporated the fight against the "monster" Bank into their political program, although serious defections occurred. Jackson's expansion of presidential power during the Bank War and his demand that Democrats follow him on the issue signaled the emergence of a national political structure with the President as the acknowledged party head and political ideologue. In short, the Bank War, whatever its economic consequences and despite the political antagonisms it generated, provided a dramatic lesson in the application of the era's new politics.

1. JACKSON'S VETO: NO RETREAT

The hesitations and doubts among Jacksonians during the early skirmishes against the Bank ended in the summer of 1832 when Jackson returned the Bank recharter bill to Congress with the single most important state paper of

139

his administration—the Bank Veto. The message had been
carefully prepared in the inner councils of the administration and was primarily the work of Amos Kendall, grey
eminence of the Kitchen Cabinet. The Bank War was
not lightly undertaken by Jacksonians for they recognized
the Bank as a formidable foe with extensive and influential support (historians now believe that the President lost
rather than gained votes because of the Bank in the election of 1832). But once opposition to the Bank recharter
had been decided upon, the Veto message became a
superb vehicle for mobilizing the fullest available support
for that policy. Faulty in logic and lacking economic
sophistication, the message fairly crackles with hard-line
politics in the best Kendall manner. All of the appeals
are there—to egalitarian prejudices, to chauvinism, to
envy, to constitutional conservatism, to fear of centralizing tyranny—and all easily mesh into an argument against
privilege that has become a meaningful part of the American political tradition, no matter how much it is ignored.
[James D. Richardson, comp., A Compilation of the Messages and Papers of the Presidents, 1789–1897 (10 vols.,
Washington, 1896–97), II: 573–91.]

Washington, July 10, 1832.

A bank of the United States is in many respects convenient for the
Government and useful to the people. Entertaining this opinion, and
deeply impressed with the belief that some of the powers and privileges
possessed by the existing bank are unauthorized by the Constitution,
subversive of the rights of the States, and dangerous to the liberties of
the people, I felt it my duty at an early period of my Administration to
call the attention of Congress to the practicability of organizing an
institution combining all its advantages and obviating these objections.
I sincerely regret that in the act before me I can perceive none of those
modifications of the bank charter which are necessary, in my opinion,
to make it compatible with justice, with sound policy, or with the
Constitution of our country.

The present corporate body, denominated the president, directors, and
company of the Bank of the United States, will have existed at the time
this act is intended to take effect twenty years. It enjoys an exclusive
privilege of banking under the authority of the General Government,
a monopoly of its favor and support, and, as a necessary consequence,
almost a monopoly of the foreign and domestic exchange. The powers,
privileges, and favors bestowed upon it in the original charter, by increasing the value of the stock far above its par value, operated as a
gratuity of many millions to the stockholders. . . . More than eight

millions of the stock of this bank are held by foreigners. By this act the American Republic proposes virtually to make them a present of some millions of dollars. For these gratuities to foreigners and to some of our own opulent citizens the act secures no equivalent whatever. They are the certain gains of the present stockholders under the operation of this act, after making full allowance for the payment of the bonus.

Every monopoly and all exclusive privileges are granted at the expense of the public, which ought to receive a fair equivalent. The many millions which this act proposes to bestow on the stockholders of the existing bank must come directly or indirectly out of the earnings of the American people. It is due to them, therefore, if their Government sell monopolies and exclusive privileges, that they should at least exact for them as much as they are worth in open market. . . .

It has been urged as an argument in favor of rechartering the present bank that the calling in its loans will produce great embarrassment and distress. The time allowed to close its concerns is ample, and if it has been well managed its pressure will be light, and heavy only in case its management has been bad. If, therefore, it shall produce distress, the fault will be its own, and it would furnish a reason against renewing a power which has been so obviously abused. . . .

. . . As little stock is held in the West, it is obvious that the debt of the people in that section to the bank is principally a debt to the Eastern and foreign stockholders; that the interest they pay upon it is carried into the Eastern States and into Europe, and that it is a burden upon their industry and a drain of their currency, which no country can bear without inconvenience and occasional distress. . . . The tendency of the plan of taxation which this act proposes will be to place the whole United States in the same relation to foreign countries which the Western States now bear to the Eastern. When by a tax on resident stockholders the stock of this bank is made worth 10 or 15 per cent more to foreigners than to residents, most of it will inevitably leave the country.

Thus will this provision in its practical effect deprive the Eastern as well as the Southern and Western States of the means of raising a revenue from the extension of business and great profits of this institution. It will make the American people debtors to aliens in nearly the whole amount due to this bank, and send across the Atlantic from two to five millions of specie every year to pay the bank dividends.

In another of its bearings this provision is fraught with danger. Of the twenty-five directors of this bank five are chosen by the Government and twenty by the citizen stockholders. From all voice in these elections the foreign stockholders are excluded by the charter. In proportion, therefore, as the stock is transferred to foreign holders the extent of suffrage in the choice of directors is curtailed. Already is almost a third of the stock in foreign hands and not represented in elections. . . .

Is there no danger to our liberty and independence in a bank that in its nature has so little to bind it to our country? The president of the bank has told us that most of the State banks exist by its forbearance. Should its influence become concentered, as it may under the operation of such an act as this, in the hands of a self-elected directory whose interests are identified with those of the foreign stockholders, will there not be cause to tremble for the purity of our elections in peace and for the independence of our country in war? . . .

Should the stock of the bank principally pass into the hands of the subjects of a foreign country, and we should unfortunately become involved in a war with that country, what would be our condition? Of the course which would be pursued by a bank almost wholly owned by the subjects of a foreign power, and managed by those whose interests, if not affections, would run in the same direction there can be no doubt. All its operations within would be in aid of the hostile fleets and armies without. Controlling our currency, receiving our public moneys, and holding thousands of our citizens in dependence, it would be more formidable and dangerous than the naval and military power of the enemy.

If we must have a bank with private stockholders, every consideration of sound policy and every impulse of American feeling admonishes that it should be *purely American*. Its stockholders should be composed exclusively of our own citizens, who at least ought to be friendly to our Government and willing to support it in times of difficulty and danger. So abundant is domestic capital that competition in subscribing for the stock of local banks has recently led almost to riots. To a bank exclusively of American stockholders, possessing the powers and privileges granted by this act, subscriptions for $200,000,000 could be readily obtained. Instead of sending abroad the stock of the bank in which the Government must deposit its funds and on which it must rely to sustain its credit in times of emergency, it would rather seem to be expedient to prohibit its sale to aliens under penalty of absolute forfeiture.

It is maintained by the advocates of the bank that its constitutionality in all its features ought to be considered as settled by precedent and by the decision of the Supreme Court. To this conclusion I can not assent. . . .

If the opinion of the Supreme Court covered the whole ground of this act, it ought not to control the coordinate authorities of this Government. The Congress, the Executive, and the Court must each for itself be guided by its own opinion of the Constitution. Each public officer who takes an oath to support the Constitution swears that he will support it as he understands it, and not as it is understood by others.

It is as much the duty of the House of Representatives, of the Senate, and of the President to decide upon the constitutionality of any bill or resolution which may be presented to them for passage or approval as it is of the supreme judges when it may be brought before them for judicial decision. The opinion of the judges has no more authority over Congress than the opinion of Congress has over the judges, and on that point the President is independent of both. The authority of the Supreme Court must not, therefore, be permitted to controll the Congress or the Executive when acting in their legislative capacities, but to have only such influence as the force of their reasoning may deserve. . . .

The principle here affirmed is that the "degree of its necessity," involving all the details of a banking institution, is a question exclusively for legislative consideration. A bank is constitutional, but it is the province of the Legislature to determine whether this or that particular power, privilege, or exemption is "necessary and proper" to enable the bank to discharge its duties to the Government, and from their decision there is no appeal to the courts of justice. Under the decision of the Supreme Court, therefore, it is the exclusive province of Congress and the President to decide whether the particular features of this act are *necessary* and *proper* in order to enable the bank to perform conveniently and efficiently the public duties assigned to it as a fiscal agent, and therefore constitutional, or *unnecessary* and *improper*, and therefore unconstitutional. . . .

The Government is the only *"proper"* judge where its agents should reside and keep their offices, because it best knows where their presence will be *"necessary."* It can not, therefore, be *"necessary"* or *"proper"* to authorize the bank to locate branches where it pleases to perform the public service, without consulting the Government, and contrary to its will. The principle laid down by the Supreme Court concedes that Congress can not establish a bank for purposes of private speculation and gain, but only as a means of executing the delegated powers of the General Government. By the same principle a branch bank can not constitutionally be established for other than public purposes. The power which this act gives to establish two branches in any State, without the injunction or request of the Government and for other than public purposes, is not *"necessary"* to the due *execution* of the powers delegated to Congress. . . .

By its silence, considered in connection with the decision of the Supreme Court in the case of McCulloch against the State of Maryland, this act takes from the States the power to tax a portion of the banking business carried on within their limits, in subversion of one of the strongest barriers which secured them against Federal encroachments. Banking, like farming, manufacturing, or any other occupation or profession, is *a business*, the right to follow which is not originally derived from the laws. Every citizen and every company of citizens in all of our States possessed the right until the State legislatures deemed it good policy to prohibit private banking by law. . . .

. . . Every private business, whether carried on by an officer of the General Government or not, whether it be mixed with public concerns or not, even if it be carried on by the Government of the United States itself, separately or in partnership, falls within the scope of the taxing power of the State. Nothing comes more fully within it than banks and the business of banking, by whomsoever instituted and carried on. Over this whole subject-matter it is just as absolute, unlimited, and uncontrollable as if the Constitution had never been adopted, because in the formation of that instrument it was reserved without qualification.

The principle is conceded that the States can not rightfully tax the operations of the General Government. They can not tax the money of the Government deposited in the State banks, nor the agency of those banks in remitting it; but will any man maintain that their mere selection to perform this public service for the General Government would exempt the State banks and their ordinary business from State taxation? Had the United States, instead of establishing a bank at Philadelphia, employed a private banker to keep and transmit their funds, would it have deprived Pennsylvania of the right to tax his bank and his usual banking operations? It will not be pretended. . . .

It can not be *necessary* to the character of the bank as a fiscal agent of the Government that its private business should be exempted from that taxation to which all the State banks are liable, nor can I conceive it *"proper"* that the substantive and most essential powers reserved by the States shall be thus attacked and annihilated as a means of executing the powers delegated to the General Government. It may be safely assumed that none of those sages who had an agency in forming or adopting our Constitution ever imagined that any portion of the taxing power of the States not prohibited to them nor delegated to Congress was to be swept away and annihilated as a means of executing certain powers delegated to Congress. . . .

Under such circumstances the bank comes forward and asks a renewal of its charter for a term of fifteen years upon conditions which not only operate as a gratuity to the stockholders of many millions of dollars, but will sanction any abuses and legalize any encroachments.

Suspicions are entertained and charges are made of gross abuse and violation of its charter. An investigation unwillingly conceded and so restricted in time as necessarily to make it incomplete and unsatisfactory discloses enough to excite suspicion and alarm. In the practices of the principal bank partially unveiled, in the absence of important witnesses, and in numerous charges confidently made and as yet wholly uninvestigated there was enough to induce a majority of the committee of investigation—a committee which was selected from the most able and honorable members of the House of Representatives—to recommend a suspension of further action upon the bill and a prosecution of the inquiry. As the charter had yet four years to run, and as a renewal now was not necessary to the successful prosecution of its business, it was to have been expected that the bank itself, conscious of its purity and proud of its character, would have withdrawn its application for the present, and demanded the severest scrutiny into all its transactions. In their declining to do so there seems to be an additional reason why the functionaries of the Government should proceed with less haste and more caution in the renewal of their monopoly.

The bank is professedly established as an agent of the executive branch of the Government, and its constitutionality is maintained on that ground. Neither upon the propriety of present action nor upon the provisions of this act was the Executive consulted. It has had no opportunity to say that it neither needs nor wants an agent clothed with such powers and favored by such exemptions. There is nothing in its legitimate functions which makes it necessary or proper. Whatever interest or influence, whether public or private, has given birth to this act, it can not be found either in the wishes or necessities of the executive department, by which present action is deemed premature, and the powers conferred upon its agent not only unnecessary, but dangerous to the Government and country.

It is to be regretted that the rich and powerful too often bend the acts of government to their selfish purposes. Distinctions in society will always exist under every just government. Equality of talents, of education, or of wealth can not be produced by human institutions. In the full enjoyment of the gifts of Heaven and the fruits of superior industry, economy, and virtue, every man is equally entitled to protection by law; but when the laws undertake to add to these natural and just advantages artificial distinctions, to grant titles, gratuities, and exclusive privileges, to make the rich richer and the potent more powerful, the humble members of society—the farmers, mechanics, and laborers—who have neither the time nor the means of securing like favors to themselves, have a right to complain of the injustice of their Government. There are no necessary evils in government. Its evils exist only in its abuses. If it would confine itself to equal protection, and, as Heaven does its rains, shower its favors alike on the high and the low, the rich and the poor, it would be an unqualified blessing. In the act before me there seems to be a wide and unnecessary departure from these just principles.

Nor is our Government to be maintained or our Union preserved by invasions of the rights and powers of the several States. In thus attempting to make our General Government strong we make it weak. Its true strength consists in leaving individuals and States as much as possible to themselves—in making itself felt, not in its power, but in its beneficence; not in its control, but in its protection; not in binding the States more closely to the center, but leaving each to move unobstructed in its proper orbit.

Experience should teach us wisdom. Most of the difficulties our Government now encounters and most of the dangers which impend over our Union have sprung from an abandonment of the legitimate objects of Government by our national legislation, and the adoption of such principles as are embodied in this act. Many of our rich men have not been content with equal protection and equal benefits, but have besought us to make them richer by act of Congress. By attempting to gratify their desires we have in the results of our legislation arrayed section against section, interest against interest, and man against man, in a fearful commotion which threatens to shake the foundations of our Union. It is time to pause in our career to review our principles, and if possible revive that devoted patriotism and spirit of compromise which distinguished the sages of the Revolution and the fathers of our Union. If we can not at once, in justice to interests vested under improvident legislation, make our Government what it ought to be, we can at least take a stand against all new grants of monopolies and exclusive privileges, against any prostitution of our Government to the advancement of the few at the expense of the many, and in favor of compromise and gradual reform in our code of laws and system of political economy.

I have now done my duty to my country. If sustained by my fellow-citizens, I shall be grateful and happy; if not, I shall find in the motives which impel me ample grounds for contentment and peace. In the difficulties which surround us and the dangers which threaten our institutions there is cause for neither dismay nor alarm. For relief and deliverance let us firmly rely on that kind Providence which I am sure watches with peculiar care over the destinies of our Republic, and on the intelligence and wisdom of our countrymen. Through *His* abundant goodness and *their* patriotic devotion our liberty and Union will be preserved.

ANDREW JACKSON

2. THE ENEMY CAMP:
CALCULATIONS AND DAYDREAMS

Meanwhile, back in Philadelphia, Nicholas Biddle, the president of the Bank, reluctantly prepared to do battle.

Biddle, in charge since 1823, was a proficient bank manager—perhaps too proficient for his own political good. The Bank had weathered minor storms in the late 1820s, and all seemed well when it managed to stay out of the presidential election of 1828. Jackson's attacks changed that. Biddle tried convincing, then placating, the President and his friends. Biddle's reluctance to gamble the Bank's fate on the outcome of national politics was based upon his insight that the Bank's success as an economic machine had increased its political vulnerability, especially when challenged by Jacksonian rhetoric. Maneuvered into a defensive position, Biddle placed the Bank's strength behind the forces of National Republicanism and its presidential candidate in 1832, Henry Clay. The following letters from the Biddle correspondence show how the Bank fought back, once cornered. Although the anti-Jackson forces increased their percentage of the popular vote over 1828, Jackson won reelection. But more importantly, Jackson interpreted his reelection as a public mandate against the Bank. The Bank War dragged on, but the election of 1832 had effectively settled the outcome. [Reginal C. McGrane, ed., The Correspondence of Nicholas Biddle . . . (Boston, 1919), 142, 145–46, 161–64, 179–81, 196.]

CLAY TO BIDDLE

Washington, 15th December 1831

MY DEAR SIR

. . . Have you come to any decision about an application to Congress at this Session for the renewal of your Charter? The friends of the Bank here, with whom I have conversed, seem to expect the application to be made. The course of the President, in the event of the passage of a bill, seems to be a matter of doubt and speculation. My own belief is that, if *now* called upon he would not negative the bill, but that if he should be re-elected the event might and probably would be different.

WEBSTER TO BIDDLE

Washington, December 18, 1831

MY DEAR SIR

The state of my health & the severity of the weather have prevented me, since my arrival here, from being much abroad. Nevertheless, I have seen a great number of persons, & conversed with them, among other things, respecting the Bank. The result of all these conversations has been a strong confirmation of the opinion which I expressed at Philadelphia that *it is* expedient for the Bank to apply for the renewal of its Charter without delay. I do not meet a Gentleman, hardly, of another opinion; & the little incidents & anecdotes, that occur & circulate among us, all tend to strengthen the impression. Indeed, I am now a good deal inclined to think, that after Gen Jackson's re-election there would be a poor chance for the Bank. I am well informed, that within three days, he has in conversation with several Gentlemen, reiterated his old opinions, somewhat vociferously, & declared them unchangeable. . . .

BIDDLE TO SAMUEL SMITH

Phil. Jany. 4, 1832

MY DEAR SIR,

You will hear, I am afraid with regret, tho' not with surprize, that we have determined on applying to the present Congress for a renewal of the Charter of the Bank & that a memorial for that purpose will be forwarded tomorrow or the next day. To this course I have made up my mind after great reflection & with the clearest convictions of its propriety. The reasons I will briefly explain. 1. The Stockholders have devolved upon the Directors the discretion of choosing the time of making the application. If we should omit a favorable opportunity we would commit an irreparable error, & would be permanently reproached with it by the Stockholders. Now these Stockholders are entirely unanimous in their opinions and in a case of such grave responsibility their wishes are entitled to great consideration. Unless therefore there should be some very strong reason against it, the application should be made. 2. Independent however of this, I believe that this is the proper time. The Charter will expire in March 1836—Unless the present Congress acts upon it, we must wait 'till the Congress of December 1833, & could not expect from them any decision before after March 1834 which would bring the Bank within two years or 18 months of the expiration of its charter. Now whether the institution is to be continued or destroyed that time is too short. . . . No man can look ahead in either public or private affairs as to the state of the currency & there will be constant anxiety about our whole monied system. The Bank too ought to know its fate so as to close its affairs without inflicting deep & dangerous wounds upon the community by sudden shocks & changes. . . . If the bank is to be continued the country ought to know it soon. If the Bank is to be destroyed the Bank & the country ought both to know it soon.

The only objection I have heard to it, is, as far as I understand, this: that in about a year hence there is to be an election for a President of the U.S.—and if the application is now made, the gentleman who is now president will take it amiss & negative the bill—while if the Bank will refrain from applying until after his election is secured, he will probably be permitted to abstain from negativing it. . . . Neither I nor any of my associates have any thing whatever to do with the President or his election. I know nothing about it & care nothing about it. The Bank has never had any concern in elections—it will not have any now. To abstain from anything which it would otherwise do, on account of an election, is just as bad as doing anything on account of an election. Both are equal violations of its neutrality. . . .

In the next place what appears to me I confess wholly inexplicable is why the friends of the present incumbent who are also friends of the Bank, if they think the Bank question likely to injure the President, do not at once take the question out of the hands of their adversaries. If the President's friends were to come forward & settle the Bank question before the election comes on, they would disarm their antagonists of their most powerful weapon. I am very ignorant of party tactics, & am probably too much biased to be a fit judge in this case, but such a course has always seemed to me so obvious that I have never been able to comprehend why it was not adopted.

But again what is the reason for supposing that the present incumbent will be offended by bringing it forward now? What possible right has he to be offended? What too has he meant by all these annual messages—declaring in 1829 that he could not "too soon present it" to Congress—repeating the same thing in 1830—and reiterating it in 1831. Was this all a mere pretence? that the moment the Bank accepts his own invitation he is to be offended by being taken at his word.

But moreover he is to negative the bill. That is to say, he will agree to the bill hereafter, but because he thinks it will interfere with his election he will negative it now. Truly this is a compliment which I trust he does not deserve from his friends, for even I who do not feel the slightest interest in him would be sorry to ascribe to a President of the United States a course much fitter for a humble demagogue than the Chief Magistrate of a great country. He will sign a bill, which of course he must think a good one, when his election is over—but he will not sign this bill, which he thinks a good one,—if it is likely to take votes from him at an election. And after all, what security is there that when his election is over, he will not negative the bill? I see none. On the contrary I am satisfied that he would be ten times more disposed to negative it then than now. Now he has at least some check in public opinion—some in the counsels of those around him—then he will have neither. . . .

BIDDLE TO CHARLES J. INGERSOLL

Phil. Feb. 11, 1832

MY DEAR SIR,

. . . Here am I, who have taken a fancy to this Bank & having built it up with infinite care am striving to keep it from being destroyed to the infinite wrong as I most sincerely & conscientiously believe of the whole country. To me all other considerations are insignificant—I mean to stand by it & defend it with all the small faculties which Providence has assigned to me. I care for no party in politics or religion. . . . I am for the Bank & the Bank alone. Well then, here comes Mr Jackson who takes it into his head to declare that the Bank had failed & that it ought to be superceded by some rickety machinery of his contrivance. . . .

It remains to see how its evil consequences may be averted. It seems to me there is no one course by which his friends may extricate him not merely safely but triumphantly. He has made the Bank a Power. He has made the Bank a deciding question as to his own selection. Now let him turn this power to his own advantage. As yet the Bank is entirely uncommitted—the Bank is neither for him nor against him. . . . If the bill passes & the President negatives it, I will not say that it will destroy him—but I certainly think it will & moreover I think it ought to. I can imagine no question which seems more exclusively for the representatives of the people than the manner in which they choose to keep & to manage the money of the people.

. . . I suppose the President has been made to believe that the Bank is busy in hostility to him—you know how wholly unfounded this is. For myself I do not care a straw for him or his rivals—I covet neither his man servant—nor even his maid servant, his ox nor any of his asses. Long may he live to enjoy all possible blessings, but if he means to wage war upon the Bank—if he pursues us till we turn & stand at bay, why then—he may perhaps awaken a spirit which has hitherto been checked & reined in—and which it is wisest not to force into offensive defence.

BIDDLE TO HENRY CLAY

Philadelphia, August 1, 1832

MY DEAR SIR,

You ask what is the effect of the Veto. My impression is that it is working as well as the friends of the Bank and of the country could desire. I have always deplored making the Bank a party question, but since the President will have it so, he must pay the penalty of his own rashness. As to the Veto message I am delighted with it. It has all the fury of a chained panther biting the bars of his cage. It is really a manifesto of anarchy—such as Marat or Robespierre might have issued to the mob of the faubourg St. Antoine: and my hope is that it will contribute to relieve the country from the dominion of these miserable people! You are destined to be the instrument of that deliverance, and at no period of your life has the country ever had a deeper stake in you. I wish you success most cordially, because I believe the institutions of the Union are involved in it.

3. VAN BUREN'S "DIVORCE" OF BANK AND STATE

To destroy the Bank was one thing. To control a nationalizing economy without effective national financial institutions was another. The second task fell to Jackson's unhappy successor, Martin Van Buren. A severe business panic occurred almost immediately after Van Buren took office in 1837 and made a political nightmare out of this professional politician's four years in the White House. When all the country's several hundred banks suspended specie payments (or refused to surrender hard money for their bank notes, at the time the nation's circulating medium), Van Buren had to act. Since the national bank's fall, the federal government had been depositing its revenues in selected state banks, but federal law required that such banks maintain specie payments. Van Buren decided to scrap the deposit banks system. In proposing to a special session of Congress that the government hold its money in its own subtreasuries, he lectured his countrymen (particularly businessmen seeking government aid) in the style of "Poor Richard." [Richardson, Messages of the Presidents, III: 324–46.]

Washington, *September 4, 1837*
Fellow-Citizens of the Senate and House of Representatives:
 . . . The history of trade in the United States for the last three or four years affords the most convincing evidence that our present condition is chiefly to be attributed to overaction in all the departments of business—an overaction deriving, perhaps, its first impulses from antecedent causes, but stimulated to its destructive consequences by excessive issues of bank paper and by other facilities for the acquisition and enlargement of credit. . . .

Proneness to excessive issues has ever been the vice of the banking system—a vice as prominent in national as in State institutions. This propensity is as subservient to the advancement of private interests in the one as in the other, and those who direct them both, being principally guided by the same views and influenced by the same motives, will be equally ready to stimulate extravagance of enterprise by improvidence of credit. How strikingly is this conclusion sustained by experience! The Bank of the United States, with the vast powers conferred on it by Congress, did not or could not prevent former and similar embarrassments, nor has the still greater strength it has been said to possess under its present charter enabled it in the existing emergency to check other institutions or even to save itself.

But it was not designed by the Constitution that the Government should assume the management of domestic or foreign exchange. It is indeed authorized to regulate by law the commerce between the States and to provide a general standard of value or medium of exchange in gold and silver, but it is not its province to aid individuals in the transfer of their funds otherwise than through the facilities afforded by the Post-Office Department. As justly might it be called on to provide for the transportation of their merchandise. These are operations of trade. They ought to be conducted by those who are interested in them in the same manner that the incidental difficulties of other pursuits are encountered by other classes of citizens. . . . [F]ew can doubt that their own interest, as well as the general welfare of the country, would be promoted by leaving such a subject in the hands of those to whom it properly belongs. A system founded on private interest, enterprise, and competition, without the aid of legislative grants or regulations by law, would rapidly prosper; it would be free from the influence of political agitation and extend the same exemption to trade itself, and it would put an end to those complaints of neglect, partiality, injustice, and oppression which are the unavoidable results of interference by the Government in the proper concerns of individuals. All former attempts on the part of the Government to carry its legislation in this respect further than was designed by the Constitution have in the end proved injurious, and have served only to convince the great body of the people more and more of the certain dangers of blending private interests with the operations of public business; and there is no reason to suppose that a repetition of them now would be more successful. . . .

Banking has become a political topic of the highest interest, and trade has suffered in the conflict of parties. A speedy termination of this state of things, however desirable, is scarcely to be expected. We have seen for nearly half a century that those who advocate a national bank, by whatever motive they may be influenced, constitute a portion of our community too numerous to allow us to hope for an early abandonment of their favorite plan. On the other hand, they must indeed form an erroneous estimate of the intelligence and temper of the American people who suppose that they have continued on slight or insufficient grounds their persevering opposition to such an institution, or that they can be induced by pecuniary pressure or by any other combination of circumstances to surrender principles they have so long and so inflexibly maintained. . . .

Under these circumstances it becomes our solemn duty to inquire whether there are not in any connection between the Government and banks of issue evils of great magnitude, inherent in its very nature and against which no precautions can effectually guard. . . .

The use by the banks, for their own benefit, of the money deposited with them has received the sanction of the Government from the commencement of this connection. The money received from the people, instead of being kept till it is needed for their use, is, in consequence of this authority, a fund on which discounts are made for the profit of those who happen to be owners of stock in the banks selected as depositories. . . .

Surely banks are not more able than the Government to secure the money in their possession against accident, violence, or fraud. The assertion that they are so must assume that a vault in a bank is stronger than a vault in the Treasury, and that directors, cashiers, and clerks not selected by the Government nor under its control are more worthy of confidence than officers selected from the people and responsible to the Government—officers bound by official oaths and bonds for a faithful performance of their duties, and constantly subject to the supervision of Congress. . . . May not Congress so regulate by law the duty of those officers and subject it to such supervision and publicity as to prevent the possibility of any serious abuse on the part of the Executive? And is there equal room for such supervision and publicity in a connection with banks, acting under the shield of corporate immunities and conducted by persons irresponsible to the Government and the people? It is believed that a considerate and candid investigation of these questions will result in the conviction that the proposed plan is far less liable to objection on the score of Executive patronage and control than any bank agency that has been or can be devised. . . .

. . . Those who look to the action of this Government for specific aid to the citizen to relieve embarrassments arising from losses by revulsions in commerce and credit lose sight of the ends for which it was created and the powers with which it is clothed. It was established to give security to us all in our lawful and honorable pursuits, under the lasting safeguard of republican institutions. It was not intended to confer special favors on individuals or on any classes of them, to create systems of agriculture, manufactures, or trade, or to engage in them either separately or in connection with individual citizens or organized associations. If its operations were to be directed for the benefit of any one class, equivalent favors must in justice be extended to the rest, and the attempt to bestow such favors with an equal hand, or even to select those who should most deserve them, would never be successful.

All communities are apt to look to government for too much. Even in our own country, where its powers and duties are so strictly limited, we are prone to do so, especially at periods of sudden embarrassment and distress. But this ought not to be. The framers of our excellent Constitution and the people who approved it with calm and sagacious deliberation acted at the time on a sounder principle. They wisely judged that the less government interferes with private pursuits the better for the general prosperity. It is not its legitimate object to make men rich or to repair by direct grants of money or legislation in favor of particular pursuits losses not incurred in the public service. This would be substantially to use the property of some for the benefit of others. But its real duty—that duty the performance of which makes a good government the most precious of human blessings—is to enact and enforce a system of general laws commensurate with, but not exceeding, the objects of its establishment, and to leave every citizen and every interest to reap under its benign protection the rewards of virtue, industry, and prudence.

I can not doubt that on this as on all similar occasions the Federal Government will find its agency most conducive to the security and happiness of the people when limited to the exercise of its conceded powers. In never assuming, even for a well-meant object, such powers as were not designed to be conferred upon it, we shall in reality do most for the general welfare. To avoid every unnecessary interference with the pursuits of the citizen will result in more benefit than to adopt measures which could only assist limited interests, and are eagerly, but perhaps naturally, sought for under the pressure of temporary circumstances. If, therefore, I refrain from suggesting to Congress any specific plan for regulating the exchanges of the country, relieving mercantile embarrassments, or interfering with the ordinary operations of foreign or domestic commerce, it is from a conviction that such measures are not within the constitutional province of the General Government, and that their adoption would not promote the real and permanent welfare of those they might be designed to aid.

The difficulties and distresses of the times, though unquestionably great, are limited in their extent, and can not be regarded as affecting the permanent prosperity of the nation. Arising in a great degree from the transactions of foreign and domestic commerce, it is upon them that they have chiefly fallen. The great agricultural interest has in many parts of the country suffered comparatively little, and, as if Providence intended to display the munificence of its goodness at the moment of our greatest need, and in direct contrast to the evils occasioned by the waywardness of man, we have been blessed throughout our extended territory with a season of general health and of uncommon fruitfulness. The proceeds of our great staples will soon furnish the means of liquidating debts at home and abroad, and contribute equally to the revival of commercial activity and the restoration of commercial credit. The banks, established avowedly for its support, deriving their profits from it, and resting under obligations to it which can not be overlooked, will feel at once the necessity and justice of uniting their energies with those of the mercantile interest.

VIII. Whig Response

Before "King Andrew" could be deposed and the virtuous American republic redeemed, the anti-Jacksonians would have to alter their political strategy. Jackson's repeated and successful appeal to "vox populi" had changed the political rules.

Back in Jefferson's day, American conservatism had undergone a partial democratization, especially after the Federalists' narrow defeat in 1800. But Federalism's apparent collapse and the subsequent blending of parties halted the process of conservative adaptation, although not the onrush of egalitarian politics. The problem of the proper relationship between political leadership and the masses was vigorously restated by Jackson's insistent claims to represent the public will. The opposition had to prove him wrong through their own reading of the public voice. The Whig majority easily adapted to the new politics, for reasons of expediency or conviction, although a conservative minority remained "unreconstructed." As a result, an effective two-party system appeared in the late 1830s, maintaining itself until the decade before the Civil War. The requirements of mass politics in Jackson's time ended any hope of sustaining an openly anti-democratic political tradition in America.

1. THE NEW WHIGS:
WEED, THE OPERATOR

A leading exponent of adaptation was Thurlow Weed, an Albany, New York, editor and former member of the Anti-Masonic party. He learned early that prissy campaigning and gentlemanly behavior toward political enemies produced election day defeats. A slashing editorialist, Weed joined the anti-Jackson forces when the Anti-Masons dis-

156

*integrated in 1834, giving Whiggery in New York a badly
needed fresh image. Weed's organizational energy and political style helped elect a governor in New York, and later
two Whig Presidents. The selection given here, from
Weed's autobiography, illustrates his disdain for issues in
favor of emphasis on organization. First, Weed tells how
practicality determined his opposition to the national bank,
despite personal preferences; he then recounts preparations
made for the election of 1840 as well as his relations with
an able but overly reform-minded young editor, Horace
Greeley. Here we see clearly the mind of the professional
political tactician at work. [Harriet A. Weed, ed., Autobiography of Thurlow Weed (Boston, 1884), 371–72,
466–68.]*

The question of a re-charter of the Bank of the United States occupied public attention as early as 1829, although the charter would
not expire until 1836. The bank had so conducted its affairs for several
years as to secure the confidence of the business men of the country.
President Jackson, however, influenced, as it was subsequently alleged,
by some of his far-seeing political friends, suggested doubts in his
message of 1829 of the constitutionality of the United States Bank.

Isaac Hill, editor of the "New Hampshire Patriot," then a leading
and influential journal, opened its columns against the bank, charging,
among other things, that by its loans to prominent politicians it was
paving the way by corrupt means for a re-charter. Other Democratic
journals followed the "New Hampshire Patriot," until, in 1832, it became the leading political issue between the friends and the opponents
of General Jackson.

My own sympathies were with the bank, believing that it was necessary to the commercial, manufacturing, mechanical, and agricultural
interests of the country, and as a means of regulating its currency and
exchanges. But I was not long in discovering that it was easy to enlist
the laboring classes against a "monster bank" or "moneyed aristocracy,"
and that as a political issue we should lose more than we could hope
to gain by it. This, however, was not the opinion of my political friends.
The opponents of the administration generally accepted the issue offered
by the friends of General Jackson, and I was drawn into the current,
though not without serious misgivings as to the result. When, however,
we were disastrously beaten, though still differing with my friends as
to the cause, I determined to cut loose from the bank, and took a
suitable occasion to avow that determination. This surprised most, and
exasperated many of my political friends. But we finally agreed to
disagree on that question, and in subsequent elections this State, out

of the city of New York, was largely exempted from the odium elsewhere attached to the "United States Bank Party."

The political success in the election of 1837 encouraged the hope that
the Whig party of the Union might carry the presidential election of
1840. We therefore determined upon inaugurating a vigorous campaign.
With that view a cheap weekly paper for extended circulation was
suggested. In casting about for an editor it occurred to me that there
was some person connected with the "New Yorker," a literary journal
published in that city, possessing the qualities needed for our new
enterprise. In reading the "New Yorker" attentively, as I had done, I felt
sure that its editor was a strong tariff man, and probably an equally
strong Whig. The chairman of our State committee, Mr. Lewis
Benedict, accompanied me to New York. I repaired to the office in
Ann Street, where the "New Yorker" was published, and inquired
for its editor. A young man with light hair and blonde complexion,
with coat off and sleevs rolled up, standing at the "case" "stick" in
hand, replied that he was the editor, and this youth was Horace
Greeley. We sat down in the composing room, when I informed him
of the object of my visit. He of course was surprised, but evidently
gratified. Nor were his surprise and gratification diminished to learn
that I was drawn to him without any other reason or information, but
such as I had derived from the columns of the "New Yorker." He
accepted an invitation to dine with Mr. Benedict and myself at the
City Hotel, where it was arranged that Mr. Greeley should, in case he
could either sell his "New Yorker," or make some arrangement that
would enable him to pass two days in each week at Albany, accept our
invitation. Mr. Greeley suggested and we adopted the "Jeffersonian"
as the name for the new paper.

The first number of the "Jeffersonian" appeared in February, 1838.
That was the opening of a career in which during the ensuing thirty-
four years he was so eminently distinguished. The "Jeffersonian" was
conducted with marked ability. It discussed measures clearly, calmly,
and forcibly, exerting during the year of its existence a wide and beneficial influence. As the canvass proceeded a more pronounced party
paper for popular circulation was needed, and in 1840, under the aus-
pices of the Whig State Committee, Mr. Greeley started the "Log
Cabin." The "Log Cabin" was zealous, spirited, and became universally
popular. The singing of patriotic songs at political meetings had its
origin in that year, which was long, and is even yet, remembered as the
"Tippecanoe and Tyler too Campaign."

It has been stated that I differed with Mr. Greeley about the new
political element, he being in favor and I against the songs. This mis-

apprehension was caused by my objection to the publication in the "Log Cabin," not of the songs, but of the words elaborately set to music, the plates taking up too much room. I saw that the songs attracted large meetings everywhere, and awakened much enthusiasm.

While at Albany during the year he was editing the "Jeffersonian," Mr. Greeley was our guest, and we became not only intimate politically but socially. I formed a high estimate of his ability and character, confidently anticipating for him a career alike honorable and useful to himself and his country. He was unselfish, conscientious, public spirited, and patriotic. He had no habits or tastes but for work, steady, indomitable work. Our sentiments and opinions of public measures and public men harmonized perfectly; our only difference was, that upon the temperance, slavery, and labor questions he was more ardent and hopeful. In this I gave him credit for fresher and less disciplined feelings.

The year following the presidential election of 1840 found Mr. Greeley at the head of a highly influential journal, "The Tribune," and possessing the friendship and confidence of the strong men of his party. Next to Hezekiah Niles, of "Niles's Register," Mr. Greeley was recognized as the best informed and most efficient tariff man in the country. After President Harrison's death, and while the Whig party was demoralized by Tylerism, the "Tribune" avowed itself in favor of Mr. Clay's nomination for the presidency in 1844, exerting an influence which contributed largely to an almost unanimous nomination of Mr. Clay by the Whig National Convention. Mr. Greeley, as its editor, by his industry, zeal, and enthusiasm extended the "Tribune" and its influence throughout the Union. We were in constant communication, and concurred heartily in the mode and manner of conducting the campaign. Time served to confirm and strengthen my early impressions of his single-eyed and single-hearted devotion to his country and his countrymen. Occasionally, when some of the "isms" which subsequently became chronic cropped out, I was enabled to repress them.

Mr. Greeley's sympathy with and friendship for the "toiling millions" led him to favor "associations" and "unions" of laborers and journeymen,—organizations which, countenanced by the widely circulating "Tribune," became as formidable as they were mischievous. But his peculiarities in this respect never turned him away from or impaired his consistent and hearty efforts in the Whig cause. Our first radical difference was after he had established the "Tribune," when under the influence of Albert Brisbane, a young man from Batavia, who returned from France with a "mission." That mission was to unsettle and remodel our social system, establishing "Fourierism" in its place. Finding Greeley imbued with that heresy, I remonstrated earnestly against his determination to espouse it in the "Tribune." Many other friends

labored to change his purpose, but all was in vain. Mr. Greeley in that
matter, as in the temperance and other questions of reform, was inflexible.

2. THE NEW WHIGS:
SEWARD, THE BELIEVER

*Weed organized the meetings, but he never addressed
them. This job fell to the "front men," the Whig orators
and candidates. In New York no Whig excelled William
Henry Seward, a small dynamo of a man whose energy
and ambition led him from Anti-Masonry to Whiggery,
the New York governorship, the U.S. Senate, and finally
to Lincoln's cabinet as Secretary of State. Seward was an
optimist. He believed profoundly in American expansion
and thought that continued moral betterment was a distinct possibility. Seward had no trouble adapting to democratic politics. Thus he defended the right of New York
City voters to choose their own mayor on grounds of
democratic principles. His views on prison conditions and
convict rehabilitation were advanced for that time. And
Seward warned that without effective, universal education
democracy could not succeed. Belief in the value of democratic government made him devote much of his time
while governor to school reforms. Seward's liberalism stood
out most clearly when he advocated state aid to all schools,
even Catholic schools. Catholic parents shunned the public
schools, which they regarded as nurseries of Protestantism.
The Governor, no friend of Catholicism per se, nevertheless
felt that education of all the young outweighed the disad-
vantage of allotting public money to sectarian schools. He
lost the battle. [George E. Baker, ed., The Works of
William H. Seward (5 vols., Boston, 1887), I: 10–13;
II: 270–72, 278–81.]*

What is the state of the question before the Senate? The provision
required by the city of New York is, that the mayor of that city shall
be elected by the people. The amendment under consideration proposes
that the legislature shall hereafter have the right to prescribe the manner
in which that officer shall be elected or appointed. . . .

. . . The tendency of all our principles of government is to democracy; the new Constitution took the appointment from the council of
appointment, and conferred it upon the immediate representatives of

the people. There is but one more change before you reach absolute democracy; that is the one now proposed, and conceded to be proper. Are gentlemen afraid that the people, once invested with this power, will come back again and sue us to relieve them from its responsibilities? Such an instance would be anomalous in the history of government.

But we are told that the appointment or election of this officer ought not to "be bound up in constitutional bonds";—that it ought to be left to the legislature. Sir, I think if there be any right of the people which ought to be bound up in constitutional bonds, it is the right of electing their magistrates. If there be any right belonging to the people of the city of New York which ought to be bound up "in constitutional bonds," it is the right guarantied to them of electing, either by their immediate representatives, or by their own ballots, the highest local magistrate in their city, without being subjected to the caprice of party in your legislature. Gentlemen who support the amendment say they are in favor of allowing the mayor to be chosen by the people; will *their* amendment carry out their views? Amend the Constitution as *they* propose, and will the people then have that right? No; but it will then be left to the legislature of the state to determine whether the mayor shall be elected by the people or by the Common Council, or appointed by the legislature, or by the governor and Senate—and to revoke that decision at pleasure.

Gentlemen do indeed assure us that the legislature will never deprive the people of that city of the privilege of electing this officer, unless at their own solicitation. We are asked if we believe any legislature would so deprive them, and we are even told that to entertain such an apprehension, is to arrogate to ourselves all the virtue and the purity of the present and future legislatures. I, sir, arrogate to myself no such extraordinary portion of virtue and purity, and yet I have less confidence in legislative bodies than is necessary to induce my consent to restore to this legislature a power, of which, within my own recollection, it has been solemnly, and for cause, deprived by the Constitution. I will not say that the legislature ever would deprive the people of New York of the right to elect the first magistrate of their city; but I can safely say that legislatures have reluctantly parted with power, and have sometimes upon poor pretexts assumed it. But, sir, the answer to the gentleman's inquiry is furnished by the Constitution. The incorporation of the provision in the Constitution which reserves the appointment of the mayor by the Common Council, shows that the people distrust the purity and virtue of the legislature. It is, I believe, a broad and living principle of democracy, that the tendency of delegated power is always to its own aggrandizement, and that the safety of the rights of the people is secured by their jealousy of encroachment. So much distrust of the legislature as the Constitution expresses, and so much as is founded in the maxims of our government, and no more, I entertain.

What was the evil which called into existence the convention which framed your Constitution? Other grounds of objection there were indeed to your old Constitution, but the crying evil was the corruption and abuses of the council of appointment, subjected to the exercise of a mighty and controlling central power at Albany. What was the great reform made by that convention? Other reforms there were, but that which was the most valuable was the abolition of the council of appointment, and the distribution among different depositories more immediately derived from and subjected to the popular will, and of the appointing power of the state. Will not the people regard this as an attempt to bring back to the central power this portion of the appointing power? Will they not regard it as a precursor of other attempts to restore that state of things which it demanded the convention of 1821 to overthrow? Yes, sir, they will so regard it, and I think I may say for that portion of them which are my constituents, that any proposition tending to increase at the expense of popular rights and privileges, the power of the legislature or executive, will be met and resisted as an encroachment.

For these reasons, I am opposed to that portion of the amendment which provides for subjecting to legislative action the mode of the appointment of the mayor of the city of New York. I am in favor of giving the election to the people, and of extending the same right of election to all the cities in the state, and I shall avail myself of a distinct motion to amend for that purpose. . . .

In regard to our penitentiaries, I have urged that discipline ought to be tempered with kindness, and that moral influences should be employed to secure the submission and promote the reformation of convicts. Although some improvement has been made in this respect, more can yet be accomplished. It is too often forgotten, that the object chiefly contemplated in the adoption of our penitentiary system, was the reformation of offenders. This object derives its importance from considerations of prudence, as well as of philanthropy. The unreformed convict, after being released, spends a brief period in committing depredations upon society, and in corrupting youth, and then returns to the prison to exercise a vicious influence upon his fellow-prisoners there. Reformation can seldom be expected, without addressing the mind. I would have the school-room in the prison fitted as carefully as the solitary cell and workshop; and although attendance there can not be so frequent, I would have it quite as regular. The recent establishment of a separate institution for female-prisoners, under the management of one of their own sex reflects much honor upon the state; and I am happy to add that it has realized the expectations of the legislature. Females convicted within the district from which criminals are received at the Auburn prison, are now sent to that penitentiary, where they remain until an executive order is made for conveying them to Mount Pleasant, and such an order can not be made for less than ten convicts. This temporary imprisonment of females in the prison at Auburn operates harshly toward them, and is inconvenient in regard to the management of that institution. I respectfully recommend that the law be modified, so that females be directly conveyed to their proper penitentiary. The chief obstacle to a reformation of this class of offenders is the inflexibility with which society rejects them after their season of penance is past. While the cause of public morals requires their exclusion, at least until they have given satisfactory evidence of reformation, humanity and expediency unite in recommending proper efforts to sustain those who are truly reformed. . . . The whole number of male convicts in the state prisons is fourteen hundred and twenty-three, of whom eleven hundred and fifty-three are white, and two hundred and seventy are colored persons. The number of female convicts is seventy-four, of whom forty are white and thirty-four are colored. The sex has a just claim to extraordinary effort for the reformation of the small number of persons it furnishes to our prisons.

The success which has crowned the benevolent efforts of the founders of the House of Refuge has induced an opinion that it would be profitable to establish a similar institution in the western part of the state, where the subjects of its discipline could be maintained at much less expense than in the city of New York.

The law which authorized the imprisonment of non-resident debtors, against whom no fraud was alleged, was repealed at the last session upon the ground that the practice operated injuriously to trade, and was inconsistent with the benign spirit of our code. There remains now only one relic of that usage in this state. Imprisonment for debt is allowed in actions brought in the federal courts; and by the laws of this state, our jails, designed only for the custody of criminals, are permitted to be used as prisons for the confinement of debtors, under process issued by the authority of the United States. If you shall be of opinion that no principle of the federal Union requires us to extend our courtesy so far, we shall no longer witness the imprisonment of honest but unfortunate debtors, with the sanction of this state.

The legislature at its last session communicated to our representatives the opinion that Congress was imperatively required to exercise its constitutional power of passing uniform laws on the subject of bankruptcy. I beg leave to refer you to the views of that interesting subject which were submitted to your predecessors, and to suggest a renewal of instructions during the present session of Congress.

Not much, however, can be accomplished by legislation to affect the relations between masses of adult citizens, and the change desired in this respect must be left chiefly to time and the operation of our institutions. But it is not so in regard to the rising generation. The census of the United States is said to show, that there are forty-three thousand eight hundred and seventy-one white persons in this state who have passed the age of twenty years without having learned to read and write. Let us make allowance for any proportion of adult foreigners, and there will yet remain a large number of uneducated native citizens. The number of children now growing up in the same manner does not fall short of thirty thousand. These are the offspring, not of prosperity and affluence, but of poverty and misfortune. Knowing, from the records of our penitentiaries, that of this neglected class, those are often most fortunate who, from precocity in vice, secure admission into the house of refuge or the stateprison through the ways of crime, and knowing too that almost every application for pardon is urged on the ground of neglected education, I have felt it an imperative duty to appeal to the legislature, to render our system of education as comprehensive as the purposes for which it was established. Of one thousand and fifty-eight children in the almshouse of the city of New York, one sixth part are of American parentage, one sixth were born abroad, and the remainder are the children of foreigners; and of two hundred and fifty children in the house of refuge, more than one half were born either abroad, or of foreign parents. The poverty, misfortunes, accidents, and prejudices, to which foreigners are exposed, satisfactorily account to my mind for the undue proportion of their children in the neglected class to which the attention of the legislature was called. Although the excellent public schools in the city of New York are open to all, and have long afforded gratuitous instruction to all who sought it, nevertheless the evil exists there in its greatest magnitude. Obviously, therefore, something more is necessary to remove it than has yet been done, unless we assume that society consents to leave it without a remedy. These circumstances led me to the reflection, that possibly a portion of those whom other efforts had failed to reach might be brought within the nurture of the schools, by employing for their instruction teachers, who, from their relations toward them, might be expected to secure their confidence. When the census of 1850 shall be taken, I trust it will show that within the borders of the state of New York, there is no child of sufficient years who is unable to read and write. I am sure it will then be acknowledged that when, ten years before, there were thirty thousand children growing up in ignorance and vice, a suggestion to seek them wherever found, and win them to the ways of knowledge and virtue by persuasion, sympathy, and kindness, was prompted by a sincere desire for the common good. I have no pride of opinion concerning the manner in which the education of those whom I have brought to your notice shall be secured, although I might derive satisfaction from the reflection, that amid abundant misrepresentations of the method suggested, no one has contended that it would be ineffectual, nor has any other plan been proposed. I observe, on the contrary, with deep regret, that the evil remains as before; and the question recurs, not merely how or by whom shall instruction be given, but whether it shall be given at all, or shall be altogether withheld. Others may be content with a system that erects free-schools and *offers* gratuitous instruction; but I trust I shall be allowed to entertain the opinions, that no system is perfect that does not accomplish what it proposes; that our system is, therefore, deficient in comprehensiveness, in the exact proportion of the children that it leaves uneducated; that knowledge, however acquired, is better than ignorance; and that neither error, accident, nor prejudice, ought to be permitted to deprive the state of the education of her citizens. Cherishing such opinions, I could not enjoy the consciousness of having performed my duty, if any effort had been omitted, which was calculated to bring within the schools all who are destined to exercise the rights of citizenship; nor shall I feel that the system is perfect, or liberty safe, until that object should be accomplished. Not personally concerned about such misapprehensions as have arisen, but desirous to remove every obstacle to the accomplishment of so important an object, I very freely declare that I seek the education of those whom I have brought before you, not to perpetuate any prejudices or distinctions which deprive them of instruction, but in disregard of all such distinctions and prejudices. I solicit their education, less from sympathy, than because the welfare of the state demands it, and can not dispense with it. As native citizens, they are born to the right of suffrage. I ask that they may at least be taught to read and write; and, in asking this, I require no more for them than I have diligently endeavored to secure to the inmates of our penitentiaries, who have forfeited that inestimable franchise by crime, and also to an unfortunate race, which, having been plunged by us into degradation and ignorance, has been excluded from the franchise by an arbitrary property-qualification incongruous with all our institutions. I have not recommended, nor do I seek, the education of any class in foreign languages, or in particular creeds or faiths; but fully believing with the author of the Declaration of Independence, that even error may be safely tolerated where reason is left free to combat it, and therefore indulging no apprehensions from the influence of any language or creed among an enlightened people, I desire the education of the entire rising generation in all the elements of knowl-

edge we possess, and in that tongue which is the universal language of
our countrymen. To me the most interesting of all our republican institutions is the common school. I seek not to disturb, in any manner,
its peaceful and assiduous exercises, and least of all with contentions
about faith or forms. I desire the education of all the children in the
commonwealth in morality and virtue, leaving matters of conscience
where, according to the principles of civil and religious liberty established by our constitution and laws, they rightfully belong.

3. AN OLD FOGY,
NORTHERN STYLE

*Many persons were unable or unwilling to adapt them-
selves to the new style and content of Jacksonian politics.
A few "silk stocking" Democrats left the party for that
reason, but most of those repelled by the political innovations were, of course, opponents of Jackson from the start.
One such critic was Philip Hone—New York City merchant, moralist, and mayor. Hone had been mayor of the
city briefly before popular election of that officer. He dis-
trusted, then came to fear, the common man, believing
as do some Americans today that "America is a republic,
not a democracy." In the selections which follow, Hone
levels his increasingly dyspeptic blasts at unworthy immigrants, the false-god Jackson, the difficulty of sustaining
"decent" political principles, the danger of trade union-
ism, and the general contagion of Locofocoism. It is a
scarifying catalog of phantoms, and one must conclude
that many a night Hone went to bed frightened. Happily
for the well-being of the "dispossessed" upper-class Americans, he suffered from an exceptionally severe case of pes-
simism. [Bayard Tuckerman, ed., The Diary of Philip
Hone, 1828–1851 (2 vols. in one, New York, 1910), I:
55–56, 64, 76–77, 117–19, 210–11, 245, 339–40.]*

JUNE 9 [1832].—A great meeting was held last evening of persons
avowedly friends to the union of the States and in favour of such a
modification of the tariff as would serve to produce that effect, together
with many violent free-trade men (as they call themselves), who would
destroy the industry of the country and discourage all improvement to
support their opinions and establish their theories. The meeting was
called to order and organized by that mild, amiable, and reasonable
gentleman, Preserved Fish. . . . The meeting was addressed and the

resolutions moved by Peter A. Jay, and they are quite unexceptionable, as was to be expected from that gentleman, who is always wise, always honest, but sometimes a little prejudiced; but would to God the affairs of our country, tariff and all, were in the hands of such men! The meeting was so large that the room was insufficient, and all the approaches to it crowded to excess. Great tumult and disorder were occasioned by some tariff men who had better have stayed away. Party spirit has unhappily been mingled with the question. The excitement increases every day. Reflecting men who love their country and would preserve its institutions are full of alarm and serious forebodings. Both sides are wrong. It is vain to talk of conciliation. Prejudice on one side, interest on the other, and intolerance on both will prevent them from approaching nearer to each other. Mr. Adams's wisdom might do something if it were seconded by General Jackson's decision. Happy would our country be if those qualifications were united in one person, and he the chief magistrate! . . .

[Sept. 20, 1832]. The distresses of the lower classes in England and Ireland have caused emigration to America in numbers so great as to cause serious alarm. Besides the immense numbers which are daily arriving here and in other parts of the United States, it is stated that forty-nine thousand five hundred and sixty-nine emigrants have arrived at Quebec since the opening of the navigation of the St. Lawrence the present year. Of these, a large proportion find their way into the United States destitute and friendless. They have brought the cholera this year, and they will always bring wretchedness and want. The boast that our country is the asylum for the oppressed in other parts of the world is very philanthropic and sentimental, but I fear that we shall, before long, derive little comfort from being made the almshouse and place of refuge for the poor of other countries. . . .

June 13 [1833].—The President is certainly the most popular man we have ever known. Washington was not so much so. His acts were popular, because all descriptions of men were ready to acknowledge him the Father of his Country; but he was superior to the homage of the populace,—too dignified, too grave for their liking; and men could not approach him with familiarity. Here is a man who suits them exactly. He has a kind expression for each,—the same to all, no doubt, but each thinks it intended for himself. His manners are certainly good, and he makes the most of them. He is a *gourmand* of adulation, and by the assistance of the populace has persuaded himself that no man ever lived in the country to whom the country was so much indebted. Talk of him as the second Washington! It won't do now. Washington was only the first Jackson. Poor Adams used to visit New York during his presidency.

The papers, to be sure, announced his arrival; but he was welcomed by no shouts, no crowd thronged around his portals, no huzzas rent the air when he made his appearance, and yet posterity, more just than ourselves, will acknowledge him to have been, in all the qualifications which constitute his fitness to fill the office of a ruler of this great Republic, twenty times superior to Jackson. He wanted tact. He gave the toast of *Ebony and Topaz*, the ungracious offspring of a mind overloaded with study and unskilful in adaptation. And the other, in a moment when we were all anxious to save the country from the mad schemes of visionary theorists whose crude principles of government seemed to threaten the welfare of our federative institution, and when we doubted what his course would be, gave in a happy moment his toast, "The Union—it must be preserved." It made a difference of five hundred thousand votes. Adams is the wisest man, the best scholar, the most accomplished statesman; but Jackson has most tact. So, huzza for Jackson! . . .

Nov. 5 [1834].—The election closed this evening. The Governor's votes were canvassed in all the wards except the sixth, and by nine o'clock enough was known to satisfy us to our heart's content that we are beaten,—badly beaten; worse than the least sanguine of us anticipated. The majority in our wards (with the exception of the 15th) have fallen off grievously, and theirs have increased in an equal ratio; the third ward has fallen off two hundred from the Spring election. The Tories will have between two and three thousand majority.

Nov. 6.—The triumph was celebrated last night by the worshippers of Jackson with the refinement and forbearance which might have been expected. I had been taken in the morning with an attack of vertigo and headache, which confined me to the house nearly the whole day, but I made out to walk up in the evening to Masonic Hall, where the news I received was not calculated to make me feel better. I returned home much indisposed, and retired to bed at an early hour, where I was kept awake during the greater part of the night by the unmanly insults of the ruffian crew from Tammany Hall, who came over to my door every half-hour and saluted me with groans and hisses. This continued until past three o'clock, and for what? Because I have exercised the right which, in common with every American citizen, I enjoy (or have enjoyed until this time), of expressing my disapprobation of a course of measures which I conceive to be dangerous to the liberties of the people, and inimical to the free institutions of my native land. This I have done with truth, zeal, and firmness, but always, I trust, with decorum and propriety; and for this I have been insulted and annoyed.

I have for many years sacrificed my comfort, exhausted my time, and abridged my enjoyments by a devotion to the service of my fellow-citizens. A member of all the public institutions, charitable, public-spirited, or patriotic, where time was to be lost, labour performed, and no pay to be had; my own affairs neglected, and my money frequently poured out like water; the friend and patron of the working-men, without regard to party;—and now my reward is found in the revilings of a mob of midnight ruffians, among whom, I have no doubt, were some of the very men whom I have assisted to support, to the exclusion of others who are proud to acknowledge themselves my personal and political friends. I believe I am rightly served. . . .

NOVEMBER 10.—I apprehend that Mr. Van Buren and his friends have no permanent cause of triumph in their victory. They have succeeded by the means of instruments which may work their own destruction; they have mounted a vicious horse, who, taking the bit in his mouth, will run away with him. The agrarian party, who have had things pretty much their own way, will not stop at Martin Van Buren,—they will dig deeper into the swamps of political depravity, and the good men of our community, the supporters of the Constitution, and the true friends of civil liberty may be soon called upon to unite in his favour, against a worse man and principles more dangerous than his. This battle had been fought upon the ground of the poor against the rich, and this unworthy prejudice, this dangerous delusion, has been encouraged by the leaders of the triumphant party, and fanned into a flame by the polluted breath of the hireling press in their employ. In the saturnalian orgies with which our streets have been disgraced, the unmannerly epithets which were so liberally bestowed upon myself and other peaceable citizens for having exercised the privilege of freemen in opposing a party whose political doctrines we thought unfavourable to the true interests of the nation, the cry of "Down with the aristocracy!" mingled with the shouts of victory, and must have grated on the ears of some of their own leaders like the croaking of the evil-boding raven. They have succeeded in raising this dangerous spirit, and have gladly availed themselves of its support to accomplish a temporary object; but can they allay it at pleasure? Will their voices be heard when they cry "Thus far shalt thou go and no farther"? Eighteen thousand men in New York have voted for the high-priest of the party whose professed design is to bring down the property, the talents, the industry, the steady habits of that class which constituted the real strength of the Commonwealth, to the common level of the idle, the worthless, and the unenlightened. Look to it, ye men of respectability in the Jackson party, are ye not afraid of the weapons ye have used in this warfare? . . .

JUNE 6 [1836].—In corroboration of the remarks which I have occasionally made of late, on the spirit of faction and contempt of the laws which pervades the community at this time, is the conduct of the journeymen tailors, instigated by a set of vile foreigners (principally English), who, unable to endure the restraints of wholesome law, well administered in their own country, take refuge here, establish tradesunions, and vilify Yankee judges and juries. Twenty odd of these were convicted at the Oyer and Terminer of a conspiracy to raise their wages and to prevent any of the craft from working at prices less than those for which they struck. Judge Edwards gave notice that he would proceed to sentence them this day; but, in consequence of the continuance of Robinson's trial, the Court postponed the sentence until Friday.

This, however, being the day on which it was expected, crowds of people have been collected in the park, ready for any mischief to which they may have been instigated, and a most diabolical and inflammatory hand-bill was circulated yesterday, headed by a coffin. The Board of Aldermen held an informal meeting this evening, at which a resolution was adopted authorizing the Mayor to offer a reward for the discovery of the author, printer, publisher, or distributor of this incendiary publication. . . .

MARCH 4 [1837].—This is the end of General Jackson's administration, —the most disastrous in the annals of the country, and one which will excite "the special wonder" of posterity. That such a man should have governed this great country, with a rule more absolute than that of any hereditary monarch of Europe, and that the people should not only have submitted to it, but upheld and supported him in his encroachments upon their rights, and his disregard of the Constitution and the laws, will equally occasion the surprise and indignation of future generations. The people's indifference will prove that the love of liberty and independence is no longer an attribute of our people, and that the patriotic labours of the men of the Revolution have sunk like water in the sands, and that the vaunted rights of the people are considered by them as a "cunningly devised fable." . . .

DECEMBER 7 [1838].—The breaking up of the Loco-foco forces in different parts of the country produces every day some new development of party atrocity; a state of things exists in Pennsylvania extremely alarming; little short, indeed, of civil war. The return of the judges of the election for the county of Philadelphia being in favor of the Whig candidates, they, as well as those on the other side, appeared at Harrisburg on Tuesday last, at the organization of the Legislature, and claimed their seats as members of the House of Representatives. . . . Confusion and disorder reigned for a time, until brutal violence was resorted to and the hall was left in possession of the Loco-focos, supported by a mob of ruffians in the galleries. The whole was a scene hitherto paralleled only by the sittings of the National Assembly of France, or the Jacobin Club of Paris in the horrid days of anarchy and bloodshed which ushered in the Revolution and led to the destruction of everything "good and lovely and of good report" in that devoted country. God grant that the same causes here may not produce the same results! Virtuous men here begin to fear the worst. Now is the critical moment of our country's fate. If the Whigs continue to grow in numbers and remain firm in the good cause they may succeed in subjecting the rabble of Loco-foco Jacobins to the power of the laws; but if not, the time is close, very close, at hand, when this noble country of ours will be subject to all the horrors of civil war; our republican institutions, theoretically so beautiful, but relying unfortunately too much upon the virtue and intelligence of the people, will be broken into pieces, and a suffering and abused nation will be compelled to submit to the degrading alternative of Jacobin misrule or the tyranny of a Cæsar, a Cromwell, or a Bonaparte.

4. A YOUNG FOGY, SOUTHERN STYLE

Northern conservatives feared that their power might slip downward into the hands of the "unwashed multitude." Southern conservatives felt secure in their more paternalistic societies. But the South had its Jeremiahs too. Southern traditionalists anxiously recorded the growing imbalance of sectional strength as political power increasingly moved northward and as the national government played an increasingly expanded role.

Thus Southern conservatism relied largely on arguments in favor of "constitutionalism," as indeed it still does today. This meant that the southern sectional interest could best be protected by constitutional views which preserved the rights of the states. Many southerners preached on this theme. The author of the selection below is Hugh Swinton Legaré, of lesser stature than his fellow South Carolinian, John C. Calhoun, but a man of talent and a Whig no less conservative than Philip Hone. Legaré, in a review of James Kent's Commentaries on the Constitution, *develops the southern viewpoint on the watering-down, if not total destruction, of the original constitution. [Mary S. Legaré, ed.,* Writings of Hugh Swinton Legaré . . . *(2 vols., Charleston, 1846), II: 123–25, 139–40.]*

The constitutional jurisprudence of the United States! Under this imposing title is presented to us, one of the most striking examples which history furnishes, to illustrate and support an opinion advanced in the course of the preceding remarks. If any one wishes to be convinced how little, even the wisest men, are able to foresee the results of their own political contrivances, let him read the constitution, with the contemporaneous exposition of it contained (even) in the *Federalist*; and then turn to this part of Chancellor Kent's work, to the inaugural speech of the present Executive of the United States, and to some of the records of Congress, during the memorable session which is just past.

He will find that the government has been fundamentally altered by the progress of opinion—that instead of being any longer one of enumerated powers and a circumscribed sphere, as it was beyond all doubt intended to be, it knows absolutely no bounds but the will of a majority of Congress—that instead of confining itself in time of peace to the diplomatic and commercial relations of the country, it is seeking out employment for itself by interfering in the domestic concerns of society, and threatens in the course of a very few years, to control, in the most offensive and despotic manner, all the pursuits, the interests, the opinions and the conduct of men. He will find that this extraordinary revolution has been brought about, in a good degree by the Supreme Court of the United States, which has applied to the constitution—very innocently, no doubt, and with commanding ability in argument—and thus given authority and currency to, such canons of interpretation, as necessarily lead to these extravagant results. Above all, he will be perfectly satisfied that that high tribunal affords, by its own shewing, no barrier whatever against the usurpations of Congress—and that the rights of the weaker part of this confederacy may, to any extent, be wantonly and tyrannically violated, under color of law, [the most grievous shape of oppression] by men neither interested in its destiny nor subject to its control, without any means of redress being left it, except such as are inconsistent with all idea of order and government. Perhaps, he will think with us, that the effect of a written constitution, interpreted by lawyers in a technical manner, is to enlarge power and to sanctify abuse, rather than to abridge and restrain them—perhaps, he will conclude that the American people have not been sufficiently careful, at the beginning of their unprecedented experiment in politics, what principles they suffered to be established—perhaps, he may look forward to the future, with anxiety and alarm, as holding forth a prospect of a rapid accumulation of power in the hands of those who have already abused it, or, on the contrary, with a strong hope that experience will teach wisdom, and diversified interests and conflicting pretensions, lead to moderation in conduct—perhaps, (and surely nothing could be more rational) he might wish to see proper means adopted to bring back the government to its first principles, and put an end to the unhappy jealousies and heart-burnings which are beginning to embitter one part of our people against another—we do not undertake to antici-pate his inferences—but we have no doubt in the world that he will agree with us as to the *fact*—that he will confess Congress to be, to all intents and purposes, omnipotent in theory, and that if, in practice, it prefer moderate counsels and a just and impartial policy, it will be owing, not to any check in the constitution, but altogether to the vigilance, the wisdom, and the firmness of a free people.

We are not, indeed, sure but that this conclusion will, in the end, be productive of much good, and that we ought rather to rejoice than com-plain that, at so early a period of our history, it has been forced upon the public mind—in one part at least of this confederacy—by evidence too strong to be resisted, and with a depth and seriousness of convic-tion which promise to make it an active, permanent and universal principle of conduct. Our political opinions, it appears to us, have been hitherto, in the last degree, wild and visionary. We have been so much accustomed to talk in a high-flown strain, of the perfec-tion—the faultless and unalterable perfection—of our institutions, that we were beginning to think that every thing had been done for us by our predecessors, and that it were impossible to mar their work by any errors of doctrine, or any defect in discipline among ourselves. We do not sufficiently reflect, what a rare and glorious privilege it is to be a free people, (in the only proper sense of that term) and how difficult it is, even under the most favourable circumstances, to keep so. We have unbounded faith in forms, and look upon a written constitution as a sort of talisman, which gives to the liberties of a nation "a charmed life." In short, no people was ever so much addicted to abstrac-tions. . . . Our statesmen are, in general, any thing but practical men —a fact that may be, in some degree, accounted for by the vast pre-dominance of mere professional lawyers, (not of the first order) and the fact, that we have a written constitution to interpret by technical rules. We look in vain for that plain, manly, unsophisticated good sense—that *instinct* of liberty, which characterizes the controversial rea-soning of the great fathers of the English constitution—the Seldens, the Sidneys, the Prynnes—and their worthy descendants and disciples, the founders of our own revolution. . . .

. . . We think the course which things are taking in this country must lead to a passive and slavish acquiescence under usurpation and abuse. Liberty is a practical matter—it has nothing to do with meta-physics—with entity and quiddity. It is a thing to be judged of altogether in the *concrete*. Like the point of honor, or the beauties of art, or the highest perfection of virtue, it addresses itself to the common sense and feelings of mankind. There is no defining it with mathematical exactness—no reducing it to precise and inflexible rules. What, for instance, does it signify, that a skilful disputant might possibly prove the tariff law to be within the words of the constitution: would that prevent its being selfish and oppressive, and, therefore, a tyrannical measure? Is there any practical difference whatever, between the usurpation of a power not granted, and the excessive and perverted exercise of one that is? If a man abuses an authority of law under which he is acting, he becomes a trespasser *ab initio*—and if it be an authority in fact, he is a trespasser for the excess. The master of a ship and other persons in authority, have a right to correct those who are subject to their control —is an act of immoderate severity less a trespass and an offence on that account? What, if the government should suspend the *habeas corpus* act, without such an overruling necessity as could alone excuse the measure, and the courts would not control its discretion, would not the people, with reason, laugh at the man who should talk of such an outrageous abuse of power as constitutional, because the judges did not pronounce it otherwise? Nor does this depend upon the express provision in the constitution. Not at all. In a free country, every act of injustice, every violation of the principles of equality and equity, is, *ex vi termini* a breach of all their fundamental laws and institutions. In the ordinary administration of the law, indeed, the distinction between usurpation and abuse, may sometimes be important, but in great questions of public liberty, in reason, and in good faith, it is wholly immaterial. The moment that this sensibility to its rights and dignity is gone, a people, be its *apparent* or nominal constitution what it may, is no longer free. A quick sense of injustice, with a determination to resist it, in every shape and under every name and pretext, is of the very essence and definition of liberty, political as well as personal. How far, indeed, this resistance to be carried in any particular instance, is a question of circumstances and discretion. So dreadful are all revolutions in their immediate effects—so uncertain in their ultimate issues—that a wise man would doubt long—that a moderate and virtuous man would bear much—before he could be prevailed upon to give his consent to extreme measures. We would be any thing rather than apostles of discord and dismemberment, sorely as the government to which South-Carolina, and the south in general, have been so loyal and devoted, is beginning to press upon all our dearest interests and sensibilities. But we feel it to be our duty to exhort our fellow-citizens to renewed exertion, and to a jealous and sleepless vigilance upon this subject. The battle must be fought inch by inch—no concession or compromise must be thought of. The courage and constancy of a free people can never fail, when they are exerted in defence of right. It is, indeed, an affecting spectacle, to look around us at the decay and desolation which are invading our pleasant places and the seats of our former industry and opulence—there is something unnatural and shocking in such a state of things. A young country already sinking into decrepitude and exhaustion—a fertile soil encroached upon again by the forests from which it has been so recently conquered—the marts and sea-ports of what might be a rich country, depopulated and in ruins. Contrast with this our actual condition, the hope and the buoyancy, and the vigor and the life that animated the same scenes only twenty-five years ago, and which have now fled away from us to bless other and more favored regions of the land. It is scarcely less discouraging to reflect upon the probable effects which the admission of an indefinite number of new states into the union, with political opinions, perhaps, altogether unsettled and unsafe, will produce. But we are yielding too much to feelings, with which recent events have, we own, made our minds but too familiar,—and we will break off here.

5. DEMOCRATIC WHIGS?
—DOUBTS OF A GERMAN SKEPTIC

How much of the Whig "conversion" was merely tactical? How many of Seward's partisan colleagues agreed with the balanced, reasonable, and liberal principles of the New Yorker? The problem admits of no precise answer, merely speculation. One such contemporary speculator was Francis J. Grund, a German immigrant. An editor like Weed, but one of Democratic connection and democratic faith, Grund wrote Aristocracy in America, largely a liberal response to Alexis de Tocqueville's best-seller, Democracy in America, written from a French, aristocratic point of view. Grund, after reading a passage from a British publication, The Edinburgh Review, mused skeptically on the new face of the American rich, and on the dangerous power of money. [Francis J. Grund, Aristocracy in America: From the Sketch-Book of a German Nobleman (London, 1839), 130–35.]

Anxious to learn the opinion of a British writer on so interesting a subject, I read on, and was struck with the following good-natured apology for the doctrines and sentiments of the old Federalists.

"The leaning of the Federalists towards monarchy and aristocracy," says the reviewer, "has probably at all times been a good deal exaggerated by their antagonists. That there is, at the present time, hardly any such feeling, may be easily admitted; and it has probably been wearing out by degrees ever since the revolution, in proportion as men saw that realised without a struggle (!), which many in America, and still more in England, had deemed impossible,—the firm establishment of a republican government over many millions of people, with sufficient power to preserve order at home, and sufficient energy to maintain the relations of peace and war. *But, at the first, no reasonable doubt can be entertained of the fondness for monarchical institutions which prevailed among the leading Federalists.*"

The perusal of this passage, after a day spent, as I have described, in the city of New York, naturally gave rise to singular reflections. "What is it," said I to myself, "that the Americans have established without a struggle? And wherein consists the stability of their republican institutions, if it be not in the fact that the people from year to year conquer them anew from the wealthy opposition? And, as regards to the predilection for monarchical and aristocratic institutions, who that has observed the higher classes of Americans, at home or abroad, can doubt but that they are at this moment as strong as at the time of Thomas Jefferson?"

The old Federalists have not given up *one* of their former pretensions,—for there is no converting men in politics by argument; but they are probably satisfied that they must *wait for a favourable opportunity* of establishing them: they have become more cautious in their actions and expressions, because they now *fear* the people over whom they once expected to rule. All that I have been able to see in the United States convinces me that the wealthy classes are in no other country as much opposed to the existing government; and that, consequently, no other government can be considered as less permanently established, or more liable to changes, than that of the United States. And this state of danger the soft speeches of the Whigs try to conceal from the people by directing their attention almost exclusively to the financial concerns of the country. Wealth, in other countries,—as, for instance, in England,—acts as the *vis inertiæ* of the state; talent from above, and the wants of the labouring classes from below, acting as motors. In America the case is the reverse: the wealthy classes wishing for a change which the labouring ones resist; and talent, I am sorry to say, acting a subordinate part, ready to serve the cause of either party that promises to reward its exertions.

This, I am aware, is a sad picture of America, but nevertheless a true one; and I appeal to the history of the last half century, and to the biography of American statesmen, if an impartial one should ever be written, in confirmation of the general correctness of my statement. Exceptions to this rule exist, of course, in every State; but, without any particular predilection in favour of democracy, it is easy to perceive that these mostly occur on the popular side.

Whenever a man of talent or wealth embraces the cause of democracy, he becomes at once the butt of society, and the object of the most unrelenting persecution with all the "respectable" editors, lawyers, bankers, and business men in the large cities. To one democratic paper published in a city, there are generally from ten to twelve, sometimes twenty, Federal or Whig journals; which I take for the best possible proof that talent loves to be rewarded, and in republics, as well as in monarchies, naturally serves those who are best *able* to reward it.

The democrats have not the means of remunerating the services of their public men in the manner of the Whigs; for, with the exception of a few government offices, with mere pittances for salaries, and the election of senators and members of Congress,—persons "hired at the rate of eight dollars a day,"—all lucrative offices of trust and emolument are in the gift of the opposition, whose patronage, therefore, is a matter of infinitely higher consideration than that of the President and his cabinet.

The little pecuniary reward which the zealots and champions of democracy meet with in the United States, is, indeed, one of the reasons for which they are despised by their aristocratic opponents. "What talents," argue the latter, "can a man possess who will give up all manner of business, and devote himself exclusively to politics, in order, near the close of his life, to sit down contented with the editorship of a penny paper, a membership of Congress, or an office of from twelve hundred to two thousand dollars a year? Success in life is the best proof of ability; and who that will look upon the respective condition of our political partisans can for one moment be doubtful as to which of them have the *best side* of the question?"

It is for such and similar reasons that they take every opportunity of railing against the increased patronage of the government; as if the government of the United States were something apart from the people, —a power which the people have to contend with, and against which, therefore, they must direct their concentrated efforts! And a considerable portion of the people are actually duped in that way; they imagine that what is taken away from the government is gained by the community, forgetting that the government is of their own choice, and that the men placed at the head of it rise or fall at their beck. They do not seem to be aware that, as long as the government of the United States remains elective, all executive power vested in it increases but the sovereignty of the people, and that the patronage of the government is essentially their own.

On the subject of patronage the aristocratic press of America is truly eloquent; that being the point for which it most contends, the lever of its patriotism. What, indeed, would become of the flower of statesmen of the present Whig party, if the government of the country, or the people who elect that government, could reward the advocacy of their cause as princely as the "wealthy and enlightened" opposition? —if *money* were at the command of the public servants, as it is at the disposal of those who manage the great financial concerns of the country? Hence the people are warned against putting the sword and the purse into the same hands. "Let the government have the sword," say the Whigs, "provided we keep the purse."

The purse is the point round which the whole system of politics turned ever since the origin of the country. The war for and against a bank did, indeed, agitate the United States before they were quite ushered into existence; and has continued to throw the elements of state into confusion, and to act in a truly corrosive manner on every true source of national grandeur. . . .

. . . The fact that the principal poets of America are really obliged to seek "a local habitation and a name" in *Europe*, may be considered as the best proof of the all-absorbing influence of the purse;—an influence which already acts restrictively on genius and talent of the highest order, and will, if it be not counteracted by a more generous system of legislation, and a different spirit diffused *among the people*, constantly absorb the main sources of thought and action, which give to every nation its individual life and character. . . .

But I trust that the good sense of the people, the intelligence pervading the masses, and, above all, the high degree of morality and virtue which distinguishes the American above all other nations in the world, will be proof against the temptations of a handful of political sceptics; and that the country, blessed with Nature's richest gifts, and selected by Providence for the noblest experiment tried by man, will fulfil its mission,—which is not only the civilization of a new world, but the practical establishment of principles which heretofore have only had an ideal existence.

Suggestions for
Further Reading

Transportation Revolution

The standard work on the Transportation Revolution and its economic repercussions is George Rogers Taylor, *The Transportation Revolution, 1815–1860* (New York, 1951).* For economic background see also Curtis P. Nettels, *The Emergence of a National Economy, 1775–1815* (New York, 1962)*; Paul W. Gates, *The Farmer's Age: Agriculture, 1815–1860* (New York, 1960) *; and Douglas C. North, *The Economic Growth of the United States, 1790–1860* (Englewood Cliffs, 1961).* Detailed and regional studies include: Edward C. Kirkland, *Men, Cities, and Transportation: A Study of New England History, 1820–1900* (2 vols., Cambridge, 1948); Robert G. Albion, *The Rise of New York Port, 1815–1860* (New York, 1939); Louis C. Hunter, *Steamboats on the Western Rivers: An Economic and Technological History* (Cambridge, 1949); Carter Goodrich (and others), *Canals and American Economic Development* (New York, 1961); Ronald E. Shaw, *Erie Water West: A History of the Erie Canal, 1792–1854* (Lexington, 1966). On railroads see Robert W. Fogel, *Railroads and American Economic Growth* (Baltimore, 1964); Albert Fishlow, *American Railroads and the Transformation of the Ante-Bellum Economy* (Cambridge, 1965); Stephen Saulsbury, *The State, the Investor, and the Railroad: The Boston & Albany, 1825–1867* (Cambridge, 1967); and Merl E. Reed, *New Orleans and the Railroads: The Struggle for Commercial Empire, 1830–1860* (Baton Rouge, 1966). The role of state governments in stimulating and regulating economic growth has been the subject of many monographs; to list but two: Louis Hartz, *Economic Policy and Democratic Thought: Pennsylvania 1776–1860* (Cambridge, 1948),* and Milton Sydney Heath, *Constructive Liberalism: The Role of the State in Economic Development in Georgia to 1860* (Cambridge, 1954).

* Books marked with an asterisk are available in paperback editions.

179

LABOR

An old work still of considerable value is John R. Commons (and others), *History of Labor in the United States* (New York, 1918); also, Norman Ware, *The Industrial Worker, 1840–1860* . . . (Boston, 1924).* Two good state studies are Hannah Josephson, *The Golden Threads: New England's Mill Girls and Magnates* (New York, 1949),* and William A. Sullivan, *The Industrial Worker in Pennsylvania, 1800–1840* (Harrisburg, 1955). For labor and politics, see Edward Pessen, *Most Uncommon Jacksonians: The Radical Leaders of the Early Labor Movement* (Albany, 1967), and Walter Hugins, *Jacksonian Democracy and the Working Class: A Study of the New York Workingmen's Movement, 1829–1837* (Stanford, 1960).* There is an abundant literature on the related theme of immigration: Marcus L. Hansen, *The Atlantic Migration, 1607–1860* . . . (Cambridge, 1940) *; Oscar Handlin, *Boston's Immigrants: A Study in Acculturation* (rev. ed., Cambridge, 1959) *; Robert Ernst, *Immigrant Life in New York City, 1825–1863* (New York, 1949); Rowland T. Berthoff, *British Immigrants in Industrial America, 1790–1950* (Cambridge, 1953); Clifton K. Yearley, Jr., *Britons in American Labor* . . . *1820–1914* (Baltimore, 1957); William F. Adams, *Ireland and Irish Emigration to the New World from 1815 to the Famine* (New Haven, 1932); Earl F. Neihaus, *The Irish in New Orleans, 1800–1860* (Baton Rouge, 1966); Mack Walker, *Germany and the Emigration: 1816–1885* (Cambridge, 1964).

RELIGION

William W. Sweet, *Religion in the Development of American Culture, 1765–1840* (New York, 1952); John R. Bodo, *The Protestant Clergy and Public Issues, 1812–1848* (Princeton, 1954); Charles I. Foster, *An Errand of Mercy: The Evangelical United Front, 1790–1837* (Chapel Hill, 1960); Ralph H. Gabriel, "Evangelical Religion and Popular Romanticism in Early Nineteenth-Century America," *Church History*, XIX (March, 1950), 34–47; Whitney R. Cross, *The Burned-Over District* . . . *Enthusiastic Religion in Western New York, 1800–1850* (Ithaca, 1950) *; Walter B. Posey, *Frontier Mission* . . . *Religion West of the Southern Appalachians to 1861* (Lexington, 1966); Timothy L. Smith, *Revivalism and Social Reform in Mid-Nineteenth America* (New York, 1957).*

Denominations

Walter B. Posey, *The [Southern] Baptist Church* . . . *1776–1845* (Lexington, 1957). For two leading Congregationalists, see Barbara M. Cross, *Horace Bushnell* . . . (Chicago, 1958); and William G. McLoughlin, ed., *Lectures on Revivals of Religion, by Charles Grandison Finney* (Cambridge, 1960). William W. Manross, *The Episcopal Church* . . . *1800–1840* (New York, 1938); Robert W. Doherty, *The Hicksite Separation*

. . . [of Quakers] (New Brunswick, 1967); David P. Edgell, *William Ellery Channing* . . . (Boston, 1955); William R. Hutchison, *The Transcendentalist Ministers* . . . (New Haven, 1959). For attempts of the dominant Protestants to proselytize within minority groups see: Clifford S. Griffin, "Converting the Catholics . . . the Ante-Bellum Crusade Against the Church," *Catholic Historical Review*, XLVII (October, 1961), 325–41; and Lorman Ratner, "Conversion of the Jews and Pre-Civil War Reform," *American Quarterly*, XIII (Spring, 1961), 43–54.

REFORM

For a useful compendium, see Alice Felt Tyler, *Freedom's Ferment: Chapters in American Social History to 1860* (Minneapolis, 1944).* General works: Clifford S. Griffin, *Their Brothers' Keepers: Moral Stewardship in the United States, 1800–1865* (New Brunswick, 1960); Clifford S. Griffin, *The Ferment of Reform, 1830–1860* (New York, 1967) *; Arthur M. Schlesinger, *The American as Reformer* (Cambridge, 1950) *; Robert E. Riegel, *Young America, 1830–1840* (Norman, 1949); Arthur A. Ekirch, Jr., *The Idea of Progress in America, 1815–1860* (New York, 1944); and John L. Thomas, "Romantic Reform in America, 1815–1865," *American Quarterly*, XVII (Winter, 1965), 656–81.

Education

Among recent critical works are: Maxine Greene, *The Public School and the Private Vision* . . . (New York, 1965) *; Michael Katz, *The Irony of Early School Reform: Educational Innovation in Mid-Nineteenth Century Massachusetts* (Cambridge, 1968); and Vincent P. Lannie, *Public Money and Parochial Education: Bishop Hughes, Governor Seward, and the New York School Controversy* (Cleveland, 1968).

Feminism

William R. Waterman, *Frances Wright* (New York, 1924); Otelia Cromwell, *Lucretia Mott* (Cambridge, 1958); Barbara Welter, "The Cult of True Womanhood: 1820–1860," *American Quarterly*, XVIII (Summer, 1966), 151–74.

Pacifism

Merle Curti, *The American Peace Crusade, 1815–1860* (Durham, 1929); Peter Brock, *Radical Pacifists in Antebellum America* (Princeton, 1968).*

Penology

Blake McKelvey, *American Prisons: A Study in American Social History* . . . (Chicago, 1936); W. David Lewis, *From Newgate to Dannemora: The Rise of the Penitentiary in New York, 1796–1848* (Ithaca, 1964);

Robert S. Pickett, *House of Refuge: Origins of Juvenile Reform in New York State, 1815–1857* (Syracuse, 1968); David Brion Davis, "The Movement to Abolish Capital Punishment in America, 1787–1861," *American Historical Review*, LXIII (October, 1957), 23–46.

Temperance

John A. Krout, *The Origins of Prohibition* (New York, 1925); Joseph R. Gusfield, *Symbolic Crusade: Status Politics and the American Temperance Movement* (Urbana, 1963)*; Frank L. Byrne, *Prophet of Prohibition: Neal Dow and His Crusade* (Madison, 1961).

Welfare

David M. Schneider, *The History of Public Welfare in New York State: 1609–1866* (Chicago, 1938); Irvin G. Wyllie, "The Search for an American Law of Charity, 1776–1844," *Mississippi Valley Historical Review*, XLVI (September, 1959), 203–21; Roy Lubove, "The New York Association for Improving the Condition of the Poor," *New-York Historical Society Quarterly*, XLIII (July, 1959), 307–33.

Utopian Communities

Arthur E. Bestor, Jr., *Backwoods Utopias: The Sectarian and Owenite Phases of Communitarian Socialism in America: 1663–1829* (Philadelphia, 1950); Edward D. Andrews, *The People Called Shakers: A Search for the Perfect Society* (rev. ed., New York, 1963)*; Edith R. Curtis, *A Season in Utopia: The Story of Brook Farm* (New York, 1961); Karl J. R. Arndt, *George Rapp's Harmony Society, 1785–1847* (Philadelphia, 1966); William E. Wilson, *The Angel and the Serpent: The Story of New Harmony* (Bloomington, 1964).

Antislavery

Philip J. Staudenraus, *The African Colonization Movement* (New York, 1961); Louis Filler, *The Crusade Against Slavery, 1830–1860* (New York, 1960)*; David Brion Davis, "The Emergence of Immediatism in British and American Antislavery Thought," *Mississippi-Valley Historical Review*, XLIX (September, 1962), 209–30. The outstanding works on the origins of American racial attitudes are: David Brion Davis, *The Problem of Slavery in Western Culture* (Ithaca, 1966) *; and Winthrop D. Jordan, *White Over Black: American Attitudes Toward the Negro, 1550–1812* (Chapel Hill, 1968).* Studies of key abolitionists include: John L. Thomas, *The Liberator: William Lloyd Garrison* (Boston, 1963); Bertram Wyatt-Brown, "William Lloyd Garrison and Anti-slavery Unity . . . ," *Civil War History*, XIII (March, 1967), 5–24; Irving H. Bartlett, *Wendell Phillips, Brahmin Radical* (Boston, 1961); Benjamin Quarles, *Frederick Douglass* (Washington, 1948) *; Betty Fladeland, *James G. Birney: Slave-*

holder to Abolitionist (Ithaca, 1955); Benjamin P. Thomas, *Theodore Weld, Crusader for Freedom* (New Brunswick, 1950). On abolitionism in the 1830s see: Gilbert H. Barnes, *The Antislavery Impulse, 1830–1844* (New York, 1933) *; Gerald S. Henig, "The Jacksonians Attitude Toward Abolitionists in the 1830's," *Tennessee Historical Quarterly*, XXVIII (Spring, 1969), 42–56; Lorman Ratner; *Powder Keg; Northern Opposition to the Antislavery Movement, 1831–1840* (New York, 1968); Leonard L. Richards, *"Gentlemen of Property and Standing": Anti-Abolition Mobs in Jacksonian America* (New York, 1970); Aileen S. Kraditor, *Means and Ends in American Abolitionism . . . 1834–1850* (New York, 1969); Robert P. Ludlum, "The Antislavery 'Gag Rule' . . ." *Journal of Negro History*, XXVI (April, 1941), 203–43.

THE NEW RULES

Suffrage

Chilton Williamson, *American Suffrage, From Property to Democracy 1760–1860* (Princeton, 1960) *: Richard P. McCormick, "New Perspectives on Jacksonian Politics," *American Historical Review*, LXV (January, 1960), 288–301; and McCormick, "Suffrage Classes and Party Alignments," *Mississippi Valley Historical Review*, XLVI (December, 1959), 397–410; J. R. Pole, "Constitutional Reform and Election Statistics in Maryland, 1790–1812," *Maryland Historical Magazine*, LV (December, 1960), 275–92.

Caucus or Convention

Some positive aspects of the congressional nominating caucus are discussed by Charles S. Sydnor, "The One-Party Period of American History," *American Historical Review*, LI (April, 1946), 439–51; see also William G. Morgan, "The Decline of the . . . Caucus," *Tennessee Historical Quarterly*, XXIV (Fall, 1965), 245–55. For the convention see James S. Chase, "Jacksonian Democracy and the Rise of the Nominating Convention," *Mid-America*, XLV (October, 1963), 229–49. Anti-Masons held the first national nominating convention. A modern study of that party is needed, but see Charles McCarthy, *The Antimasonic Party* (Washington, 1903).

Parties

On early parties see: William N. Chambers, *Political Parties in a New Nation* (New York, 1963) *; and Richard P. McCormick, *The Second American Party System* (Chapel Hill, 1966).* The acceptance of the existence of parties is the subject of Richard Hofstadter, *The Idea of a Party System: The Rise of Legitimate Opposition* (Berkeley, 1969); and Michael Wallace, "Changing Concepts of Party in the United States: New York, 1815–1828," *American Historical Review*, LXXIV (December,

1968), 453–91. On two key Republican-Democratic machines, see: Robert V. Remini, "The Albany Regency," *New York History*, XXXIX (October, 1958), 341–55; and Harry Ammon, "The Richmond Junto," *Virginia Magazine of History*, LXI (October, 1953), 394–418.

THE NEW MEN

Jacksonian Takeover

Robert V. Remini, *The Election of Andrew Jackson* (Philadelphia, 1963).* For the preceding decade, see George Dangerfield, *The Awakening of American Nationalism* (New York, 1965) * ; and Richard H. Brown, "The Missouri Crisis, Slavery, and the Politics of Jacksonianism," *South Atlantic Quarterly*, LXV (Winter, 1966), 55–72.

Patronage

Carl R. Fish, *The Civil Service and the Patronage* (Cambridge, 1904); Howard L. McBain, *DeWitt Clinton and the Origin of the Spoils System in New York* (New York, 1907); Erik M. Erikson; "The Federal Civil Service Under President Jackson," *Mississippi Valley Historical Review*, XIII (March, 1927), 517–40. Leonard D. White's studies, *The Jeffersonians* (New York, 1951) * and *The Jacksonians* (New York, 1954) * contain much material on patronage and problems of administration generally.

Presidency

In addition to general histories and analyses of the presidential office and its powers, see: Carlton Jackson, *Presidential Vetoes* (Athens, Ga., 1967); Richard P. Longaker, "Was Jackson's Kitchen Cabinet a Cabinet?" *Mississippi Valley Historical Review*, XLIV (June, 1957), 94–108; Longaker, "Andrew Jackson and the Judiciary," *Political Science Quarterly*, LXXI (September, 1956), 341–64; Albert Somit, "Andrew Jackson as Administrative Reformer," *Tennessee Historical Quarterly*, XII (September, 1954), 204–23. For the Jackson mystique, see: John W. Ward, *Andrew Jackson: Symbol for an Age* (New York, 1955).*

Biographies of leading Jacksonians include: William N. Chambers, *Old Bullion Benton, Senator from the New West* (Boston, 1956); Russel B. Nye, *George Bancroft, Brahmin Rebel* (New York, 1945); John A. Garraty, *Silas Wright* (New York, 1949); Philip S. Klein, *President James Buchanan* (Univ. Park, Pa., 1962); Carl B. Swisher, *Roger B. Taney* (New York, 1935); Charles H. Ambler, *Thomas Ritchie* (Richmond, 1913). The leading defector is treated gently by Charles M. Wiltse, *John C. Calhoun* (3 vols., Indianapolis, 1944–51); Gerald M. Capers, *John C. Calhoun, Opportunist* (Gainesville, 1960),* more than redresses the balance.

Some general analyses of the Jacksonian years: Arthur M. Schlesinger, Jr., *The Age of Jackson* (Boston, 1945) *; Glyndon G. Van Deusen, *The Jacksonian Era, 1828–1848* (New York, 1959) *; and Edward Pessen,

Jacksonian America (Homewood, Ill., 1969).* Every student should read the model historiographical essay by Charles Sellers, "Andrew Jackson versus the Historians," *Mississippi Valley Historical Review,* XLIV (March, 1958), 615–34.

THE BANK WAR

The best interpretative overview of early American banking is Fritz Redlich, *The Molding of American Banking: Men and Ideas* (2 vols., New York, 1947–51). Robert V. Remini, *Andrew Jackson and the Bank War* (New York, 1967) * stresses politics over economics. For attacks on Jacksonianism, see Bray Hammond, *Banks and Politics in America* (Princeton, 1957) * and Thomas P. Govan, *Nicholas Biddle* (Chicago, 1959). Marvin Meyers probes the Democrats' economic dilemma in *The Jacksonian Persuasion* (Stanford, 1957).* Specialized studies include: Frank Otto Gatell, "Sober Second Thoughts on Van Buren . . . and the Wall Street Conspiracy," *Journal of American History,* LIII (June, 1966), 19–40; Lynn L. Marshall, "The Authorship of Jackson's Bank Veto Message," *Mississippi Valley Historical Review,* L (December, 1963), 466–77; Jacob P. Meerman, ". . . Biddle's Contraction of 1833–34," *Journal of Political Economy,* LXXI (April, 1963), 378–388; Gatell, "Spoils of the Bank War: Political Bias in the Selection of Pet Banks," *American Historical Review,* LXX (October, 1964), 35–58. Jacksonian financial policy after 1833 can be followed in Charles G. Sellers, *James K. Polk: Jacksonian* (Princeton, 1957).

WHIG RESPONSE

Glyndon G. Van Deusen is the author of several works which seek to rehabilitate the Whig Party as something more than a mere foil for Jacksonians. His biographies include: *Henry Clay* (Boston, 1937) * ; *Thurlow Weed: Wizard of the Lobby* (Boston, 1947); *Horace Greeley* (Philadelphia, 1953).* See also Van Deusen, "Some Aspects of Whig Thought and Theory in the Jacksonian Period," *American Historical Review,* LXIII (January, 1958), 305–22. Party beginnings are treated in E. Malcolm Carroll, *Origins of the Whig Party* (Durham, 1925); and Lynn L. Marshall, "The Strange Stillbirth of the Whig Party," *American Historical Review,* LXXII (January, 1967), 445–68. Robert G. Gunderson details the hoopla of the 1840 election in *The Log-Cabin Campaign* (Lexington, 1957).